THE STOIC PHILOSOPHY OF SENECA

MOSES HADAS (1900-1966) was Professor of Greek and Latin at Columbia University. He is the author of *A History of Greek Literature*, *A History of Latin Literature*, and *Hellenistic Culture;* editor of the *Complete Works of Tacitus,* the *Basic Works of Cicero,* and *The Greek Poets;* and translator of many works of classical literature.

p. 198:
"Creative Reason = God

THE
STOIC PHILOSOPHY OF
SENECA

b. 4 – 65 ce. (spanish birth)

Essays and Letters of Seneca

Translated and with an Introduction

by Moses Hadas

note:
repeatedly cites
Aeneid on gods

W · W · NORTON & COMPANY

New York · London

Books That Live
The Norton imprint on a book means that in the publisher's
estimation it is a book not for a single season but for the years.
W. W. Norton & Company, Inc.

ISBN 0-393-00459-7

PRINTED IN THE UNITED STATES OF AMERICA

2 3 4 5 6 7 8 9 0

CONTENTS

THE STOIC PHILOSOPHY OF SENECA

INTRODUCTION

1. THE SHADOW OF A GREAT NAME

Bookish people know that Seneca has a large responsibility for the configuration of Elizabethan tragedy and that he was Montaigne's main point of departure for his Essays; they may also be aware that he was the favorite pagan of the Latin Church, so that the zealot Tertullian called him *"our* Seneca," that the austere Calvin commented on his *On Clemency;* and they may have heard that Stoic egalitarianism, as communicated by Seneca, contributed significantly to the ferment which exploded in the French Revolution. Here, then, is an ancient author who appreciably affected European prose and poetry and European politics, who was surely one of the three Romans most widely, continuously, and favorably known in subsequent centuries; and yet the twentieth-century reader who turns from Seneca's reputation to his works is bound to be puzzled if not completely disillusioned. Even the warmest partisan of Seneca must admit to serious inadequacies in his author from the point of view of current taste, and even a lukewarm partisan must be reluctant to expose him to scrutiny likely to be unsympathetic without preliminary word of defense.

Broadly speaking, there are three categories under which a writer of an earlier age can claim attention. There are, in the lowest category, innumerable deservedly forgotten littérateurs whose contemporaries acclaimed them as immortal because they originated or suited an ephemeral vogue. These were sham giants strutting among authentic pygmies, and we sometimes look at them because sham giants and pygmies are quaint and provide a gauge for recognizing true giants and true men. At the other extreme are the writers, relatively a handful in number, who have a continuing validity and a continuing vogue as literature, not curiosities. They tend to cluster at luminous periods of history, and though their origins may be remote, they require a minimum of antiquarian introduction but are susceptible of endless discussion in contemporary terms. Between these extremes are creators of stature whose innovations in matter and form have in fact determined or influenced the direction of subsequent writing, to the degree that they have themselves been swallowed up in the stream they fed and are of interest mainly as a basis for plotting the course of the stream and assessing its divagations. It is to this category, so far as he is susceptible of categorization, that Seneca belongs. His influence on posterity is indubitable, and if he did not himself create the ideas he transmitted he did collect them and make them persuasive and shape them into a transmissible form.

2. BELLES-LETTRES AND A GUIDING PROVIDENCE

The main obstacle to a just appreciation of Seneca is chronology. In time he belongs to the first third of European literary history, but in certain essential criteria to the last, and these criteria are so impressive that we read him as if he in fact belonged to the last third and so are offended by what seems a want of sophistication. The movement from Homer to the present is indeed a continuum, in the sense that seeds for every new development can be found in what went before, but its pace is by no means constant; there are moments when the stream ran very thin indeed or when it shifted direction very sharply. The sharpest shift of all can be dated to the period between the death of Alexander the Great and the death of Augustus, and Seneca belongs on the modern side of the divide. The change in life and letters manifested itself and can be examined in various aspects; for our present purpose it will be sufficient to glance at two new attitudes of the writer, first toward his work, and then toward the world.

It was the Alexandrians who created the concept of belles-lettres, the doctrine of art for art's sake, which to a classic Greek would have been meaningless or absurd. Where the classic poets considered themselves, and were considered by their community, as responsible and, in a sense, inspired teachers, and made their work beautiful because Greek craftsmen made their products beautiful, the Alexandrians had no real community to address but were royal pensioners who wrote to impress each other with their artistic sophistication. They were wholly indifferent to the materials to which they gave so high a polish, and were not aware that their predecessors had been otherwise motivated. An Apollonius of Rhodes doubtless thought he was doing with more recondite materials and higher professional skill what Homer had done naïvely and with obvious materials. On the other hand, writers who were concerned to propagate significant doctrine were quite indifferent to style in the knotty philosophic treatises they wrote. It is a real merit of the Roman essayists, Cicero and Seneca alike, that they made the Hellenistic philosophers presentable and intelligible. In another century, during the so-called Second Sophistic, prose "orators" succumbed to stylishness more completely than even the Alexandrian poets had done. Seneca is mannered but not bizarre, and is obviously deeply concerned to communicate doctrine.

The more important change has to do with a new con-

cept of the world which, so far as belief in a ruling providence and in external sanctions for conduct are concerned,
is virtually Christian. This concept underlies all of Seneca's
writing, and that is why the reader unconsciously approaches and judges him as he would an author in the
Continental tradition rather than as he would a classic
Greek. Though he is immediate heir to the Greeks and uses
their modes of expression, mythology, and literary canons,
he is not a Greek at all, not even a bad Greek; it would
be more accurate to call him a bad Elizabethan.

The tragedies will serve to illustrate the point, because
the comparison is easier, and because the essays will be
treated for their own sake in the sequel. Superficially the
tragedies look Greek: the plots and personages are Greek,
the dialogue is in iambic and the choruses in lyric meter,
the unities are observed, and the length and general form
of Greek tragedy are closely imitated. But they are essentially closer to Shakespeare, and not merely because they
are stark and rhetorical and use witches and ghosts and
clanking chains. True pagan tragedy has no villains because it has no unquestioned code of morality. Each of two
alternative courses of conduct has powerful sanctions, and
the hero must make his choice and take the consequences
imposed by the rejected sanction. In this sense Christian
tragedy is impossible; when there can be only one right, the
man who defies it is a villain. We may have melodrama or
a tableau showing right triumphant and villainy requited,
but this is not *Greek* tragedy. (Needless to say, not all non-
Greek tragedy is Christian.) Seneca's Stoic universe is also
controlled by an all-pervasive and exigent intelligence and
is also sure of its categories of right and wrong.

Seneca's affinity to the Shakespearean rather than the
Greek mode may be exemplified by his concept of history
as a single directed totality rather than as a congeries of
events in which temporal relationships are irrelevant. The
difference in their respective views of time appears in the

respective verb forms of Hebrew and Greek. The characteristic tense of the Hebrew verb is the preterit; its only
other tense is the future, and the present can be expressed
only by an awkward participial phrase. The characteristic
tense of the Greek verb is the aorist, which indicates a
single act unspecified in time. The Hebrew regards history
as a continuum, with datable events such as the Creation,
the Fall, the revelation at Sinai, the Crucifixion as manifestations of a single will which orders events and requires a
specified standard of human conduct. For the Greeks, man
is the measure and each new moral problem is confronted
on its own terms. It is not necessary to maintain—though
there are arguments in favor and it was believed until modern times that he was in correspondence with St. Paul—
that Seneca was influenced by Eastern ideas; the change
he manifests is characteristic of the climate of his time,
East or West. But the climate his works illustrate is the
climate we breathe—and sometimes find a little stale. The
Greek is alien, and therefore offers a fresh challenge and, it
may be, fresh insights. Derogatory criticism of Seneca is
posited on the assumption that he is a corrupted Greek; it
is fairer to look upon him as an embryonic Elizabethan.

3. LIFE

Like most of our Latin authors, Seneca was not Roman, or
even Italian, by birth. He belonged to a wealthy and cultivated Spanish family which produced other writers of distinction. Seneca's father, after whom he was named, was
an influential rhetorician, whose handbooks on debating
(*Suasoriae* and *Controversiae*) can still be read with interest and profit. One of his brothers was Gallio, the procura-
tor of Achaea mentioned in Acts, and another was father
of the gifted poet Lucan, whose *Civil War,* commonly
called *Pharsalia,* is easily the second Latin epic after the

Aeneid. Seneca himself was born at Cordova about 4 B.C. He was taken to Rome in infancy by an aunt, who nursed him through a sickly childhood and helped launch him on his official career. He achieved high success as a lawyer and quickly amassed a huge fortune; critics ancient and modern have been disturbed by the discrepancy between his own pursuit of wealth by sometimes dubious means (e.g., usurious interest rates, though the practice was general) and his repeated advocacy of a simple life which disdains all externals. His principal avocation (no Roman gentleman could acknowledge that he was a professional) was philosophy; of his productions as a philosopher and writer we shall speak more fully presently. About A.D. 33, under the Emperor Tiberius, he held the quaestorship, the first step in the Roman's career in office. By the time of Caligula's accession (A.D. 37) Seneca's reputation as an orator and writer was great enough to arouse the emperor's jealousy. Caligula refrained from killing him only because he was given to understand that the sickly intellectual would soon die a natural death. Certain traits in Seneca's character and his works are doubtless due to his persistent valetudinarianism; we may speculate that if Seneca had had a robust constitution Elizabethan tragedy might not have been so strained and passionate.

In Claudius' first year (A.D. 41) Claudius' third wife, Messalina, procured Seneca's banishment to Corsica on the improbable charge of adultery with Julia Livilla. Again his abject despondency and his groveling pleas for restoration make a melancholy contrast with his Stoic insistence that situation is a thing indifferent and that a man is equally at home anywhere in the world. In 49 Agrippina procured his recall and made him, together with the praetorian prefect Afranius Burrus, tutor to her son Nero. Nero succeeded in 54, and the beneficent administration of the first five years of his reign is attributed to the tutelage of Burrus and especially of Seneca, who was now of consular rank and virtually prime minister. But in 59 Nero asserted his true character; Seneca and Burrus were reluctant accessories to the murder of Agrippina in that year, and Seneca wrote Nero's dishonest exculpation to the senate. Relations with the emperor grew strained, and when Burrus died, in 62, Seneca offered his enormous fortune to the emperor and went into virtual retirement on his estates. Upon apparently dubious evidence of implication in the abortive Pisonian conspiracy of A.D. 65 Seneca was bidden to take his life, and he did so, with a theatrical gesture becoming to his tragic heroes, but with a fortitude of which the course of his life had given no evidence. This is the description of the last scene in Tacitus (*Annals* 15.62), who did not much like Seneca:

Seneca calmly requested tablets for making a will, and on the centurion's refusal turned to his friends and declared that as he was prevented from showing gratitude for their deserts he would leave them his only, but fairest, possession, the pattern of his life; if they heeded this they would win a reputation for good character and the reward of steadfast friendship. At the same time, now by persuasion and now by rebuke, he led them from tears to fortitude, asking them repeatedly, "Where are those philosophical precepts, where the logic you have so long studied for just such an event? Has Nero's savagery been a secret? After the murders of mother and brother it is natural that he should add the death of his guardian and tutor."

When he had discoursed in this fashion to all in common he embraced his wife. He relaxed his stern fortitude to beg and implore her to temper her grief and not nourish it forever but rather to find honorable solace for the loss of her husband by contemplation of a life spent in virtue. In return she declared that she too had resolved to die, and asked for the executioner's stroke. Seneca would not oppose her nobility and would not leave behind for insult one he had dearly loved. "I have shown you a cushioning for life," said he, "but you prefer the glory of death. I do not begrudge you the gesture. Let the constancy of our departure be alike for both of us, but greater fame in your end." Then with the same stroke they severed the arteries of their arms.

The pattern of life which Seneca recommended to his survivors others have not found so exemplary. Here is a sketch by Dio Cassius (61.10):

While denouncing tyranny, Seneca was making himself the teacher of a tyrant; while inveighing against the associates of the powerful, he did not hold aloof from the palace himself; and though he had nothing good to say of flatterers, he himself had constantly fawned upon Messalina and the freedmen of Claudius, to such an extent, in fact, as actually to send them from the island of his exile a book containing their praises, a book that he afterwards suppressed out of shame. Though finding fault with the rich, he himself acquired a fortune of 300,000,000 sesterces; and though he censured the extravagances of others, he had 500 tables of citrus wood with legs of ivory, all identically alike, and he served banquets on them. In stating thus much I have also made clear what naturally went with it—the licentiousness in which he indulged at the very time that he contracted a most brilliant marriage, and the delight that he took in boys past their prime, a practice which he also taught Nero to follow.

We may write Dio's denigration down to senatorial bias and the scandalmongering penchant of his age (his dates are A.D. 155–235); elsewhere (59.19) he is ready to say that Seneca was "superior in wisdom to all the Romans of his day and to many others as well." Personal character may be irrelevant in a metaphysician, but in a moralist of the Senecan type it is of the first importance. Socrates' arguments for the immortality of the soul are empty verbiage without the enormously persuasive example of his life and death, and if his life suggested that he actively disbelieved in his doctrines the arguments would be worse than merely unpersuasive. Seneca is perhaps most offensive in his satire on the deification of Claudius (called *Apocolocyntosis,* or "Pumpkinification"), written apparently to curry favor with Claudius' successor. Here he makes a particular butt of measures which a professing Stoic must have approved because they were central to the Stoic program—care for the integrity of the judiciary, extension of the franchise, study of history. Cleavage between profession and practice is a common phenomenon, but seldom is the gap so yawning, because Seneca was an artist both in his preaching and his malefactions. It may be that his intensity in either direction is a kind of excrescence of a clinical morbidity connected with his general ill health.

4. THE CORPUS

Seneca the poet and Seneca the philosopher were thought, until modern times, to be distinct persons, and the manuscript traditions of the two groups of writings are independent of each other. The sole (but sufficient) external evidence that the philosopher also wrote the tragedies is Quintilian's ascription of a line of the *Medea* to our Seneca. In any case, internal evidence makes it reasonably clear that the tragedies and essays derive from the same hand. Scholars have long labored to establish a chronology of the writings but have reached no unanimity, and the matter is of no great importance, for there seems to be little change

in Seneca's thought or manner. Seneca wrote more than has
survived. All his oratory is lost, as are a number of philosophical treatises which we know only from references to
them. The surviving writings attributed to Seneca are the
following:

[A] *Dialogues.* There are ten treatises, in twelve "books"
grouped together under this title in the manuscript tradition. They are not, strictly speaking, dialogues, but occasionally an interlocutor is imagined as raising a direct
question and receiving a direct reply. Of the ten, three are
formal "Consolations," a genus well established in later
antiquity, employing stock arguments in a fairly fixed order.
There are extant specimens of the genus in other writers,
too; perhaps the most attractive is Plutarch's consolation to
his wife on the death of their infant daughter. Seneca's consolations include:

[i] *To Marcia.* This is addressed to the daughter of the
Stoic Cremutius Cordus, a victim of Sejanus, on the loss of
her son three years before. It offers the standard prescriptions for the control of grief, with citations of the examples
of other bereaved mothers.

[ii] *To Helvia* (included in the present collection). Here
Seneca writes from his exile in Corsica to console his mother
for being deprived of himself. His argument is based upon
Stoic indifference to externals, so that a man can be, as he
in fact is, happy under any circumstances, and, indeed, he
has leisure to pursue his philosophic studies. His mother
must therefore not grieve for his unhappiness and must remember her proven strength of character to endure her own
deprivation.

[iii] *To Polybius.* This, too, was written in exile, to an
influential freedman at Claudius' court upon the death of
his brother, and employs the grossest adulation of Polybius
and his master (whom Seneca would ridicule after his
death) for an abject plea for restoration. The treatise con-

tains brilliant apothegms and sensible Stoic advice, which the reader must regret the author did not apply to his own case.

The longest of the "Dialogues" is

[iv] *On Anger,* in three books. This is addressed to Seneca's brother Novatus, who was subsequently called Gallio, and deals with one of the major "perturbations" of which the Stoic endeavored to rid his soul. The book is not well organized but is filled with perennially relevant observations and advice and enlivened by good illustrative anecdotes.

[v] *On the Happy Life.* This, too, is addressed to Gallio. The prescription for happiness is the Stoic principle of "life according to nature," which necessarily involves the traditional canon of virtues. The program can be followed even amidst wealth if a man will retain his detachment from its appurtenances.

There are three related treatises addressed to Serenus:

[vi] *On the Constancy of the Sage,* which bears the subtitle "That the sage can receive neither injury nor insult." This is an admirably eloquent sermon on Stoic self-sufficiency.

[vii] *On Tranquillity* (included in the present collection). This opens with Serenus' request for a remedy to cure his vacillation of spirit: despite his intellectual convictions he finds himself susceptible to the attractions of luxury and a public career. Seneca's response forms the body of the treatise. He is at his most charming and most helpful in suggesting a point of view and a way of life which will bring contentment.

[viii] *On Leisure.* This advocates renunciation of the active life, especially for older men, in favor of philosophic contemplation and scientific inquiry.

[ix] *On the Shortness of Life* (included in the present collection), addressed to Paulinus, who directed the Roman grain supply. This again is an admirable homily. True

length of life cannot be measured in years, for so much of our time is frittered away in essentially futile occupations and squandered in trivial pleasures. Philosophy can make even a short life long, for it enables a man to share all the experience of the past and commune with the great of all ages.

[x] *On Providence* (included in the present collection) bears the subtitle "Why misfortunes befall good men when there is a providence." The answer, since the Stoic believes that the world is governed for the best, must be that suffering serves good purposes. The principal ones suggested are spiritual discipline and scope for exercising virtue.

[B] There are two longer treatises which are not included in the "Dialogues," though their character is much the same:

[xi] *On Clemency,* originally in three books, of which only the first (included in the present collection) and a fragment of the second are extant. This is addressed to Nero in his eighteenth year, and seems actually intended to make him a humane ruler; the adulatory addresses to him, therefore, are only cloying, not repulsive. The treatise is, in effect, an exegesis, point by point, on Portia's glorification of the quality of mercy in *The Merchant of Venice,* with particular concern for " 'Tis mightiest in the mightiest; it becomes the throned monarch better than his crown." It is altogether possible that the speech derived, perhaps indirectly, from Seneca's treatise.

[xii] *On Benefits,* in seven books. This is a discursive treatment, written intermittently, of what constitutes a benefit, how it should be conferred and how received, and of the nature of gratitude and ingratitude. Its informality gives this work a special attraction, and it may still be read for pleasure and edification.

[C] The most attractive of Seneca's works for the general reader is doubtless the collection of

[xiii] *Letters to Lucilius,* 124 in number (of which eighteen are included in the present collection). Because they are generally shorter than the formal treatises and generally confine themselves to a single topic, they make an ideal bedside book, which can be read or browsed as the spirit moves. The subjects include not only philosophic themes (generally treated with greater conciseness than in the "Dialogues") but such personal experiences as journeys, bouts of illness, visits to circuses and seaside resorts, and the like. Few Roman writings transport readers to the Roman scene so effectively. But the homiletic tone persists throughout. The letters read, in fact, like the midweek chats of a skillful and alert modernist preacher. In his relaxed mood, especially in the earlier letters, Seneca can so far abate his Stoicism as to include, with high approbation, choice tidbits from the Epicurean school.

[D] The orderly grandeur of astronomical phenomena seemed to the Stoics a most immediate proof of the direction of the universe by a rational and powerful providence, and hence study of celestial and other natural phenomena was an essential part of their program. Seneca repeatedly recommends it, not only as a means for assimilating man's reason to the great directing reason from which it derives, but also as an ethical exercise. Stargazing gives a sense of proportion; as Seneca's admirer Emerson said, its moral is, "Why so hot, little man?" The connection between ethics and celestial phenomena is close because both are guided by an undifferentiated Nature. One of the advantages the soul will enjoy upon its release from the body is nearer association with the stars. To matters of this sort Seneca devoted his

[xiv] *Natural Questions.* The seven books, whose proper order is disputed, deal with thunder and lightning, snow, rain, and hail, earthquakes, comets, and like subjects. This book was not less influential than Seneca's other writings;

until Aristotle became known to the West, it was the accepted authority on cosmology. And though its "science" is antiquated and valuable only as a curiosity, the book is still interesting for its numerous sidelights and for its humanistic approach to a subject where humanism is usually at a discount.

[E] Quite different in content and manner from all the rest of Seneca's productions is the

[xv] *Apocolocyntosis,* a satire on the deification of the Emperor Claudius. The form is that of the Menippean Satire, that is, a mingling of prose and verse, like Boethius' *Consolation* or *Aucassin and Nicolette,* whose object was to communicate truth with a smile. The form may exculpate the questionable taste of the satire; it is indubitably funny.

[F] The other main division of Seneca's works are the

[xvi] Tragedies. There are nine: *Hercules Mad, Trojan Women, Phoenician Women* (fragmentary), *Medea, Phaedra, Oedipus, Agamemnon, Thyestes, Hercules on Oetaea* (probably expanded by another hand). A tenth play, included in one manuscript tradition, is the *Octavia;* it is quite in the Senecan manner, but deals with a contemporary historical subject and is generally considered to be another's. All of Seneca's plays are adaptations of Greek models, some of which are extant. They differ from the Greek in that their object seems to be to demonstrate the limits of intense passion rather than to examine questions of moral choice. But the plays are Stoic nevertheless, not only in detachable quotations and choral odes advocating the simple life or the Stoic rather than the oriental principle of kingship, but also in illustrating the disastrous effects of the various emotional "perturbations" which the Stoic aimed to suppress.

[G] Two other items are listed in the Senecan corpus: a number of rather trivial short poems, some amorous, and an exchange of correspondence between Seneca and St. Paul, which is certainly spurious but which the Latin Fathers regarded as genuine. Jerome, for example, says (*On Famous Men,* 12):

> Lucius Annaeus Seneca of Cordova . . . lived a most continent life. I should not be placing him in the catalogue of saints were I not impelled to do so by those widely read letters of Paul to Seneca and of Seneca to Paul. Though he was a minister and the most powerful personage of his day, he said that he would prefer to have among his own people the place which Paul had among Christians.

Just as misinterpretation of Vergil's Fourth Eclogue as a prophecy of the birth of Christ assured esteem of Vergil in the Middle Ages, so the supposed connection with St. Paul assured Seneca a place of honor.

It is always instructive to know what critics in a writer's own tradition thought of him. Suetonius (*Caligula* 53.2) records Caligula's disparaging remarks, uttered before Seneca had become politically important:

> Caligula used to say that Seneca, who was very popular just then, composed "mere school exercises," and that he was "sand without lime."

Similar judgments of later critics are reported in Aulus Gellius (12.2); the fullest statement is in the pedestrian but always sound Quintilian (10.1.125 ff.):

> I have deliberately postponed the discussion of Seneca . . . owing to the fact that there is a general, though false, impression that I condemn and even detest him. It is true that I had occasion to pass censure upon him when I was endeavoring to recall students from a de-

praved style, weakened by every kind of error, to a severer standard of taste. But at that time Seneca's works were in the hands of every young man, and my aim was not to ban his reading altogether but to prevent his being preferred to authors superior to himself but whom he was never tired of disparaging; for, being conscious of the fact that his own style was very different from theirs, he was afraid that he would fail to please those who admired them. . . . Seneca had many excellent qualities, a quick and fertile intelligence with great industry and wide knowledge, though as regards the last quality he was often led into error by those whom he had entrusted with the task of investigating certain subjects on his behalf. . . . If he had only despised all unnatural expressions and had not been so passionately fond of all that was incorrect, if he had not felt such affection for all that was his own and had not impaired the solidity of his matter by striving after epigrammatic brevity, he would have won the approval of the learned instead of the enthusiasm of boys. But even as it is, he deserves to be read by those whose powers have been formed and firmly molded on the standards of a severer taste, if only because he will exercise their critical faculties in distinguishing between his merits and his defects. For, as I have said, there is much in him which we may approve, much even that we may admire.

It must be remarked that Quintilian's strictures apply only to form; ancient critics are regularly and sometimes exasperatingly blind to content. Even so, it must be noted that it is not the manner which Seneca shares with other writers of Silver (or post-Augustan) Latin that is objected to, but the extremes to which he went. And since form is so essential to an appreciation of Seneca, a word of amplification may be in place.

5 · SILVER POINT

The most obtrusive characteristic of Seneca's writing, bound to strike the reader's notice on every page and, in our current antipathy to "elegant" writing, to arouse his distrust, is his propensity to rhetorical expression. Seneca uses every rhetorical device that Greek and Roman theorists had elaborated, but his special hallmark is what has been called the "pointed" style. This Professor Summers has defined as "a kind of writing which, without sacrificing clearness or conciseness, regularly avoids in thought or phrase or both, all that is obvious, direct, or natural, seeking to be ingenious rather than true, neat rather than beautiful, exercising the wit but not rousing the emotions or appealing to the judgement of the reader."[1] The Roman development is paralleled in other literatures; in English the full-blooded genius of the Elizabethans was succeeded by the conceits of Donne and Cowley, which led in their turn to the more intellectualized epigrammatic style of Dryden and Pope. Pope's Homer is un-Homeric because of Pope's predilection for the pointed style. Lines like "Be still yourselves and Hector asks no more," "Achilles absent was Achilles still," "In all my equal but in misery," might have come straight out of Seneca.

But the genius of the Latin language and of Seneca's age make the pointed style less artificial, or at least more appropriate, to first-century Rome. Several factors are involved. In the first place, no language falls so naturally into *sententiae;* its brevity gives apothegms, antitheses, paradoxes, a crystalline conciseness, and the facets of the jewel receive an easy glitter from the natural alliterations and homoioteleuta of the language. *Sententiae* occur in ev-

[1] W. C. Summers, *Select Letters of Seneca* (London, 1910), p. xv.

ery Latin author from Livius Andronicus onward, mainly
as decorations; in the first century they became central, because censorship actual or tacit stifled matter and the writer
perforce concentrated on form. Earlier writers were mainly
sober men concerned with inculcating Roman virtues and
Roman pride; Silver Age writers were mainly belletrists
who eschewed dangerous thoughts. When other avenues
of achievement were blocked, literature became fashionable
and elegance and art usurped the place of vigor and independence in literature as in life. Style was of the essence,
and style meant highly polished rhetorical jewels intended
to pre-empt attention from the fabrics they might legitimately have set off.

The appeal of Latin literature had always been to the
cultivated few; the Latin author could address himself only
to readers with sufficient education to appreciate alien
forms and grasp allusions to an alien history and mythology.
Artificiality was encouraged and heightened by the doctrines of the rhetorical schools. Connected with the standards of excellence propagated by the schools was a social
institution which did much to give Silver literature its peculiar character—the practice of giving public readings or
recitationes. Writers had always listened to and criticized
each other's work, and among the Greeks, at least, readings
were recognized as a form of publication. But in first-
century Rome the recitation became a fashionable mania
and was the only means of obtaining a public hearing.
With crowded calendars and keen rivalries, it was natural
that each performer should strive for the most numerous
rounds of applause. It was "point" that would bring the
house down, and literature came to be studded with points
calculated to elicit applause even when it was not intended
for oral delivery. Whole paragraphs in Seneca are conglom-
erates of disparate *sententiae*. Line-for-line dialogue in his
tragedies is often a game of batting apothegms back and

forth, and the reader finds his head oscillating from one player to the other as at a game of Ping-pong.

It has not been the object of these paragraphs to make the reader like Seneca's manner but rather to minimize the distaste which that manner is likely to provoke. Where writers are self-conscious, literature has its own rules, like football or chess, and we cannot play or follow the game unless we are aware of and give tentative acceptance to the rules. We now turn to what should chiefly concern us, the "what" rather than the "how" of Seneca's writings.

6. STOICISM

It is his propagation of Stoicism, which a respectable body of opinion regards as the principal achievement of the Hellenistic Age, that gives Seneca his importance, and if Stoicism were a metaphysical system whose validity did not depend on the circumstances of an age or the eloquence of an expositor, Seneca's peculiarities of style or character would be irrelevant. But though Stoicism equipped itself with a logic and a cosmology, like rival schools, the impelling motive out of which it was originated and perpetuated through several centuries was not so much philosophical as evangelical. Its program was at all times more important than the scaffolding of logic and physics erected to support it, and could adapt itself to changing conditions as a metaphysics could not. Its original intention was nothing less than to revolutionize the political organization of the known world, but when its unworldly perfectionism and the intransigence of practical politics made revolutionary change impossible, the Stoic teachers were willing to abate its perfectionism and to seek, by a gradualistic approach, to implement as much of the program as was possible, eventually to content themselves with propagating a Stoic attitude or even maintaining it in their own lives.

But the fact that an ideal has been modified need not mean that it has been wholly frustrated. The design for the Augustan principate was shaped by Stoic theory, and though the imperial implementation of the theory may seem as perverse as the implementation of Marxism in the Comintern, yet enough of the Stoic spirit survived ultimately to spread Roman citizenship and the equality of Roman law over the whole empire. Even today "Stoic" comes nearer being a common adjective than "Platonic" or "Aristotelian," and though its meaning is vestigial and distorted (a man is Stoic if he resigns himself to the dentist's drill) it is not so distorted as the meaning of "Platonic."

For the term Stoic to have any precision, therefore, we need to be told whether the Early, Middle, or Late Stoa is intended, and to understand the movement at all, as to understand any gospel, we should know the circumstances out of which it originated, and especially what it found in the existing order that impelled to opposition or reform. Stoicism, then, was called into being when the political revolution effected by Alexander the Great stripped the individual of the insulated shelter of his little city-state and forced him to come to terms with and find a place in an enormously expanded polity. The city-state had absorbed all his energy and all his loyalty and was the channel for his self-expression and his relations with the rest of the world. Not individuals but types are the subject of the literature and the plastic art of the classical period; now, paradoxically in view of the sudden crowding of his world, his idiosyncrasies, physical and mental, come to be studied, and means are sought for reconciling the claims of his individuality with the demands of his overwhelmingly enlarged environment.

To redress the imbalance between little man and huge world, to restore dignity to the little man, one of two paths could be taken; either man could be made more important or the world less important. The first was, in effect, the technique of Stoicism, the second of Epicureanism, which arose to confront the same problem at the same time. The Epicureans rested their ethics on a thoroughgoing materialism. The world and all in it is composed of void, fortuitous concatenations of atoms, and nothing else. There is no design, no providence, no sanction external to man. Gods exist, but they too are made of chance atoms and have no concern whatever with man; they would not be gods if they were burdened with surveillance over man. Death is merely dispersion of atoms and so final. Man is therefore his own sole guide to a satisfactory life, and should pursue his own pleasure, which is defined as freedom from pain, but must not become so involved in pleasure or any other activity as to interfere with his *ataraxy*, or unruffledness. "Eat, drink, and be merry, for tomorrow you may die" is really a travesty of Epicureanism; the revels in the Garden seem mainly to have centered on mathematics, which can be pursued without emotional involvement and entail no hang-over. The uncompromising independence of Epicureanism naturally provoked all believers in authority, including the Stoics.

The Stoic universe was as precisely ordered as the Epicurean was anarchic. Nature is the guiding principle, but, as we shall see, nature is synonomous with god (Spinoza regularly said *deus sive natura*); and the most familiar of the Stoic precepts is that enjoining "life in accordance with nature." To understand the range of meanings implied in this prescription we must glance at part of its background. The Sophists, perhaps following a suggestion of the Hippocratic medical men, used the concept of nature (*physis*), as opposed to convention (*nomos*), as a basis for questioning all traditional institutions. In nature there are no distinctions among men: noble or commoner, Hellene or barbarian, function alike physically and so must belong to the same species, and distinctions between them, like other social traditions, are matters of convention. The conventions

were doubtless expedient when established, but, unlike nature, they are susceptible to change and indeed should be
changed if re-examination shows they are no longer expedient. Man is the measure.

Upon the basis of this distinction the Cynics carried their
flouting of convention to the extreme: Diogenes, as the
stories tell, showed no deference to Alexander's exalted
position nor to the requirements of conventional decency
(which is why he was called *Cynic,* or "Doggish"). When
he was asked to what city he belonged he answered that
he was a citizen of the world (*cosmopolites*), implying that
he rejected the cherished superiority of Athens or Corinth
as being without basis in nature. Diogenes may have acted
out of doggish surliness; his well-born disciple Crates gave
up riches and family, and took scrip and staff to preach
the brotherhood of the simple life out of love. And Crates
was the teacher of Zeno.

It was Zeno who gave form to the vision of a world which
should be a single *oikoumene* "in which all men should be
members one of another, citizens of one state without distinction of race or institutions, subject only to and in harmony with a common law immanent in the universe, and
united in one social life not by compulsion but only by
their own willing consent, or (as he put it) by Love"
(W. W. Tarn, *Alexander the Great* 147 f.). The vision, at
least, persisted to the end of Stoicism. Marcus Aurelius, ad-
dressing himself, says, "I say 'dear city of Cecrops' (Athens); shall I not say 'dear city of Zeus'?" The stages by
which a doctrine proclaimed to the world was reduced to
an exhortation of a contemplative emperor to himself may
be marked by the declining effectiveness of efforts to give
the doctrine practical realization. It came nearest to being
realized in Zeno's own age by Alexander's conscious efforts
to unify his world. At the end of the third century B.C.
we read of a gallant social revolution in Sparta, where the
teacher of the reforming kings Agis and Cleomenes was

Zeno's disciple Sphairos of Borysthenes. At the end of the second century the Gracchi in Rome attempted similar reforms; their teacher was the Stoic Blossius of Cumae.

Natura, or *physis*, means more than our "nature," and living according to it more than leading an unpretentious life. Both words are derived from verbs (*phyein*, *nascor*) which signify "to be born," "to burgeon," and imply a realization of a potential. "Life according to nature" is not merely a life stripped of non-essentials but one which strives toward consummation. The peculiar potentiality of man as distinct from the rest of natural creation is reason, which subsumes all the traditional virtues; a man can be brave and continent and just only if he understands the folly of their opposites. Man's goal is therefore the achievement of perfect reason, but nothing less than perfection will do; a miss is as good as a mile, a man is drowned whether he is submerged in three inches of water or three fathoms. The goods men commonly value are classed as things indifferent; no matter if he possesses none of them and his work is menial, the sage is a king and perfectly happy, and the actual king is not happy, unless he is a sage, no matter how much he possesses. Place and possessions are external to man and do not affect his true self.

In the absolute scale of good, then, the king is not privileged, the pauper under no disabilities. Both are equally important in the scheme of nature, which has assigned a necessary role to each. The figure of the stage role is invoked repeatedly. Each man must play out to the best of his ability the role assigned him; he is as worthy a performer if he plays a slave well as if he had played a king well, and neither role affects his inward self. Or, each man is given a number of counters with which to play; more counters might enable him to win, but playing well, not winning, is the object, and he can play well with few or with many. Essential in every man's role is obedience to the naturally ordained overseers of the grand plan; in other words, the Stoic is bound to do his duty to the state. It was this aspect of Stoicism which made it sympathetic to Rome, even to such Romans as Cicero, who objected to its impractical perfectionism; on the other hand, emperors inclined to absolutism chafed at the Stoic concept of king as minister rather than master, and sometimes began their reigns by expelling the "philosophers."

Like Epicureanism, then, Stoicism sought to give man self-sufficient freedom, but the Stoic achieved his freedom not by rejecting the divine but by identifying himself with it. This is the source of his patience under suffering. The body itself is a mere encumbrance to the divine part of him, and therefore also a thing indifferent. Under a benevolent providence all that happens must be good for the whole; since the sufferer's body is part of the whole, the pain that afflicts it must be good for him. The leg or tooth that hurts is not really or merely his own. Nor, if he is to cultivate reason, must he allow emotions, not only fear and envy and vengefulness but even love and grief for loved ones, to impinge upon his soul. This is Stoic *apathy*, which means not listlessness but imperviousness to perturbations. A man must keep his soul free, and cleaving to reason will help him do so; but when he has done all that a man can for the ideal, when his pains are intolerable and hopeless, the door is always open and he is invited to step out of life. With this alternative always available, a man can never be enslaved.

These ethical principles are what mainly concern Seneca, but he also makes reference to the other divisions of the philosophy, logic and physics, and to its leading teachers. To make these references intelligible we shall take a brief survey of teachers and doctrines. After Zeno (300–263 B.C.) the heads of the Early Stoa were Cleanthes (the author of the most famous pagan hymn; 263–232 B.C.), Chrysippus (called the second founder; 232–207), Zeno of Tarsus and Diogenes the Babylonian (not the famous Cynic; together 207–150), and Antipater of Tarsus (150–129). The preponderance of men from the East is noticeable. The interesting point in their logic is their theory of the criterion. Sense impressions conveyed by objects (which, in opposition to Plato, they regarded as real) produce concepts which irresistibly force conviction upon the mind if they are true. Their physical theory was pantheistic materialism. The whole universe is an embodied spiritual force. Its active portion is the soul, a fiery ether which pervades the whole but has its principal seat in heaven, and the passive portion the inferior elements, mainly earth and water. The latter proceed from the former and are periodically reabsorbed into it in the world conflagration. The universe itself, as a perfect living creature, is rightly called god. The gods of popular religion represent different activities of the true god, and the foolish or immoral stories told about them are allegories intended to convey some moral truth.

The Middle Stoa is represented by Panaetius of Rhodes (185–109 B.C.) and his pupils Posidonius and Hecaton. Panaetius, who had many aristocratic Roman disciples, adapted the system to their practical requirements. He rejected the notion of the periodic world conflagration and the tenet that only the perfect sage could be happy, and stressed the active virtues of magnanimity and benevolence as against the passive virtues of fortitude and justice. Virtually all Romans of position were trained in the law, and to their practical minds it was absurd to make no distinction, as the perfectionism of the Early Stoa did not, between a felony and a misdemeanor. Hecaton further diminished the old perfectionism by suggesting desirable choices when there was an apparent conflict in duties. Posidonius (135–50 B.C.) was a polymath who has been judged to be second only to Aristotle in the influence he exerted in many fields, especially in political theory. It was he, apparently, who definitely equated Roman imperialism with the Stoic mission; all the world, accordingly, must welcome the rule of the empire, and the empire, for its part, must discharge its high obligation as the vicar of the divine.

In its final, or Roman, phase theoretical questions became purely academic and interest centered on ethics. Seneca, who is the outstanding Roman Stoic, illustrates this tendency, though he urged study of science and wrote the *Natural Questions*. In Epictetus and Marcus Aurelius (both of whom used Greek) theory recedes wholly into the background. Epictetus (A.D. 55–135), who was born a slave, at least preached Stoicism to the many; Marcus Aurelius (A.D. 121–180), who was born an emperor, applied it to his own comfort and guidance. After his time the school as such faded out, but its doctrines perceptibly influenced later Neoplatonism and some of the Church Fathers and became a substantial strand in the skein of European thought.

ON PROVIDENCE

WHY ANY MISFORTUNES BEFALL GOOD

MEN WHEN A PROVIDENCE EXISTS

Our manuscripts and editions normally give this treatise first place. There is no conclusive evidence to fix the date of its composition, and some editors place it at the beginning of Seneca's exile while others put it near the end of his life. It serves as an appropriate introduction in any case, for its opening summarizes the arguments for a belief in providence (which the Stoics equated with nature or god) and the remainder seeks to answer the objection which has disturbed adherents of all systems which posit a providence: Why, if god is all-powerful and all-good, do the righteous suffer? The answers given can also be paralleled in other systems. Evils are not punishment but paternal correctives. They are like exercise to the athlete or medicine to the sick. Good men accept them willingly, for they offer themselves freely to the decrees of eternal fate. Moreover, good men must serve as examples of strength and endurance to weaker members of society. Finally (and this, of course, is peculiar to Stoicism), if suffering is really intolerable and hopeless, man is given the liberty to end it by suicide. The Lucilius to whom the essay is addressed is a literary friend to whom Seneca also addressed the Letters and the Natural Questions.

[1] You have asked me, Lucilius, why it is that many evils befall good men if the world is governed by providence.

The answer could more conveniently be supplied in an organized treatise in the course of which we would demonstrate that providence rules all things and that god is concerned for our welfare. But since it is your pleasure to pluck one member from the whole and reconcile a single objection without impinging on the problem in its totality I shall acquiesce; the task is not difficult, for it is the gods' cause I shall be pleading.

For our present purpose it is superfluous to point out that so mighty a structure does not persist without some caretaker; that the concourse and dispersal of the heavenly bodies is not an effect of a fortuitous impulse; that whereas what chance sets into motion is without direction and is likely to run into collisions, the course which is guided by the rules of eternal law moves speedily and without running foul and carries with it the multitudes of objects on land and sea and of brilliant lights shining forth according to a fixed plan; that this orderliness is not a property of matter moving at random; and that fortuitous conglomerations cannot arrange their balance so skillfully that the earth, which is heaviest in weight, should abide unmoved and, as spectator, observe the rapid flight of the surrounding sky, how the seas are distilled into the valleys to soften the earth, how huge growths burgeon from tiny seeds. Even those phenomena which seem irregular and anarchic—I mean clouds and rain and the flashes of crashing thunder and flames shot up from riven mountain peaks and the tremors of quaking earth and the other manifestations of the turbulent workings of nature upon earth—even these phenomena do not happen without a plan, though their coming may be unexpected; they have their own causes, as do those phenomena whose incongruous location gives them an aspect of the miraculous, as, for example, hot springs in the midst of the waves or new stretches of island springing up in the vast ocean. Indeed, if a man observe how the shore is laid bare when the sea withdraws into

itself and is then flooded again in a short time, he might
suppose that it is some blind turbulence which causes the
waves at one time to contract with an inward motion and
at another to burst forth with a great rush to recover their
normal position. In point of fact, their growth is strictly allotted; at the appropriate day and hour they approach in
greater volume or less according as they are attracted by
the lunar orb, at whose sway the ocean wells up. But such
questions as these must be reserved for their proper occasion, especially since you are merely complaining of providence, not questioning its existence. I shall reconcile you
with the gods, who prove best to men who are best. Nature
never suffers the good to be harmed by the good; between
good men and the gods there subsists a friendship, with
virtue as its bond.

Did I say friendship? It is rather a kinship and a close
resemblance, for the only difference between the good man
and god is in the matter of time. Man is god's disciple and
emulator and true progeny, whom the glorious parent, who
insists upon virtue, educated very strictly, like a stern father. When you see men who are good and acceptable to
the gods toil and sweat and climb laboriously upward,
therefore, while the wicked run riot and luxuriate in wantonness, remember that in our sons it is modesty that
pleases, whereas pertness pleases us only in home-born
slaves; and that our sons we restrain by severe discipline,
whereas we encourage the slaves' sauciness. Be sure that
god's course is the same. He does not treat the good man
like a toy, but tries him, hardens him, and readies him for
himself.

[2] "Why do many misfortunes fall to the lot of good
men?" It is not possible that any evil can befall a good
man. Opposites cannot combine. Just as the influx of so
many streams and the downpour of so much rain and the
flavor of so many mineral springs do not change the tang
of the sea or even so much as dilute it, just so the assaults

of adversity do not affect the spirit of a stalwart man. He maintains his poise and assimilates all that falls to his lot to his own complexion, for he is more potent than the world without. I do not maintain that he is insensible to externals, but that he overcomes them; unperturbed and serene, he rises to meet every sally. All adversity he regards as exercise. Is not every upstanding man who is intent upon what is right eager for appropriate exertion and ready for service which involves danger? Does not any diligent man regard idleness as a punishment? In the case of athletes, whose concern is for physical strength, we observe that they employ very strong adversaries in their practice bouts and insist that their trainers use all their strength against them. They submit to blows and bruises, and if they cannot find individuals strong enough to match with them, they take on several at once. Without an antagonist prowess fades away. Its true proportions and capacities come to light only when action proves its endurance. You must know that good men should behave similarly; they must not shrink from hardship and difficulty or complain of fate; they should take whatever befalls in good part and turn it to advantage. The thing that matters is not what you bear but how you bear it.

Observe how differently fathers and mothers show their affection. Fathers make their children get up to attend to their tasks betimes; even on holidays they do not suffer them to be idle but drive them to sweat and sometimes to tears. Mothers want to cuddle them in their laps, keep them in the shade, never let them be disappointed or cry or work hard. God's attitude to good men is a father's; his love for them is a manly love. "Let them be harassed by toil and sorrow and loss," says he, "that so they may acquire true strength." Pampered bodies grow sluggish through sloth; not work but movement and their own weight exhausts them. Prosperity unbruised cannot endure a single blow, but a man who has been at constant feud with misfortunes acquires a skin calloused by suffering; he yields to no evil and even if he stumbles carries the fight on upon his knee.

Do you find it strange that god, who so loves good men that he wishes them to attain pre-eminent goodness, should allot them a fortune on which to exercise themselves? I myself do not find it strange that the gods are sometimes moved to enjoy the spectacle of great men wrestling with some disaster. It gives us pleasure, on occasion, when a young man of steadfast courage meets a wild beast's charge with his hunting spear or faces a rushing lion without flinching, and the spectacle is the more pleasing in the degree that the hero is a man of position. Yet those are not achievements to attract the attention of the gods but the childish amusements of human frivolity. But look you upon this spectacle worthy the attention of a god intent upon his own work, look you upon this bout worthy a god—a stalwart man matched with evil fortune, especially when the man takes the initiative. I cannot see, I declare, what fairer spectacle Jupiter could enjoy on earth, if he should wish to direct his attention there, than Cato still standing upright amidst his country's ruins after his party had repeatedly been crushed. "Though all the world has yielded to one man's sway," says he, "though Caesar's legions guard the dry land and his fleets the sea, though his soldiers beset the city gates, yet does Cato possess a way of egress; with a single hand he can open a wide path to freedom. This sword which has remained untainted and guiltless even in civil war shall at last perform a good and noble deed; it shall give Cato the freedom it could not give his country. Take up, my soul, the task you have long studied; deliver yourself from the world of men. Petreius and Juba have already run their race, and each lies slain by the hand of the other. That was a brave and noble compact with fate, but not seemly for my stature; for Cato it is as ignominious to beg death of anyone as it is life."

I am sure the gods looked on with great satisfaction when that man who was so uncompromising in maintaining his own freedom took measures to secure the safety of others and arranged the escape of those who were leaving, when he spent even his last night in study, when he thrust his sword into his hallowed bosom, when he pulled his vitals apart and with his own hand released that holy spirit which was too pure to be defiled by steel. That is why, I should suppose, the wound was badly aimed and ineffectual: for the immortal gods it was not enough to look on Cato but once; he was encored and kept on the stage to exhibit his character in a more demanding role, for it wants a loftier spirit to seek death a second time. How could the gods fail to be pleased when they viewed their charge making his way to freedom by so glorious and memorable a departure? Death hallows men whose mode of dying is praised even by those who dread it.

[3] As my discourse proceeds I shall show that what seem to be evils are not actually such. For the present, I will say so much of the eventualities which you style harsh, unfortunate, and detestable: in the first place, they benefit the individuals to whose lot they fall, and, in the second place, they benefit the whole body of mankind, for which the gods are more concerned than they are for individuals; next, good men receive these eventualities willingly, and deserve ill fortune if they do not; further, these things are destined, and befall good men by the same law that makes them good. And finally I shall persuade you never to commiserate a good man; he may be called unhappy, he cannot be unhappy.

Of all these propositions the most difficult, apparently, is the first in the list, that the objects of our dread and horror are actually advantageous to the persons to whose lot they fall. "Is it for the victim's advantage," you object, "to be driven into exile, to be reduced to poverty, to bury wife and children, to be branded with ignominy, to be made

a cipher?" If you find it strange that these things are bene-
ficial, you will find it no less strange that certain maladies
are treated by surgery and cautery and by hunger and
thirst as well. But if you reflect that for the sake of a cure
some persons have their bones scraped or removed, their
veins pulled out, or members whose presence would be
deleterious to the organism as a whole amputated, you will
also allow yourself to be convinced that certain misfortunes
work to the advantage of those whom they befall—precisely, by Hercules, as certain things which are praised and
sought after work to the disadvantage of those who delight
in them; overeating, drunkenness, and other indulgences,
for example, kill through giving pleasure. Among the many
magnificent sayings of our friend Demetrius is the following, which I have just heard; it still rings and reverberates
in my ears. "No one is more unhappy, in my judgment,"
says he, "than a man who has never met with adversity."
He has never had the privilege of testing himself. Everything has come easily to him according to his wish; yet
the gods' judgment of him has been unfavorable. He was
deemed unworthy of ever vanquishing Fortune, which
shuns any cowardly antagonist, as if to say, "Why should
I take on that kind of opponent? He will lay his arms down
at once, and I will not need to use my full strength against
him. A threatening gesture will rout him; he cannot face
my grim expression. I must look around for someone else
with whom to match my strength; I am ashamed to fight
a man who is ready to be beaten." A gladiator counts it
a disgrace to be matched with an inferior; he knows that
a victory devoid of danger is a victory devoid of glory. Fortune follows the same principle: she searches out stalwart
adversaries, and passes some by in disdain. It is the upstanding and inflexible that she challenges, for against them
she can exert all her force. She tries Mucius by fire, Fabricius by poverty, Rutilius by exile, Regulus by torture,

Socrates by poison, Cato by death. Only misfortune can reveal such outstanding models.

Is Mucius unfortunate because he grasped the enemy's fire with his right hand and himself exacted punishment for his own mistake? Because the hand burned routed the king whom his hand armed could not? Would he have been more fortunate, then, if he had been coddling his hand in his mistress' bosom? Is Fabricius unfortunate because he tilled his own field when he was not engaged in affairs of state? Because he waged war alike against Pyrrhus and against riches? Because, though an old man with a triumph to his credit, he dined by his own fireside upon roots and herbs he himself plucked as he cleared his field? Would he have been more fortunate, then, if he had gorged his belly with fish from a distant shore and fowl imported from abroad? If he had stimulated his jaded and cloyed appetite with sea food from the upper and lower seas? If he had been served prime game, taken at the cost of many hunters' lives, garnished with heaps of fruit? Is Rutilius unfortunate because those who condemned him will have to defend themselves before all posterity? Because he was more indifferent to losing his country than to losing his exile? Because he was the only man to say no to the dictator Sulla, and when he was invited to return all but drew back and went to deeper exile? "That," says he, "is the business of those whom your Happy Reign has caught at Rome. It is for them to look upon the Forum drenched with blood and the heads of senators above the pool of Servilius (it was there that the victims of Sulla's proscriptions were stripped) and bands of assassins roaming through the city, and many thousands of Roman citizens massacred in a single spot after they had received a pledge, indeed by means of that pledge. Those are sights for men who cannot go into exile." Is Sulla happy, then, because his way down to the Forum is cleared by the sword, because he has the hardihood to inspect the heads of consulars which are exhibited to him and pays out blood money from the public exchequer through the treasurer? All these things Sulla did, Sulla who passed the Cornelian Law!

We come now to Regulus. How did Fortune harm him when she made him a model of loyalty, a model of endurance? Nails pierce his skin, and wherever he leans his tormented frame he inflicts a wound; his eyes stare open, forever sleepless. But the greater the torment, the greater shall the glory be. Would you learn how little he regrets the price he set upon virtue? Make him whole again and send him back to the senate: he will urge the same course. Would you count Maecenas more fortunate because, when he was lovesick and bewailing the repulses of his disagreeable wife, he wooed slumber through the strains of music sounding softly in the distance? Though he drug himself with strong wine and divert himself with the rippling of water and beguile his distraught mind with a thousand delights, he will be as sleepless on his bed of down as Regulus upon his cross. But Regulus has consolation: the hardship he endures is for honor's sake, and he looks away from his suffering to its cause; whereas Maecenas, enervated by pleasure and sick with excess of prosperity, suffers greater torment from the cause of his suffering than from the actual suffering. Vice has not taken such complete possession of the human race as to leave any doubt that, if men could choose their destiny, more would prefer to be born a Regulus than a Maecenas. Or if anyone should have the effrontery to declare that he would rather be born a Maecenas than a Regulus, that same man, though he might not admit it, actually prefers to be born a Terentia.

Do you judge that Socrates was badly used because he drained that potion the state compounded as though it were a specific for immortality and discoursed on death until death came? Was he badly dealt with because his blood cooled and, as the chill gradually spread, the pulsing of his veins stopped? How much more enviable is he than are they who are served in jeweled cups, whose drink some catamite trained to every abuse, a creature unsexed or sexless, dilutes with snow dropped from a golden vessel! Such men will measure back in vomit all they have drunk, with the sour taste of their own bile, whereas Socrates quaffs his poison willingly and cheerfully.

Touching Cato, enough has been said; general consensus acknowledges that Nature's choice for her formidable sparring has attained the pinnacle of happiness. "The enmity of men in power is a serious handicap," says Nature. "Cato must face Pompey, Caesar, and Crassus simultaneously. It is a hard thing to be defeated for office by an inferior: Cato must run second to Vatinius. It is a hard thing to be involved in civil war: Cato shall fight for the good cause the whole world over, with as ill success as perseverance. It is a hard thing to do violence to oneself: Cato shall do so. What shall I gain by all this? All men shall know that these things of which I deem Cato worthy are not evils."

[4] Prosperity can come to the vulgar and to ordinary talents, but to triumph over the disasters and terrors of mortal life is the privilege of the great man. To be lucky always and to pass through life without gnawing of the mind is to be ignorant of the half of nature. You are a great man, but how can I know, if Fortune has never given you a chance to display your prowess? You have entered the Olympic games but have no rival; you gain the crown but not the victory. I felicitate you, not as a brave man, but as one who has obtained a consulship or praetorship; your dignity is enhanced. I can say the same of a good man whom no difficult conjuncture has afforded an occasion for displaying the force of his mind. "I account you unfortunate because you have never been unfortunate. You have passed through life without an adversary; no one can know your potentiality, not even you." For self-knowledge, testing is necessary; no one can discover what he can do

except by trying. That is why some men have voluntarily exposed themselves to misfortune when it was reluctant, and have sought an opportunity for their prowess, which would otherwise pass into obscurity, to shine forth. Great men, I insist, sometimes rejoice in adversity precisely as brave soldiers rejoice in war. I once heard Triumphus, a gladiator in the days of Caligula, complain of the scarcity of performances. "It was fine in the old days," he said.

Prowess is avid for danger and thinks rather of the goal than of its trials, for these too are part of glory. Soldiers glory in their wounds and gladly vaunt themselves over the blood they were privileged to shed; though those who returned from the fray unhurt may have fought as well, the man who brings back a wound is more respected. To those men he desires shall achieve the highest excellence, god shows his favor whenever he affords them a field for spirited and courageous action, and for this some particular exertion is requisite. You assay a pilot in a storm, a soldier in the battle line. How can I know with what spirit you would confront poverty if you are running over with riches? How can I know with what constancy you will confront disgrace, dishonor, and public contumely if you reach old age amidst acclamations, if you are always attended by an inexpugnable popularity which gravitates in your direction by general inclination? How do I know how serenely you would endure bereavement when all the children you have raised are present to your sight? I have heard you offering condolences to others; I might have glimpsed your true character if you had been consoling yourself, if you had been bidding yourself not to grieve.

Do not, I beseech you, dread the things which the immortal gods apply to our souls like goads; disaster is virtue's opportunity. Those whom an excess of prosperity has rendered sluggish may justly be called unfortunate; a dead calm holds them fast, as it were, on a motionless sea, and whatever befalls them comes as a surprise. Cruelty presses hardest on the inexperienced; the tender neck chafes at the yoke. The recruit pales at the thought of a wound; the veteran can look at his flowing gash with composure, for he knows that he has often won the victory after losing blood. So god hardens and scrutinizes and exercises those he approves and loves; but those he appears to indulge and spare he is only keeping tender for disasters to come. If you suppose that anyone is immune you are mistaken. The man who has long prospered will get his share one day; the man you thought discharged has only been reprieved. Why does god afflict every good man with sickness or grief or other misfortune? Because in the army, too, the most hazardous duties are assigned to the bravest soldiers. It is only the picked men that the general sends to surprise the enemy by a night attack, to reconnoiter the road, or to dislodge a garrison. And no man in such a detachment will say, "The general has treated me badly," but rather, "The general thinks well of me." Similarly, those told off to undergo what cowards and weaklings would weep over should say, "God has judged us fit subjects to try how much human nature can endure."

Avoid luxury, avoid debilitating prosperity which makes men's minds soggy and which, unless something intervenes to remind them of the human condition, renders them comatose as in unending inebriation. If a man has always been protected from the wind by glass windows, if his feet have been kept warm by constant relays of poultices, if the temperature of his dining room has been maintained by hot air circulating under the floor and through the walls, he will be dangerously susceptible to a slight breeze. All excesses are injurious, but immoderate prosperity is the most dangerous of all. It affects the brain, it conjures empty fantasies up in the mind, and it befogs the distinction between true and false with a confusing cloud. Is it not better to endure everlasting misfortune, with virtue's help, than to burst with endless and immoderate prosperity? Death by starvation comes gently, gluttony makes men explode.

In the case of good men, accordingly, the gods follow the plan that teachers follow with their pupils: they demand more effort from those in whom they have confident expectations. Can you imagine that the Lacedaemonians hate their children because they try their mettle by public flogging? Their own fathers urge them to bear up under the scourge and, when they are mangled and half dead, beg them to persevere and offer their wounds for further wounding. What wonder, then, if god tries noble spirits with sternness? The demonstration of courage can never be gentle. Fortune scourges and rends us: we must endure it. It is not cruelty but a contest, and the oftener we submit to it the braver shall we be. The most robust part of the body is that which is most frequently put to active use. We must offer ourselves to Fortune so that we may be inured against her through her own agency; gradually she will make us her peers, and constant exposure to peril will beget contempt for danger. So sailors' bodies are hardened by enduring the sea, and farmers have calloused hands, and soldiers' biceps are powerful for hurling missiles, and runners have nimble legs; the member each exercises is the most robust. By suffering misfortune the mind grows able to belittle suffering.

You will realize how effective this can be in our case if you observe how profitable labor is to naked tribes whom poverty makes rugged. Consider all the nations beyond the bounds of the Roman peace—I mean the Germans and the nomad tribes that infest the Danube. Endless winter and dismal skies weigh them down and the barren earth grudges them food. They keep the rain off with thatch or leaves, they bound over marshes hardened into ice, they hunt wild animals for their food. Do you think them wretched? There is no wretchedness where habit has restored men to nature; what they begin out of necessity gradually becomes a pleasure. They have no homes and no lodgings except those which weariness appoints for the day. Their victuals are vile and must be obtained by their own hands, their brooding climate is repulsive, their bodies uncovered. What you regard as disastrous is the daily life of many races. Why do you wonder that good men are shaken to make them strong? No tree stands firm and sturdy if it is not buffeted by constant wind; the very stresses cause it to stiffen and fix its roots firmly. Trees that have grown in a sunny vale are fragile. It is therefore to the advantage of good men, and it enables them to live without fear, to be on terms of intimacy with danger and to bear with serenity a fortune that is ill only to him who bears it ill.

[5] Consider further that it is to the common interest for the best men to be soldiers, so to speak, and do our service. It is god's purpose, and the sage's as well, to show that what the crowd desires or fears is neither good nor evil; things will evidently be good if god bestows them upon none but good men, and evil if he inflicts them only upon evil men. Blindness would be execrable if no one lost his eyes except the man who deserved to have them gouged out. That is why Appius and Metellus must be deprived of light. Riches are not a good; that is why the pimp Elius must have riches, so that men who sanctify money in temples may see that it is in the brothel also. God can discredit the objects of our concupiscence in no more effective way than by bestowing them upon vile characters and withholding them from the best. "But," you object, "it is unfair for a good man to become invalid or be pierced or fettered while rogues mince about carefree and dainty and in sound health." Why so? Is it not unfair for brave men to take up arms and spend their nights in camp and stand guard before the rampart with bandaged wounds while perverts and professional profligates loll at ease in the city? Why so? Is it not unfair for the noblest of our maidens to be aroused before daylight to perform the Vestal rites while tainted women enjoy sound sleep? The best men are con-

scripts of toil. Frequently the senate is in session the live-
long day while nobodies are taking their pleasure in the
sporting field or lurking in some tavern or passing their
time with cronies.

The same thing happens in the commonwealth of the
world. Good men toil, spend and are spent, and willingly;
they are not dragged along by Fortune but follow her and
keep in step. If they knew how, they would have out-
stripped her. Here is another spirited utterance of that
stalwart Demetrius which I remember hearing: "This one
complaint I can make of you, immortal gods," said he, "you
did not make your will known to me sooner, for I would
then myself have long ago reached the state to which I
am now called. Do you wish to take my children? It was
for you I reared them. Do you want some part of my body?
Take it; it is no great boon I grant, for soon I shall leave
the whole of it. Do you want the breath of my life? Why
not? I shall not balk at your taking back what you have
given. Whatever you ask you shall obtain from a willing
giver. What then is my complaint? I should have preferred
to offer rather than to surrender. What need was there for
you to take it when I would have handed it to you? But
even now you will not really be taking it, for nothing can
be wrested from a man if he does not cling to it."

I am not under duress, I do not submit against my will,
I am not god's slave but his follower, and the more willingly because I know that all things proceed according to
a law that is fixed and eternally valid. Fate directs us, and
the first hour of our birth determines each man's span.
Cause is linked with cause, and a long chain of events governs all matters public and private. Everything must therefore be borne with fortitude, because events do not, as we
suppose, happen but arrive by appointment. What would
make you rejoice and what would make you weep was determined long ago, and though individual lives seem to differ in a wide range, the sum amounts to the same thing:

FATE

what we receive is perishable and we shall ourselves perish. Why then are we indignant? Why do we complain? It is for this we were born. Nature may use her own bodies as she will; we must be cheerful and steadfast whatever befalls, in the thought that nothing that is ours is lost.

NB

What is the duty of the good man? To offer himself to Fate. It is a great consolation that our rapid course is one with the universe's. Whatever it is that has ordained the mode of our life and the mode of our death has bound the gods, too, by the same necessity. The course that carries human affairs and divine alike is irrevocable. The very founder and ruler of all things has prescribed the fates indeed, but he follows them; he obeys always, he commanded but once. "Yet why was god so unfair in distributing destinies as to allot good men poverty and wounds and painful death?" The artisan cannot transform his material; such is its nature. Certain elements cannot be separated from others; they cohere and are indivisible. Languid constitutions that are prone to sleep or to a wakefulness indistinguishable from sleep are compounded of sluggish elements; it requires more vigorous endowment to produce a man who merits careful study. His path will not be level, he must go uphill and down, he must be wave-tossed and steer his craft through troubled waters, he must maintain his course in the face of Fortune. Much that is hard and rough will befall him, but he will himself soften it and smooth it down. Gold is tried by fire, brave men by misfortune. See how high virtue must mount: you will realize the perils that beset the ascent.

Steep is the way at first, and the steeds in their morning freshness
Must strain for the climb. The crest is heaven's center.
Thence to look down upon lands and sea has often terrified even me,
And my bosom has quaked with panic.

Sheer downward is the last stretch, and wants a firm
    rein.
Even Tethys who spreads her waves for my descent
Will often fear for my headlong fall.[1]

When he had heard this plea the spirited young man
said: "I like the road and shall climb it. It is worth a fall
to travel through those regions." Phoebus persisted in his
attempt to cow Phaethon's bold spirit with terrors:

Even if you hold your course and are not pulled astray
Yet must you go through the fierce horns of the Bull,
Through the Archer's bow, the maw of raging Leo.[2]

Whereupon Phaethon said: "Harness the chariot you promised. The adventures you suppose will frighten me prick
me on. I want to stand where Sun himself trembles." To
stick to safety is the part of the puny and the spiritless;
virtue marches on high.

[6] "Yet why does god allow evil to happen to good
men?" But in fact he does not. From good men he keeps
every evil away—sin and crime and wicked thoughts and
greedy schemes and blind lust and avarice which covets
another's property. The good man himself, god protects
and defends; should anyone expect that god will look after
the good man's baggage also? Good men release god from
this care, for they themselves despise externals. Democritus
cast his riches away in the belief that they were a burden
to a good mind. Then why should you wonder that god
allows a good man to light upon a lot which a good man
would sometimes himself choose to light upon? Good men
lose their sons: why not, when they sometimes leave their
country of their own accord never to return? They are slain:
why not, when they sometimes lay hands upon themselves?

[1] Ovid, *Metamorphoses* 2.63–69. This is the story of Phaethon,
whom his father Phoebus is here attempting to dissuade from
driving the chariot of the Sun.
[2] Ovid, *Metamorphoses* 2.79–81.

to
serve
as
models

> Why do they suffer certain hardships? To teach others to endure them; they were born to serve as models.

Imagine that god speaks as follows: "What grounds do you have to complain of me, you who have opted for righteousness? Other men I have surrounded with spurious goods, I have beguiled their empty minds, as it were, with a long and deceptive dream. I have adorned them with gold and silver and ivory, but there is nothing good inside. The men you look upon as happy, if you could see not their outward appearance but their inward nature, are wretched, squalid, mean, well groomed on the surface, like their own house walls; that is no solid and genuine happiness but only a veneer, and a thin one. And so, as long as they can keep their feet and give the impression they desire, they glitter and carry it off; but when something happens to set them awry and uncover them, then one can see what a mass of genuine foulness their adventitious glitter concealed. But to you I have given goods that are sure and abiding, goods which are better and greater the more one turns them about and scrutinizes them from every side. To you I have granted scorn of terrors and disdain of passions. You do not shine outwardly because all your goods are turned inward. So does our world scorn what lies without and rejoice in the contemplation of itself. Your whole good I have bestowed within yourselves: your good fortune is not to need good fortune.

"'But,' you object, 'many things which are sad and dreadful and hard to bear do happen.' Because I could not make you evade their assault, I have given your minds armor to withstand them; bear them with fortitude. In this respect you can surpass god: he is exempt from enduring evil, you rise superior to it. Scorn poverty: no one is as poor as he was at birth. Scorn pain: either it will go away or you will. Scorn death: either it finishes you or it transforms you. Scorn Fortune: I have given her no weapon with which to strike your soul. Above all, I have taken pains that noth-

ing should detain you against your will: the way out lies
open. If you do not wish to fight you may escape. Of all
the things which I deemed necessary for you, therefore, I
have made none easier than dying. The soul I have placed
on a downgrade, where it is pulled by gravity: only observe and you will see what a short and direct road leads
to freedom. I have imposed no such long delays at your
egress as at your entry. Otherwise, if a man were as slow
in dying as he is in being born, Fortune would have enormous power over you. Let every occasion and every situation teach you how easy it is to renounce Nature and
throw her gift in her face. At the very altars and the solemn
rites of sacrifice, even as you pray for life, study death.
Massive bulls fall by a paltry wound, and the blow of a
man's hand fells powerful animals. A thin blade severs the
joints of the neck, and when the articulation of head and
neck is cut the whole mass collapses. The seat of life is not
buried at a great depth and need not be rooted out with
steel, the vitals need not be searched out with deep wounds;
death is near at hand. For the lethal blow I have appointed
no specific spot; whatever way you choose will serve. The
process called dying, whereby the soul departs from the
body, is so short that its passing is imperceptible. Whether
the noose strangles the throat, or water suffocates the
breath, or the hard ground which breaks the fall crushes
the skull, or fire sucked in blocks respiration—whatever the
means, it is swift. Do you not blush at fearing so long a
thing that happens so quickly?"

ON THE SHORTNESS
OF LIFE

The Paulinus to whom this essay is addressed held the ex-
tremely important position of supervisor of Rome's grain
supply; the probable date of its composition is A.D. *48–50.*
The theme is the great cost in time of futile occupations
and meaningless social duties, particularly degrading and
thankless attendance upon the rich. With this Seneca con-
trasts the delightful and profitable intercourse which any
man who can read may enjoy at any time with the choice
spirits of the past. But one may question Seneca's honesty
as Stoic and statesman when he suggests that philosophic
contemplation is a worthier employment than the useful
task which Paulinus was performing for the service of the
state.

[1] It is a general complaint among mankind, Paulinus,
that Nature is niggardly: our allotted span is brief, and
the term granted us flies by with such dizzy speed that
all but a few exhaust it just when they are beginning to
live. And it is not only the unthinking masses who bemoan
what they consider the universal evil: the same sentiment
has evoked complaints even from men of distinction. Hence
the cry of that prince of physicians (Hippocrates), "Life
is short, art long." Hence Aristotle's grievance against Nature—an incongruous position for a philosopher: Nature has
been so lavish to animals that they vegetate for five or ten

human spans, whereas man, with his capacity for numerous and great achievements, is limited by so much shorter a tether.

It is not that we have so little time but that we lose so much. Life is long enough and our allotted portion generous enough for our most ambitious projects if we invest it all carefully. But when it is squandered through luxury and indifference, and spent for no good end, we realize it has gone, under the pressure of the ultimate necessity, before we were aware it was going. So it is: the life we receive is not short but we make it so; we are not ill provided but use what we have wastefully. Kingly riches are dissipated in an instant if they fall into the hands of a bad master, but even moderate wealth increases with use in the hands of a careful steward; just so does our life provide ample scope if it is well managed.

[2] Why do we complain of Nature? She has behaved handsomely; life, if you know how to use it, is long. One man is possessed by an insatiable avarice, another by assiduous application to trifling enterprises. One man is sodden with wine, another benumbed by sloth. One man is exhausted by an ambition which always depends on the votes of others, another is driven over every land and sea by the trader's urge to seek profit. Some are plagued by a passion for soldiering, and are incessantly bent upon threatening others or anxious about others' threats. Some are worn out by self-imposed and unrequited attendance upon the great; many busy themselves with the pursuit of other men's estates or in complaints about their own. Some follow no plan consistently but are precipitated into one new scheme after another by a fickleness which is rambling and unstable and dissatisfied with itself; some have no objective at all at which to aim but are overtaken by fate as they gape and yawn. I cannot, therefore, question the truth of the great poet's dictum, uttered with oracular impres-

siveness: "Slight is the portion of life we live." All the residue is not living but passing time.

On all sides we are surrounded and beset by vices, and these do not permit us to rise and lift our eyes to the discernment of truth but submerge us and hold us chained down to lust. The prisoners are never allowed to return to their true selves; if they are ever so lucky as to win some respite they continue to roll, as the sea swells even after the storm is over, and secure no release from their lusts. Do you suppose I am referring to wretches whose failings are acknowledged? Look at the men whose felicity is the cynosure of all eyes; they are smothered by their prosperity. How many have found riches a bane! How many have paid with blood for their eloquence and their daily straining to display their talent! How many are sallow from constant indulgence! How many are deprived of liberty by a besieging mob of clients! Run through the whole list from top to bottom: this man wants a friend at court, that man serves his turn; this man is the defendant, that man his lawyer, and the other the judge: but no one presses his claim to himself, everyone is used up for the sake of someone else. Investigate the personages whose names are household words and you will find they can be classified by the following criteria: A is B's sycophant and B is C's; no one shows solicitude for himself. And then some of them give vent to the most irrational indignation: they complain of their superiors' snobbery, because they were too busy to receive them when they wanted to call. Dare a man complain of another's pride when he is too busy to receive himself? The nabob has after all sometime condescended to look at you, however offensive his expression, and has stepped down to listen to you, and has let you walk at his side; but you have never deigned to look in upon yourself or listen to yourself. You cannot debit anyone with those attentions of yours, because you showed them not out of a desire to commune with another but out of inability to commune with yourself.

[3] Though all the luminaries of the ages devoted their combined genius to this one theme, they could never satisfactorily expound this phenomenal fog that darkens men's minds. Men will never allow anyone to take possession of their estates, and at the slightest dispute on boundary lines they pick up stones and rush to arms; but they do allow others to trespass on their lives, and themselves introduce intruders who will eventually claim full possession. Nobody on earth is willing to distribute his money, but everybody shares out his life, and to all comers. Men are very strict in keeping their patrimony intact, but when it comes to squandering time they are most lavish of the one item where miserliness is respectable.

I should like to buttonhole one of the oldsters and say to him: "I see that you have reached the highest life expectancy and are now close to a century or more; please give us an itemized account of your years. Calculate how much of that span was subtracted by a creditor, a mistress, a patron, a client, quarreling with your wife, punishing your slaves, gadding about the city on social duties. Add to the subtrahend self-caused diseases and the time left an idle blank. You will see that you possess fewer years than the calendar shows. Search your memory: how seldom you have had a consistent plan, how few days worked out as you intended, how seldom you have enjoyed full use of yourself, how seldom your face wore an inartificial expression, how seldom your mind was unflurried, what accomplishments you have to show for so long a life, how much of your life has been pilfered by others without your being aware of it, how much of it you have lost, how much was dispensed on groundless regret, foolish gladness, greedy desire, polite society—and then realize that your death will be premature."

Why should this be? It is because you live as if you

would live forever; the thought of human frailty never enters your head, you never notice how much of your time is already spent. You squander it as though your store were full to overflowing, when in fact the very day of which you make a present to someone or something may be your last. Like the mortal you are, you are apprehensive of everything; but your desires are unlimited as if you were immortal. Many a man will say, "After my fiftieth year I shall retire and relax; my sixtieth year will release me from obligations." And what guarantee have you that your life will be longer? Who will arrange that your program shall proceed according to plan? Are you not ashamed to reserve for yourself only the tail end of life and to allot to serious thought only such time as cannot be applied to business? How late an hour to begin to live when you must depart from life! What stupid obliviousness to mortality to postpone counsels of sanity to the fifties or sixties, with the intention of beginning life at an age few have reached!

[4] You will find that men of great power and high position let fall phrases which indicate their desire for leisure and the high value they set upon it, to the point of preferring it to their present advantages. They sometimes crave to step down from their pedestal, if they could safely do so, for greatness comes crashing down of its own weight even with no impingement or shock from without.

The deified Augustus, whom heaven endowed more richly than any other man, never ceased praying for rest and begging for release from affairs of state. His conversation always came round to his hope for leisure. The thought that he would one day live for himself was the sweet if unreal solace which gave savor to his labors. He wrote a letter to the senate in which he promised that his retirement would not involve abdication of dignity or contrast with his former high position, and then continued, as I find, in the words following: "But such conduct is more impressive in execution than in promise. But my anticipa-

tion of that period so earnestly prayed for has led me to
sample some of its delight by the pleasure of words, since
the happy reality is still slow in coming." So precious a
thing was leisure in his sight that he hastened it in thought
when he could not in fact. That man who saw that the
world hung upon him alone, who determined the fortunes
of men and nations, was happiest in the thought of the
day upon which he would lay his greatness aside. He had
experienced how much sweat that felicity which shone
brilliant the world over had wrung out, how much secret
anxiety it veiled.

He was forced to the decision of arms first with his countrymen, then with his colleagues, and lastly with his kin,
and he shed blood by land and sea. War took him through
Macedonia, Sicily, Egypt, Syria, Asia, and almost every
country in the world, and when his armies were weary of
Roman bloodshed he turned them to foreign wars. While
he was subduing the Alps and subjugating enemy en-
claves within an empire at peace, while he was extending
its boundaries beyond Rhine and Euphrates and Danube,
in the capital itself Murena, Caepio, Lepidus, Egnatius,
and others were whetting their blades against him. Before
he had escaped their conspiracy, when he had grown old
and feeble, his daughter and the band of aristocratic para-
mours whom adultery bound to her service like a military
oath repeatedly terrified him. Then there was Paulus, and
another Antony in league with a woman to alarm him.
Hardly had he cut these cankers away, limbs and all, when
others sprouted in their place; as in a body overloaded with
blood, there was always a hemorrhage at some point. That
is why Augustus longed for leisure, why he found relief
for his labors in hoping for it and imagining it. This was
the unfulfilled prayer of a man who could fulfill the prayer
of others.

[5] Marcus Cicero was storm-tossed among Catilines
and Clodiuses, Pompeys and Crassuses, some open enemies

and others dubious friends; he foundered with the ship of state, which he tried to keep on an even keel, but was in the end swept away. Cicero was never at ease in prosperity and could not tolerate adversity; how often did he curse that consulship which he had praised, justifiably to be sure, but so tirelessly! How piteous the language of the letter he addressed to Atticus when the elder Pompey was beaten and the younger recruiting his shattered forces in Spain! "You ask," he says, "what I am doing here? I am lingering in my Tuscan estate, half a prisoner." The rest of the letter is filled with lamentations for his past life, complaints for the present, despair of the future. "Half a prisoner," Cicero called himself. But, by Hercules, a sage would never give himself so groveling a style; he could never be half a prisoner, because his freedom is always complete and solid, unbeholden to others, master of itself, and towering above others. What can rise higher than a man who is higher than Fortune?

[6] Livius Drusus was an intense and energetic man who, supported by masses of unenfranchised Italians, agitated for radical measures of the Gracchan type. He was unable to carry his measures through, and no longer at liberty to abandon the enterprise once started, and when he saw there was no prospect of success, he is said to have cursed the life of harassment he had led from infancy, remarking that he was the only person who had never had a holiday even as a boy. The fact is that when he was still a ward and not yet of age he ventured to appear in court on behalf of defendants, and that his pleading was so effective that certain acquittals are commonly attributed to him. Such premature ambition might have landed Drusus anywhere, but one could guess that such half-baked audacity would result in some disaster to himself and the state. It was too late for him to complain, then, that he had never had a holiday, when he had been factious and a public nuisance from boyhood. It is a moot point whether he was

a suicide; he died suddenly of a wound in the groin, and some doubt that his death was self-inflicted. But everyone agrees that it was well timed.

It is idle to extend the list of men whom others looked upon as very happy but who have themselves testified in good faith that they loathed every act of their lives. But these plaints reformed neither their audience nor themselves, for no sooner have their feelings burst into expression than they backslide to their old habit. Even if you live a thousand years, by Hercules, your span will shrink into a trifle, for your vices will devour any amount of time. Your actual span, though Nature speeds its passing, can be stretched out by reason; but inevitably it slips quickly from your grasp, for you do not seize it and hold it back, you do nothing to brake the speediest thing in the world but let it go as if it were useless and replaceable.

[7] Among the worst offenders I count those who give all their time to drink and lust; that is the sorriest abuse of time of all. Though the phantom of glory which possesses some men is illusory, their error, at all events, has a creditable look. And even if you cite the avaricious, the wrathful, and those who prosecute unjust hatreds and even unjust war, these too are more manly kinds of sin. But the stain upon men abandoned to their belly and their lusts is vile. Open their schedules for examination and note how much time they spend on bookkeeping, on machinations, on protective measures, on courting the powerful, on being courted, on obtaining or providing collateral, on banquets (which have now become a business routine), and you will see how little time their distractions, call them good or bad, leave them for drawing breath.

It is universally agreed, moreover, that no pursuit, neither eloquence nor the liberal arts, can be followed by a man preoccupied, for the mind can take nothing in deeply when its interests are fragmented, but spews back everything that is crammed into it. The least concern of the preoccupied man is life; it is the hardest science of all. Experts in other disciplines are numerous and common; some of them mere boys have been able to master so thoroughly that they could even play the teacher. But the science of life requires a whole lifetime, and the science of dying, which you may find more surprising, requires a whole lifetime. Many fine people have abandoned all their encumbrances, have renounced riches and business and pleasure, and have made it their one object, during the remainder of their span, to learn how to live. Even so, the greater number died confessing that they had not yet learned the art—still less have those others learned it. It takes a great man, believe me, and one who rises high above human frailty, to allow none of his time to be frittered away; such a man's life is very long because he devotes every available minute of it to himself. None of it lies idle and unexploited, none of it is at the disposal of another. The frugal steward finds nothing worth trading his time for; that is why he has enough of it. The supply is necessarily short for those who allow the public to abstract quantities of it.

And you may be sure that those people occasionally realize the damage. At least you can hear many who are burdened with great prosperity sometimes cry out amidst their throngs of clients or their pleadings at court or their other respectable afflictions: "I have no chance to live!" Of course not. All who retain you distrain you from yourself. How many days has that defendant purloined? How many that candidate? How many that rich old lady who has buried all her natural heirs? How many the malingerer who shams sickness to whet the greed of hopeful beneficiaries? How many the powerful friend who uses you not as a friend but as an accessory to his pomp? Balance your account, I say, and tot up the days of your life: you will see that the residue is very small and mostly dregs.

The man who got the office he prayed for is eager to lay it down and repeatedly sighs, "When will this year be

over!" The man who thought the chance of providing public spectacles a great privilege says, when he gives them,
"When will I be rid of them?" There is a lawyer for whose
services every litigant eagerly competes; the crowd he at-
tracts fills every cranny, far beyond earshot. "When," he
complains, "will the courts adjourn?" Everyone accelerates
life's pace, and is sick with anticipation of the future and
loathing of the present. But the man who puts all of his
time to his own uses, who plans every day as if it were his
last, is neither impatient for the morrow nor afraid of it.
Is there some new kind of pleasure that an hour might
bring? All are familiar, all have been experienced to the
full. The rest Lady Fortune may dispose of as she will; his
life is now impregnable. Additions may be made but no
diminution, and the additions are like the food a man can
hold but does not want after he has eaten his fill. You cannot, therefore, accept a hoary head and wrinkles as proof
of a long life; the man has existed a long time, he has not
lived a long time. Would you think a man had traveled a
long voyage if he had been caught in a savage gale immediately on leaving port and had been buffeted to and
fro by alternate blasts from opposite directions so that he
was running circles in the same spot? That man has had
not a long voyage but a long floundering.

[8] I am always astonished when I see people asking
for time and those of whom they ask it very ready to
oblige. Each focuses his attention on the object for which
time is asked, but neither on the time itself, as if the thing
actually asked for and bestowed were a cipher. They trifle
with the most precious of all commodities. They take no
notice of it because it has no substance and is not a visible
entity, and therefore it is reckoned very cheap, or rather
completely valueless. Annuities and bonuses men are very
glad to receive, and hire their labor and effort and industry
out to obtain them. But upon time no value is set; men
use it as carelessly as if it came gratis. But see how these

same people supplicate their doctors when they fall sick
and death looms large, see how ready they are to spend
their all for life if they are threatened with a capital charge!
So utterly inconsistent are their moods. If men could see
their future years numbered as precisely as their past, what
a flutter there would be among those who saw that their
remaining years were few, how sparing of them would they
be! With a fixed amount, however small, it is easy to econ-
omize; but when you cannot know when what you have
will be gone you must husband your store very carefully.

But you must not think those people are not aware what
a precious thing time is. If they love someone very much
it is their habit to declare that they are ready to give them
part of their own years. They do give them part, without
realizing it; but their mode of giving subtracts from their
own store without adding to their friends'. They do not, in
fact, know that there is any diminution, and the loss causes
no qualms because it is not noticed. But no one can restore
years, no one can give you back to yourself. Time marches
on and will neither repeat nor halt its course; it will make
no bustle, it will not call attention to its speed. Its movement is silent; it will play no encore either at royal command or for popular applause. It will run the course specified at the starting post, with no diversions and no slowing
down. What is the upshot? You are preoccupied; life hur-
ries on. Meanwhile death draws nearer, and for it, willy-
nilly, you must find time.

[9] Certain people who brag of their foresight are the
stupidest of all. They are always preoccupied with work
so that they may be in position to live better; they spend
life in making provision for life. Their plans are designed for
the future, but procrastination is the greatest waste of life.
It robs us of each day as it comes, and extorts the present
from us on promises of the future. Expectancy is the greatest impediment to living: in anticipation of tomorrow it
loses today. You operate with what is in Fortune's hand

but let go what is in your own. What is your range? What
is your objective? Everything future is uncertain; live now!
The greatest of our bards sings us this wholesome strain,
as if by divine inspiration (Vergil, *Georgics* 3.66):

> First to flee in wretched mortals' life
> Is ever the day that is best.

"Why do you hesitate?" he says. "Why are you idle? If
you do not grasp the day, it flies away." It will fly anyhow,
even if you do grasp it, and so your speed in using time
must compete with time's own rapid pace; you must quaff
quickly, as from an intermittent spurt of water. By writing
"day that is best" rather than "age that is best," Vergil
again admirably reproves remote anticipation. How can
you be indifferent to time's rapid pace and reach out, in
complete unconcern, for as long a series of months and
years as your greed fancies? It is about the day the poet
speaks, and about a day fleeing. Can there be any doubt
that in the life of wretched mortals, which is to say, of preoccupied mortals, the best day is the first to flee? Their
minds are still childish when they are surprised by old age,
which they reach without preparation and without weapons, for they have stumbled upon it suddenly and unexpectedly without realizing that it was stealing upon them
day by day. Just as conversation or reading or some deep
thought beguiles travelers, so that they reach their destination before they are aware they were drawing near, so are
we, if we are preoccupied, unaware of our ceaseless and
rapid journey through life, which proceeds at the same rate
whether we are awake or asleep, until we reach its end.

[10] If I should choose to divide my subject into heads,
with evidence for each, I could find many arguments to
prove that the life of men preoccupied is the shortest of all.
Fabianus, who was a true philosopher of the old-fashioned
kind and not one of your professional lecturers, used to say:
"Against the passions we must fight by main force, not by

logic-chopping; the line must be turned by frontal attack, not by pinpricks. Casuistry will not do, for the adversary must be smashed, not scratched." But we must not give the victims up as hopeless; they must be taught, and the faults peculiar to each censured.

Life falls into three divisions—past, present, and future. Of these, the present is transitory, the future uncertain, the past unalterable. This is the part over which Fortune has lost her power, which cannot be subjected to any man's control. But this part men preoccupied lose, for they have no leisure to look back on the past, and if they had there would be no pleasure in recollecting a regrettable episode. They are unwilling to call to mind time badly spent, therefore, and have no stomach for traversing again passages whose faults are obvious in retrospect though they were disguised at the time by the pander pleasure. No one willingly turns his mind back to the past unless his acts have all passed the censorship of his own conscience, which is never deceived; a man who has coveted much in his ambition, behaved arrogantly in his pride, used his victory without restraint, overreached by treachery, plundered out of avarice, squandered out of prodigality, must inevitably be afraid of his own memory. And yet that is the part of our time which is hallowed and sacrosanct, above the reach of human vicissitudes and beyond the sway of Fortune, impregnable to the vexations of want and fear and the assaults of disease; it is the part which is not subject to turmoil or looting; its possession is everlasting and free from anxiety. The days of our present come one by one, and each day minute by minute; but all the days of the past will appear at your bidding and allow you to examine them and linger over them at your will. Busy men have no time for this. Excursions into all the parts of its past are the privilege of a serene and untroubled mind; but the minds of the preoccupied cannot turn or look back, as if constricted by a yoke. And so their life vanishes into an abyss.

However much water you pour on will do no good if there is no vessel ready to receive and hold it; and similarly it makes no difference how much time is given you if there is no place for it to settle and it passes through the cracks and holes of the mind. The present is fleeting, to the degree that to some it seems non-existent. It is always in motion, it flows on headlong; it ceases to be before it has come, and will no more brook delay than the firmament or the stars, whose incessant drive never allows them to remain stationary. It is only with the present that busy men are concerned, and the present is so transitory that it cannot be grasped; but because their attention is distracted in many directions they are deprived of even this little.

[11] Here is a summary indication that these men's lives are short: see how eager they are for a long life! Decrepit old men beg and pray for the addition of a few more years; they pretend they are younger than they are; they flatter themselves with a lie, and are as pleased with their deception as if they were deluding Fate at the same time. And in the end, when some sickness reminds them of their mortality, they die in a panic, not as if they were departing from life, but as if they were being dragged out of it. They cry out that they were fools not to have lived and declare they will live at leisure if only they survive their sickness. Only then do they reflect how futile was their acquisition of things they would never enjoy, how vain was all their labor. But life is ample, of course, for men who keep themselves detached from involvement. None of their time is transferred to others, none is frittered away in this direction and that, none is committed to Fortune, none perishes of neglect, none is squandered in lavishness, none is idle: all of it, so to speak, produces income. A very little is therefore amply sufficient, and hence, when his last day comes, the philosopher goes to meet his death with a steady step.

[12] You may wish to know whom I mean when I speak of men preoccupied. Do not suppose I mean only those

who leave the law court only when the watchdogs take
over; those who are crushed in an admiring crowd, with
a show of grandeur if the retinue is their own, or of contempt if they are part of another's; those whom formal calling gets out of their own house to bump against the doors
of others'; or yet those whom the praetor's auction keeps
intent on profits that are disreputable and will one day fes-
ter. Some men are preoccupied even in their leisure. In a
country house, upon a couch, in the midst of solitude,
though they are inaccessible to others, they are troublesome to themselves; their life cannot be called leisurely but
rather a busy idleness. Would you call a man at leisure
when he sets out his Corinthian bronzes with anxious
finesse and spends most of each day pottering with bits of
metal whose value is inflated by the mania of a few collectors? When he sits at the ringside (our vices are not
even Roman!) to watch boys wrestling? When he matches
the pack animals in his own herds in terms of like age and
color? When he keeps the most modern stable of athletes?
How? Would you call men at leisure when they pass many
hours at the barber's to be cropped of last night's growth,
to hold formal consultation over each individual hair, to
rearrange hair that is rumpled, and draw it over the fore-
head from this side and that where it has grown thin? How
angry they get if the barber is a little careless, as if it were
a real man he was shearing! How livid they get if a bit
of the mane is snipped off, if a hair is out of place, if it
does not all fall into proper ringlets! Not one of that crew
but would rather see the state disordered than his hair. To
a man they are more concerned for the style of the head
than its soundness, to a man they prefer spruceness to re-
spectability. Would you say that men busy with comb and
mirror are at leisure?

And what would you say of those preoccupied with com-
posing, hearing, and learning songs? The voice, which is
naturally simplest and best when it is used in a straight-

forward way, they torture into the twistings of some footless air. Their fingers are always snapping to mark the time
of some tune in their heads, and they hum their obbligato
as they assist at any serious or even melancholy function.
It is not leisure such men have, but idle occupation. Their
banquets, save the mark, I would certainly not class as
leisurely pastime when I see how anxiously they set out
their silver plate, how carefully they gird their footmen's
tunics, how they are on tenterhooks to see that the chef
garnishes the boar in proper style, how deftly the depilated
waiters take up their posts at the signal, how artistically
the fowl is carved into portions of prescribed shape and
size, how scrupulously the wretched little pages wipe away
the hawking of the drunks. These performances are a bid
for a reputation for elegance and grandeur, and so far do
these abuses follow them into the intimate recesses of life
that they cannot eat or drink without ostentation.

Nor would I class as leisured the men who gad about
in sedan chair or litter and are as punctual for these rides
as if it were sin to omit them, and who have to be notified
of their scheduled hour for bathing, for swimming, for dining. So enervated are they by the extreme languor of the
pampered spirit that they cannot find out for themselves
whether they are hungry. I have heard of one of these
delicate creatures—if you can call unlearning the habits of
ordinary life delicacy—who, when he was lifted out of the
bath and deposited in his sedan chair, asked, "Am I sitting
down?" Do you suppose that a man who does not know
whether he is sitting down can know whether he is alive,
whether he can see, whether he is at leisure? It is hard to
decide whether he is more to be pitied if he really did not
know or if he pretended not to know. They are really oblivious to many things, but to many they pretend oblivion.
Certain failings they consider choice, as being proofs of
their felicity; to know what you are doing would prove you
lowly and contemptible. The mimes, you may be sure, do

not have to resort to imagination for their burlesques on luxury. They pass over more than they invent, by Hercules; our age, whose ingenuity is fertile only in this one direction, has produced such an abundance of unbelievable vices that we may charge the mimes with overlooking them. To think that a man can be so comatose with luxury that he must take another's word on the question of his sitting or standing! That is not a man at leisure; you must apply a different term to him. He is sick, or rather he is dead; a man is at leisure only if he is aware that he is. But a man who needs a guide to know what posture his body is in is only half alive; how can he be master of any of his time?

[13] It would be tedious to list the types who spend their lives on backgammon or ball or toasting in the sun. Men whose pleasures involve much business are not at leisure. It is perfectly clear that those who spend their time on profitless literary questions—of whom Rome, too, now has a large number—are busy over nothing. It used to be a Greek aberration to inquire into the number of Ulysses' rowers, whether *Iliad* or *Odyssey* was written first and also whether they are by the same author, and other problems of the same description, which, if you kept them to yourself, would give your inward consciousness no pleasure, and if you published them would give you the character not of a scholar but of a bore. And now this inane passion for useless knowledge has infected the Romans also. The other day I heard someone reporting what Roman general was the first to do what: Duilius was the first to win a naval engagement, Curius Dentatus was the first to have elephants in his triumphal procession. Still, even if such details contribute nothing to true glory, they do involve examples of patriotic achievement; there is no profit in such research, but for all its uselessness the theme is attractive and holds our interest. We will be indulgent also to inquiries on who first persuaded the Romans to take to the sea. The man was Claudius, and he was styled Caudex for

his innovation, because the ancients called any structure made of individual boards *caudex;* that is why the Tables of the Law are called *codices,* and the boats which carry grain up the Tiber are still called *codicariae,* in keeping with ancient usage. There may be relevance, too, in the fact that Valerius Corvinus was the first to conquer Messana, and was the first of the Valerian family to bear the name Messana, adopted from his conquest; gradually vernacular usage changed the consonants, and the name became Messala.

But would you countenance research to establish that Lucius Sulla was the first to give a show of unleashed lions in the circus, whereas the usual practice was to have them chained, and that marksmen for dispatching them were supplied by King Bocchus? Perhaps this, too, is allowable; but can it serve any useful purpose to determine that Pompey was the first to give a circus exhibition in which eighteen elephants were matched against a number of convicts in battle formation? The leading personage in the state, and a man who stood out among the principal figures of the era for his extraordinary kindliness, made an entertainment of killing human beings after a novel fashion. Have them fight to the death? Not enough. Have them torn to pieces? Not enough; they must be reduced to pulp by beasts of enormous bulk. It would be better to consign the episode to oblivion for fear some future potentate might hear of it and emulate its barbarity. With how thick a mist does great prosperity blind our minds! When he was casting troops of wretches before monsters spawned under an alien sky, when he was proclaiming war between creatures so ill matched, when he was shedding rivers of blood before the eyes of the Roman people and would soon force them to shed even more, then that man thought himself above the laws of nature. But later that same man was deceived by Alexandrian treachery and must needs offer his bosom to be pierced by the meanest of slaves; then at last he realized the empty braggadocio of his title "the Great."

But I must return to the point where I digressed and exhibit the utter futility of the pains some people bestow on subjects of this kind. The same author tells us that Metellus, in celebrating his triumph over the Carthaginians defeated in Sicily, was the only Roman to have 120 captive elephants walk in procession before his chariot; and that Sulla was the last Roman to enlarge the sacred boundary of the city, a measure the ancients took only upon the acquisition of Italian, not provincial, territory. This information is of the same degree of usefulness as that the Aventine Hill is outside the sacred boundary, as he states, for one of two reasons: either it was the plebeian rallying point in their secession, or the birds had not proved propitious when Remus took the auspices there. He has countless other tidbits which are of the same quality, or altogether false. But even if they write in good faith and vouch for their facts, how can their tales reduce anyone's errors? Whose covetousness will they suppress? Whom will they make braver or more just or more liberal? My friend Fabianus used to say that he was sometimes in doubt whether it would not be better to leave off studying altogether than to become involved in such subjects as these.

[14] The only people really at leisure are those who take time for philosophy. They alone really live. It is not their lifetime alone of which they are careful stewards: they annex every age to their own and exploit all the years that have gone before. Unless we prove ingrate, it was for us that the illustrious founders of divine schools of thought came into being, for us they prepared a way of life. By the exertions of others we are led to the fairest treasures, raised to the light out of the darkness in which they were mined. No age is forbidden us, we have admittance to all, and if we choose to transcend the narrow bounds of human frailty by loftiness of mind, there is a vast stretch of time

for us to roam. We may dispute with Socrates, doubt with Carneades, repose with Epicurus, transcend human nature with the Stoics, defy it with the Cynics. Since Nature allows us to participate in any age, why should we not betake ourselves in mind from this petty and ephemeral span to the boundless and timeless region we can share with our betters?

Men who gad about town on errands of politeness, who agitate themselves and others, when they have duly done their silly business, when they have crossed every threshold every day and have passed no open doors by, when they have delivered their venal greetings to houses at opposite ends of town, how few will they be able to see in a city so vast and so fragmented by disparate passions? How many will deny them admittance because they are asleep or disinclined for activity or merely rude! How many, after tormenting them with long waiting, will dash by with a pretense of urgent business! How many will avoid going out through the reception hall which is crowded with callers and escape by an inconspicuous back door, as if it were not ruder to dodge visitors than not to admit them at all. How many still groggy and stupid from yesterday's debauch will yawn offensively to a man who has broken his own sleep to wait upon another's finishing his and mumble a greeting through half-open lips and only after the butler has whispered the visitor's name into their ears a thousand times!

Only men who make Zeno and Pythagoras and Democritus and the other high priests of liberal studies their daily familiars, who cultivate Aristotle and Theophrastus, can properly be said to be engaged in the duties of life. None of these will be "not at home," none will send his visitor away without making him happier and better contented with himself, none will allow a visitor to leave him empty-handed, and they are accessible to all comers, night and day.

[15] None of these will force you to die, but all will teach you how. None of these will wear your years away, but rather add his own to yours. Conversation with them is not subversive, association not a capital offense, and no great expense is involved in cultivating them. You can carry home whatever you like: it will not be their fault if you do not draw as deeply as you like from their wellsprings. What felicity awaits the man who has enrolled as their client, what a fair old age! He will have friends with whom he can deliberate on matters great and small, whom he may consult about his problems every day, from whom he can hear truth without offense and praise without flattery, after whose likeness he may mold himself.

It is a common saying that a man's parents are not of his own choosing but allotted to him by chance. But we can choose our genealogy. Here are families with noble endowments: choose whichever you wish to belong to. Your adoption will give you not only the name but actually the property, and this you need not guard in a mean or niggardly spirit: the more people you share it with, the greater will it become. These will open the path to eternity for you and will raise you to a height from which none can be cast down. This is the sole means of prolonging your mortality, rather of transforming it into immortality. Honors, monuments, all that ambition has blazoned in inscriptions or piled high in stone will speedily sink to ruin; there is nothing that the lapse of time does not dilapidate and exterminate. But the dedications of philosophy are impregnable; age cannot erase their memory or diminish their force. Each succeeding generation will hold them in ever higher reverence; what is close at hand is subject to envy, whereas the distant we can admire without prejudice. The philosopher's life is therefore spacious; he is not hemmed in and constricted like others. He alone is exempt from the limitations of humanity; all ages are at his service as at a god's. Has time gone by? He holds it fast in recollection. Is time

now present? He utilizes it. Is it still to come? He anticipates it. The amalgamation of all time into one makes his
life long.

[16] But for those who are oblivious to the past, negli-
gent of the present, fearful of the future, life is very short
and very troubled. When they reach its end they realize
too late, miserable creatures, that all this while they have
been preoccupied in doing nothing. The fact that they
sometimes pray for death is no proof that they find life long.
Their folly tosses them to and fro with shifting feelings
which compel them to the very things they dread; it is because they fear death that they often pray for it. Nor is
the fact that the day so often seems long to them any proof
that their life is long. They complain of the dragging hours
until the time appointed for dinner, for when their usual
preoccupations fail them and they are left idle, they fret
and are at a loss for something to do with their leisure or
how to make it pass. And so they betake themselves to
some other preoccupation, and all the time intervening is a
burden, precisely, by Hercules, as they wish to leap over
the intervening days when a gladiatorial show has been advertised or the date of some other spectacle or other entertainment is in the offing. Any postponement of something
they are waiting for seems long. But the time they enjoy
is short and passes quickly, and their own fault makes it
shorter, for they run from one pleasure to another and cannot linger in any one desire. Their days are not long but
hateful. On the other hand, how short they find the nights
they spend in a harlot's embrace or over wine! Hence that
aberration of poets who feed human frailty by stories representing Jupiter as impelled by sexual pleasure to double
the length of the night. To write the gods down as precedents and to give free license to corruption by citing the
example of a deity is nothing else than to add fuel to our
vices. How can the nights for which they pay so dear seem

other than short to these men? They lose the day in expectation of night, and night in fear of dawn.

[17] The very pleasures of these men are uneasy and disturbed by various alarms; in the very moment of triumph they are assailed by the anxious thought, "How long will this last?" It is this mood which has made kings weep over their power; the extent of their might gave them no pleasure, its inevitable ending terrified them. The high and mighty king of the Persians who marshaled his army over wide plains because he could number his men only by measuring, not counting, shed tears at the thought that within a century not one of that vast army would be alive. But the very man who wept for them was destined to hasten their doom, to destroy some on the sea, some on land, some in battle, some in flight, and within a brief span bring death upon those for whose hundredth year he was so solicitous.

Why are their pleasures uneasy? Because the motives upon which they are founded are not stable and they totter with the frivolity which gave them birth. How wretched do you suppose are the hours they confess are wretched when there is so little solidity in the hours in which they vaunt and exalt themselves above humanity? All very great blessings involve anxiety; good fortune is less to be trusted than any other. To preserve felicity, new felicity is needed, and we must offer prayer on behalf of prayers that have turned out well. Anything that comes by chance is unstable, and the higher it rises the more liable it is to fall. But what must inevitably fall can give no one pleasure; therefore the life of those who acquire with toil what requires greater toil to hold must be not only very short but also very miserable. Laboriously they attain what they desire, anxiously they hold what they have attained, and in the meanwhile irrecoverable time is not taken into consideration.

New preoccupations take the place of old, one hope leads to another, one ambition arouses another. There is no effort to end wretchedness; only its composition is changed. Are we done with the torments of winning public office? Other office seekers take more of our time. Are we free of the exertions of candidacy? We begin to canvass for others. Have we laid aside the vexations of the prosecutor? We acquire those of the judge. Is a man no longer a judge? He is now chairman of an investigating committee. Has he retired from managing estates for a fee? He is kept busy managing his own. Is Marius done with army service? The consulship keeps him busy. Is Cincinnatus in a hurry to have done with his dictatorship? He will be recalled from the plow. Scipio proceeds against the Carthaginians before he is old enough for such an assignment; he conquers Hannibal, conquers Antiochus, is the great glory of his own consulship and the surety of his brothers', and if he had not objected his statue would have been put alongside Jove's. But then sedition among the citizens harasses their savior, and the man who in his youth disdained honors matching the gods' will please his old age by posing as a rebellious exile. Be our lot prosperous or wretched, causes of anxiety will never be wanting; life is pushed along through one preoccupation after another. Leisure will always be longed for, never attained.

[18] Raise yourself above the crowd, then, my dearest Paulinus. You have seen more rough weather than suits your years; retire, at last, to a more tranquil haven. Think how many waves have buffeted you, how many gales you have had to weather, some in your private life, and some which your public career brought upon you. Long enough has your virtue been displayed in toilsome and vexatious proofs: try how it will behave in leisure. The greater part of your life, certainly the better part, has been given to the state: take a bit of your time for yourself as well. It is not to a dull and lazy sloth I invite you; I do not urge you to drown your lively energy in sleep and the pleasures dear to the crowd. That is not rest. You will find problems larger

than any you have so vigorously dealt with to occupy you
in your serene retirement. You manage the revenues of the
whole world, to be sure, as scrupulously as you would a
stranger's, as diligently as you would your own, as conscientiously as you would the state's. You win love in a post
in which it is hard to avoid hatred. But believe me, it is
still better to know the balance sheet of one's life than of
the public grain supply.

Recall that keen mind of yours, which is so capable of
grappling with the largest of problems, from a post which
is indeed eminent but hardly fitted for the happy life. Reflect that it was not the object of your long and compre-
hensive education in the liberal arts to make you a reliable
steward of so much grain; you gave promise of something
greater and nobler. There will be no lack of respectable
managers and hard workers. But plodding pack animals are
better suited to carrying burdens than thoroughbreds; who
would cumber their high-bred fleetness with a heavy pack?
Think, too, how risky it is to subject yourself to so heavy a
burden. Your business is with the human belly, and a hungry people neither listens to reason nor is softened by justice
nor swayed by prayer. A short time ago, a few days after
Caligula's death—while he was still bitterly distressed, if the
dead have consciousness, at the thought that the Roman
people had survived and had enough food for at most seven
or eight days—while he was making bridges of boats and
playing with the resources of the empire, there was a short-
age of food, the worst disaster that can befall even during
a siege. His imitation of a crazy, outlandish, and ruinously
arrogant king had very nearly cost ruin and famine and the
general catastrophe which follows famine. What was the
mood of the officials in charge of the grain supply when
they were threatened with stones, steel, fire—and Caligula?
With artful dissimulation they concealed the evil gnawing
at the vitals of the state, and with good reason, you may
be sure. Some diseases must be treated without the pa-

tient's knowledge; knowing what ailed them has brought
death to many.

[19] Betake you to these serener, safer, larger realms. Do
you think there is no difference whether you see that grain
is delivered to the granary by the carriers in good condition, without pilferage or damage, that it tallies in weight
and measure, or whether you approach these sacred and
sublime studies which will teach you the substance, will,
environment, and shape of god, what destiny awaits your
soul, where Nature lays us to rest when we are released
from our bodies, what the power is which sustains the
heaviest matter at the center of our world, suspends the
lighter above, carries fire to the highest part, causes the
stars to move with their proper changes, and other similar
matters full of great marvels? Leave the ground, won't you,
and turn your mind to these things! You must make your
way to them now, while your blood is warm and your per-
ceptions keen. In this mode of life there awaits you a quantity of goodly accomplishments, the love and practice of
the virtues, forgetfulness of the passions, knowledge of living and dying, a life of profound repose.

Wretched is the state of all men who are preoccupied,
but especially wretched are those who suffer with preoccupations not even their own, who regulate their rest by
another man's sleep, who adjust their gait to another man's
pace, and whose loves and hates, where freedom is of the
essence, are prescribed by order. If such men wish to know
how short their life is, let them think how small a fraction
of it is their own.

[20] When you see a man often take up the robe of
office, therefore, or hear his name bruited in the law courts,
do not envy him; the price of these distinctions is life. They
waste all their years to have one dated by their name. Some
lose their lives at the bottom of the climb, before they reach
the height to which they aspire. Some crawl up through a
thousand indignities to reach the crowning dignity, only to

realize that the object of their toil was their epitaph. Some shape new aspirations in old age as in youth, and find their vital energy at its end amidst large and ambitious undertakings. It is a shameful ending for an old man to faint away in court while representing perfect strangers and courting the applause of an ignorant gallery. It is disgraceful for a man exhausted by his life rather than his work to collapse in the midst of his duties. It is disgraceful to die in the act of collecting accounts, as the long-expectant heir jeers.

One example that occurs to me I cannot pass over. Sextus Turannius was a very efficient and conscientious administrator, and when he passed the age of ninety Caligula, on his own initiative, relieved him of his charge. Turannius ordered his household to lay him out and stand wailing about his bed as if he were dead. The household went into mourning for the unemployment of their aged master and did not lay their mourning aside until his work was restored to him. Can it be such a pleasure to die in harness? Many are convinced that it is, and their eagerness to work outlasts their capacity for it. They struggle against physical infirmity, and they consider old age a hardship for no other reason than that it removes them from active life. The law does not draft a soldier after his fiftieth year nor require a senator's attendance after his sixtieth; it is harder for men to obtain release from themselves than from the law.

In the meanwhile, while they are robbing and being robbed, while they disrupt each other's repose and make one another miserable, life remains without profit, without pleasure, without moral improvement. No one keeps death in view, everyone focuses on remote hopes. Some even make posthumous provisions—massive sepulchres, dedications of public buildings, gladiatorial shows, and pretentious obsequies. But the funerals of such people should be conducted by torch and taper light, as though they had in fact died in childhood.

ON TRANQUILLITY
OF MIND

Dialogue

The *Serenus* to whom this piece is addressed was Nero's
police commissioner and died during Seneca's latter years.
Of the date of the dialogue we can say only that it falls
after Seneca's return from exile (A.D. 49). The dialogue
opens with a letter from Serenus requesting a philosophic
remedy for his spiritual vacillation. In response, Seneca supplies sensible and undoctrinaire prescriptions against ennui
and nerves. Intellectual pursuits, for example, and friendship are good; footless globe-trotting and book-collecting
bad. The artificialities of the social round must be assayed
at their true value. Perhaps the most interesting prescription is for an occasional excursion into drinking and nonsense.

SERENUS'S QUERY

[1] *Serenus:* When I look into my faults, Seneca, I find
that some are on the surface, so openly exposed that I can
lay my hand upon them, while others are under cover and
less distinct, and still others are not continuous but recur at
intervals. These last I should say are the most troublesome,
like enemy bands that make surprise descents, for which a
man cannot be on guard, as in war, nor yet free of apprehension, as in peace. This latter condition I find my particular weakness. I must be as frank with you as with a
physician: I am not unrestrictedly free of the faults I hate
and fear, nor yet under lien to them. My situation is not

absolutely bad, but very fretful and sulky: I am neither sick or well.

I do not need to be told that all virtues are fragile in the beginning and acquire toughness and stability in time. But I also know that the impulses directed toward outward show—I refer to prestige and reputation for eloquence and other distinctions subject to outsiders' judgment—are also toughened by time. Both the qualities which afford us real strength and those which trick us out with a specious veneer require long years until the colors are fixed, and I am afraid that habit, which conduces to stability, will only root this vice of mine the deeper. Long association induces love of evil as well as good. The nature of this infirmity, when the hesitant mind veers markedly neither to right nor wrong, I can show you better piecemeal than all at once. I will tell you my symptoms; you find the disease a name.

I have, I confess, a deep love of frugality. I do not like a couch pretentiously decked out, clothing brought out of the chest and pressed with heavy irons and repeatedly mangled to make it glossy, but prefer cheap and homely wear which does not need to be tended or worn with such care. I do not like food prepared and gaped at by a troupe of chefs, ordered many days in advance and served up by many hands, but something handy and easy to prepare with nothing recherché or costly about it, something available everywhere, burdensome neither to purse nor body, and not likely to take the same route out of the body it took in. I like my servant homebred and simple in manner and dress; my plate the heavy silver my country-bred father used, with no craftsman's hallmark; my table not conspicuous for the variety of its grain or known to the town for the long succession of fashionable owners through whose hands it has passed, but made simply for use and not calculated to attract the appreciative scrutiny of any guest or kindle his envy.

But though I like all these things, my mind is entranced

by the elaborate outfits of page boys, slaves trimmed out with gold fittings and more carefully dressed than for a procession, a troupe of well-groomed servants; by a mansion where the floor underfoot is of costly stones, and riches are scattered in every corner, where the very ceiling is jeweled and there is a whole multitude to flatter and dance attendance upon the fortunes that are being dissipated. Need I mention the channels of water, transparent top to bottom, which flow around the guests as they dine, or the viands worthy of such décor?

I come to these things from a long sojourn with frugality, and the luxury overwhelms me with its splendor and rings in my ears from every side. My sight falters a little; it is easier to encounter it with mind than with eye. I am no worse when I return, but sadder. I do not walk among my commonplace possessions with head so high, and a gnawing, if unspoken, doubt creeps in: Can that life be better? My convictions are not altered, but I am disturbed.

I resolve to follow the precepts of our school and take up a political career. I resolve to seek public office not, of course, for the allurement of the purple and mace, but to be more serviceable and useful to my friends and relatives, to all my fellow citizens, and eventually to all mankind. Ready and determined I follow Zeno, Cleanthes, and Chrysippus, all of whom urged a public career though none of them followed one. When a problem assaults my mind, which is unused to being pounded, when something disagreeable comes up, as come it must, and frequently, in every life, or when a problem proves recalcitrant, or when trivialities demand excessive application, I turn back to my leisure, and with a livelier pace, like tired cattle homeward bound.

I resolve to confine my life within its own walls. "No one not prepared to offer adequate recompense for so great a loss shall rob me of a single day," I say. "My mind shall be absorbed with itself, shall cultivate itself, shall apply itself to nothing external, to nothing which depends upon the approval of others. My devotion shall be to tranquillity exempt from public or private troubles." But when some spirited book has made my mind tingle and noble examples have applied spurs, I want to spring into the forum, lend my voice to one man, my efforts to another, to try to help though the effort may be fruitless, to curb the pride of some public figure whose success has exalted him dangerously.

In literary pursuits I hold it better, by Hercules, to keep my eye on the subject and to treat it for its own sake; the words must be subordinate to the subject, and the composition will follow where the subject leads without elaboration. "What need to compose a classic for the ages?" say I. "Why try so hard to make yourself known to posterity? You were born to die, and a quiet funeral is less of a nuisance. And so, to use the time, write in a simple style, for your own benefit, not as an advertisement. Less labor is needed when your concern is for the present." But then, when my mind has been uplifted by lofty ideas, it becomes ambitious of words and strives for language to match its aspirations; then the composition rises to the dignity of the subject. I disregard my own rule and my decision for economy and soar aloft in speech no longer my own.

Not to multiply examples, this same lack of firmness in implementing good intentions pursues me everywhere. Actually, I am afraid I may be losing ground little by little, or, what is more disturbing, that I am on the verge of falling for unsteadiness and that my situation may be worse than I realize. Our view of our own condition is always friendly, and favoritism blinds judgment. Many people, I imagine, could attain wisdom if they were not convinced they had already attained it, if they did not dissemble some of their failings and turn a blind eye to others. It is a mistake to think that the flattery of others is more harmful to us than our own flattery of ourselves. Who has the courage to tell himself the truth? Who that finds himself in a crowd of eulogizers and flatterers is not his own most enthusiastic courtier?

I beg you, therefore, if you have some remedy to halt this vacillation of mine, kindly make me obliged to you for tranquillity. These currents of my mind are not dangerous, I know, and will cause no violent upset; a proper figure to express my complaint is that I am suffering not from a storm but from seasickness. Relieve me, then, of this trouble, whatever it may be, and rescue a voyager in distress in sight of land.

[2] *Seneca:* I have long been searching my own mind for some parallel to your mental state, Serenus, and the nearest analogy I can find is the situation of persons who have recovered from some long and severe illness but are occasionally visited by twinges and light attacks, and even when they have got rid of these sequelae are disquieted by mistrust and take their pulse to a physician when they are perfectly well and think the worst when their body shows any trace of warmth. It is not that their health is not sound, Serenus, but that they are not used to sound health. Even a calm sea shows a ripple, especially when it has quieted after a storm. What you need, therefore, is not the drastic measures we have already been through—opposing yourself at one juncture, showing anger at another, being peremptory at another—but the crowning measure of all: have faith in yourself and believe that you are traveling the right road and not being led astray by the zigzag tracks of hurrying wayfarers, many of whom go astray at the very roadside. What you desiderate is something great and lofty and of a nighness to god—to be inaccessible to impingement.

The Greeks have a word for this stability of mind—*euthymia* ("well-being of soul")—and there is a fine treatise on the subject by Democritus. My term is tranquillity, for there is no need to ape the Greek usage in a literal translation; the quality in question should be given a designation which conveys the force, not the form, of the Greek. Our question, then, is how the mind can maintain a consistent and advantageous course, be kind to itself and take pleasure in its attributes, never interrupt this satisfaction but abide in its serenity, without excitement or depression. This amounts to tranquillity. We shall inquire how it may be attained in general, and from the general prescription you may appropriate as much as you choose. Meanwhile the whole stock of evil must be dragged into the light, and individuals will recognize their own share. Incidentally you will realize how much less troubled you are with self-depreciation than individuals who are manacled to some specious profession and weighed down by some grandiloquent title and enact their role out of shame rather than choice.

All are in the same case, both those who are afflicted with fickleness and ennui and continual shifting of aim, who are always fondest of what they have given up, and those who are languid and yawn. Subjoin those who turn from side to side like insomniacs trying to settle down, until they find rest in weariness. After constantly reshaping their mode of life, they retain the latest mode not for dislike of change but because they have been overtaken by old age, which abhors innovation. Subjoin those who are immutable not by excess of constancy but of indolence; they live not as they choose but as they have begun. The malady has countless symptoms but its effect is uniform—dissatisfaction with self. This arises from an imbalance in the mind and from fainthearted or unrealized desires, when men dare not or cannot attain as much as they crave and rest wholly on hopes. They are unstable and vacillating, as is inevitable for persons in suspense. They strive for their objectives by every means, and teach and force themselves to do dishonorable and difficult things, and when their exertion fails of its end they are vexed by the fruitless ignominy: they are sorry, not because their desires were bad, but because they were frustrated. Then regret for what they have begun possesses them, and fear of beginning again, and there steals over them the vacillation of a mind that can find no outlet, because they can neither control nor yield to their passions; then comes the hesitancy of a life that is baffled, and then the inertia of a soul unnerved amidst disappointed hopes. The process is aggravated when loathing of laborious failure drives these victims to leisure and private studies, for a mind alert to politics, eager for activity, naturally restless, and obviously without internal resources, cannot tolerate such studies. And so, when the entertainment which busy people find even in business is withdrawn, their mind cannot endure home, loneliness, walls, and cannot abide itself left to itself.

This is the source of that ennui and self-dissatisfaction and vacillation of a mind never at rest and of morose impatience with leisure. When the victim is ashamed to confess his malady and bashfulness forces its pangs inward, the cravings confined in a narrow space without vent strangle one another. Hence sadness and melancholy and the thousand fluctuations of an unsure mind which hope not yet fulfilled holds in suspense and hope despaired of dejects; hence the mood of loathing leisure, complaining of nothing to do, and bitterest jealousy of the progress of others. For an unhappy sloth nurtures envy, and because they have themselves been unable to advance they wish everyone else ruined. From this aversion to the success of others and despair of their own, the mind becomes angry at Fortune, complains of the times, and withdraws into a corner to brood over its abuse until it becomes sick and tired of itself. The human mind is naturally agile and susceptible to movement. Any basis for excitement or diversion is welcome, and all the more welcome to those bad characters which are glad to be worn out in activity. Just as certain sores invite the hands that must hurt them and are pleased at their touch, just as a foul itch finds satisfaction in anything that scratches, just so would I say that toil and vexation are pleasurable for those minds upon which passions have broken out like malignant pustules.

Some things do give pleasure along with a certain pain, as, for example, to change over from one side to the other before it is tired, or to change from one position to another to get a breath of air. Achilles is like that, in Homer, lying now on his face and now on his back, trying to settle in various postures, able to stand no position long, as sick men can't, and using changes as a remedy.

That is why people go roaming abroad, wander over untrodden shores, and demonstrate their moody impatience with what they have by land and sea. "Let's go to Campania." But luxury soon cloys: "Let's visit uncivilized country, let's trek through the wilds of Bruttium and Lucania." But amid the desolation they miss the element of the agreeable to relieve their pampered eyes from the unbroken squalor of the wild wastes: "Let's go to Tarentum; it has a famous water front and mild winters and an opulence which was adequate to a population of voluptuaries in the old days." But their ears have too long missed the plaudits and the din, and human blood would be an agreeable diversion: "Let's go back to town." One junket comes on the heels of another, and one spectacle gives way to another. As Lucretius says (3.1068): "Each man always flees himself." But what is the good if he cannot get away from himself? He follows close and is his own most burdensome companion. We ought to understand that it is not the locale whose shortcomings vex us but our own. We are too unstable to put up with anything, and cannot bear hardship or pleasure or ourselves or anything else very long. Some men have been driven to death by this failing; frequent changes of plan brought them back to their starting point and exhausted the possibility of novelty. Life and the world itself began to cloy, and out of their disintegrating self-indulgence came the thought, "How long must this routine go on?"

[3] You ask what remedy I would prescribe against this tedium. The best course, as Athenodorus says, is to be employed in some active career, in political activity and civic functions. Just as some people pass their days in sunbathing, exercise, and care of the body, just as athletes find it most useful to spend most of their time nurturing their biceps and the toughness to which they have dedicated themselves wholly, so for you whose minds are in training for the political arena it is far best to be at work. For when a man's declared object is to make himself useful to his fellow citizens and to all mankind, he will exercise and improve his abilities by participating fully in demanding activities, serving both public and private interests as best he can. "But," continues Athenodorus, "since human ambition is unscrupulous and many detractors stand ready to twist right into wrong, since ingenuousness is defenseless and will always be more likely to be tripped than to succeed, it is best to withdraw from the forum and public life. But even in private life a large mind has ample scope for development. Man is not like lions and other creatures whose energies are restricted by being caged; man's greatest achievements are carried out in private.

"But retirement should be of such a nature that, however insulated a man keeps his leisure, he must still be willing to be of service to individuals and to mankind by his intelligence, his voice, his counsel. The man who brings candidates forward, defends the accused, votes on war and peace, is not the only one who serves the state; he who exhorts the youth, who, when good preceptors are so rare, imbues their minds with virtue, who seizes them as they race for money and luxury and holds them back, slowing them down, at least, if nothing else—he, too, is working for the community, albeit in a private station. Is the judge in the aliens' or citizens' court of arbitration performing a higher service when he delivers his assistant's verdict to suitors than the man who defines justice, piety, patience, fortitude, contempt of death, knowledge of the gods, and shows what a safe and easy asset a good conscience is? If, then, you bestow the time you abstract from public business upon study, you will not be deserting or shirking your duty. The man on the firing line, posted on the right wing or left, is not the only soldier in the army; the guard at the gates (a less dangerous but certainly not an idle function), the picket on watch, the keeper of the armory also serve, and though their duties are bloodless they still count as soldiers.

"If you devote yourself to study you will escape your distaste for life; you will not wish for night to come because you are weary of light, and you will not be a burden to yourself and useless to others. You will draw many people to become your friends; good men will flock to you. For however unadvertised virtue may be, it is never wholly unknown but gives signs of its presence, and the worthy will track it down. But if we give society up altogether, renounce the human race, and live wrapped up in ourselves, solitude with no serious objective will beget a vacuum for activity of some sort. We shall begin to put up buildings, pull down buildings, dam out the sea, channel water through natural obstacles, and squander the time which Nature vouchsafed us for use. Some of us use it sparingly and some prodigally; some can render a strict accounting of their expenditure of time and others have no balance left, which is the most disgraceful of all. Often an old man will have nothing but the calendar to prove that he has lived a long time."

[4] In my judgment, dearest Serenus, Athenodorus surrendered to the modern climate too easily and retreated prematurely. I would not deny that a withdrawal is sometimes indicated, but it should be a gradual retreat, without surrender of colors or of the soldier's honor; even the enemy shows higher respect and consideration for those who yield with weapons in hand. This, I think, is the proper course

for virtue and Virtue's partisan. If Fortune gets the upper
hand and interdicts action, he should not at once turn his
back and fly defenseless to seek a hiding place, as if there
were any place where Fortune could not reach him; let him
rather participate in public affairs more discreetly and carefully choose some capacity in which he can be useful to
the state. Is a military career impossible? Let him aspire to
office. Is the private station mandatory? Let him become
an orator. Is he condemned to silence? Let him support his
fellow citizens without speechmaking. Is it dangerous for
him even to enter the forum? Then he must show himself
a good companion, a faithful friend, a temperate guest in
people's houses, at public shows, at dinner parties. Has he
lost the functions of a citizen? Let him exercise those of a
man.

The reason we Stoics have high-heartedly refused to confine ourselves within the walls of a single city but have
sought relations with the whole earth and claimed the
whole world for our fatherland was to afford virtue a
broader scope. Is the judge's bench barred to you and are
you shut out from the rostrum and the hustings? Look at
the great populations and broad countries stretching out behind you; never can so large a portion be barred to you but
that an even larger will be left open.

But make sure that the fault is not your own. You are
unwilling to undertake public service except as consul or
president or premier or khalif; what if you were unwilling
to serve in the army except as general or colonel? Even if
others shall be shock troops and your lot assigns you to the
reserve line, play the soldierly part from there with voice,
encouragement, example, spirit. A man who has his hands
cut off can help his side by keeping his position and shouting. You must behave similarly. If Fortune has removed
you from the first rank in public affairs, stand your ground
anyhow and help with the shouting. The efforts of a good
citizen are never useless; by being heard and seen, by his

expression, gesture, silent determination, by his very gait he is of service. Just as certain medicines work by odor without taste or touch, so Virtue, at a distance and unseen, radiates usefulness. Whether she walks at her ease and exercises her rights, or whether her appearances are on sufferance and she is forced to shorten sail, whether she is inactive and mute and pent up within narrow bounds, or whether she is open to the world, whatever her state, Virtue does useful service. Why do you think the example of a man in useful retirement has no value? Whenever chance impediments or the political situation make our active career impossible, far the best course is to season your leisure with activity; for never can all pursuits be so blocked off that there is no room left for honorable action.

[5] Never could you find a city more miserable than Athens when the Thirty Tyrants were tearing it to pieces. They had killed the thirteen hundred best men in the city, and this did not end their savagery but only whetted it. In the city which was the seat of that hallowed tribunal the Areopagus, which had a senate and an assembly as august, there foregathered daily a melancholy commission of hangmen, and the unhappy senate house was too little to hold the crowd of tyrants. Could there be calm in a city which had as many tyrants as a tyrant has henchmen? No slightest hope of recovering liberty could be entertained, and there appeared to be no possible remedy against such a mass of disaster. Where could the wretched state find enough Harmodiuses? But Socrates was on the spot. Socrates consoled the senior citizens, encouraged men who despaired of their country, reproached the wealthy, who now feared their wealth, for their tardy repentance for their avarice, and presented to any who wished to imitate him the magnificent example of a free man walking unafraid amid thirty autocrats. But this same Socrates, Athens killed in jail: liberty could not tolerate the liberty of the man not afraid to scorn a crew of tyrants. This will give you to un-

derstand that in a commonwealth under oppression there is opportunity for a wise man to assert himself, and in one flourishing and prosperous willfulness, envy, and a thousand other unmanly vices hold sway.

According to the state's attitude toward us, therefore, and according as Fortune allows, we shall spread sail or shorten it, but in any case we shall move and not freeze in the fetters of fear. On the contrary, the true man will not impair his virtue or hide it away when danger threatens from all sides, when weapons and chains clang all about him. Burying one's self is not saving one's self. Curius Dentatus was right, I think, when he said he would rather be dead than a living cipher; the worst fate of all is to be stricken from the roster of the living before you die. But your proper course of conduct, if you happen upon a refractory political conjuncture, is to claim more time for leisure and letters, just as you might seek a haven in a perilous voyage, and step out of harness yourself without waiting for formal dismissal.

[6] Our first duty will be to examine ourselves, next the career we shall undertake, and finally our associates in the work and its beneficiaries. [7] You must consider whether your nature is better suited for busy activity or for leisurely study and contemplation, and must turn as your character directs. Isocrates intervened to take Ephorus away from the forum, in the conviction that Ephorus would be more usefully employed in compiling the records of history. Talent responds badly to coercion; where nature is reluctant, labor is vain.

A correct estimate of self is prerequisite, for we are generally inclined to overrate our capacities. One man is tripped by confidence in his eloquence, another makes greater demands upon his estate than it can stand, another burdens a frail body with an exhausting office. Some are too bashful for politics, which require aggressiveness; some are too headstrong for court; some do not control their temper and break into unguarded language at the slightest provocation; some cannot restrain their wit or resist making risky jokes. For all such people retirement is better than a career; an assertive and intolerant temperament should avoid incitements to outspokenness that will prove harmful.

Next we must appraise the career and compare our strength with the task we shall attempt. The worker must be stronger than his project; loads larger than the bearer must necessarily crush him. Certain careers, moreover, are not so demanding in themselves as they are prolific in begetting a mass of other activities. Enterprises which give rise to new and multifarious activities should be avoided; you must not commit yourself to a task from which there is no free egress. Put your hand to one you can finish or at least hope to finish; leave alone those that expand as you work at them and do not stop where you intended they should.

In our choice of men we should be particularly careful to see whether they are worth spending part of our life on and whether they will appreciate our loss of time; some people think we are in their debt if we do them a service. Athenodorus said he would not even go to dine with a man who would not feel indebted for his coming. Much less would he dine with people, as I suppose you understand, who discharge indebtedness for services rendered by giving a dinner and count the courses as favors, as if their lavishness was a mark of honor to others. Take away witnesses and spectators and they will take no pleasure in secret gormandizing.

But nothing can equal the pleasures of faithful and congenial friendship. How good it is to have willing hearts as safe repositories for your every secret, whose privity you fear less than your own, whose conversation allays your anxiety, whose counsel promotes your plans, whose cheerfulness dissipates your gloom, whose very appearance gives you joy! But we must choose friends who are, so far as possible, free from passions. Vices are contagious; they light upon whoever is nearest and infect by contact. During a plague we must be careful not to sit near people caught in the throes and burning with fever, because we would be courting danger and drawing poison in with our breath; just so in choosing friends we must pay attention to character and take those least tainted. To mingle the healthy with the sick is the beginning of disease. But I would not prescribe that you become attached to or attract no one who is not a sage. Where would you find him? We have been searching for him for centuries. Call the least bad man the best. You could not have a more opulent choice, if you were looking for good men, than among the Platos and Xenophons and the famous Socratic brood, or if you had at your disposal the age of Cato, which produced many characters worthy to be his contemporaries (just as it produced many unprecedentedly bad, who engineered monstrous crimes. Both kinds were necessary to make Cato's quality understood: he needed bad men against whom he could make his strength effective and good men to appreciate his effectiveness). But now there is a great dearth of good men, and your choice cannot be fastidious. But gloomy people who deplore everything and find reason to complain you must take pains to avoid. With all his loyalty and good will, a grumbling and touchy companion militates against tranquillity.

[8] We pass now to property, the greatest source of affliction to humanity. If you balance all our other troubles —deaths, diseases, fears, longings, subjection to labor and pain—with the miseries in which our money involves us, the latter will far outweigh the former. Reflect, then, how much less a grief it is not to have money than to lose it, and then you will realize that poverty has less to torment us with in the degree that it has less to lose. If you suppose that rich men take their losses with greater equanimity you are mistaken; a wound hurts a big man as much as it does

a little. Bion put it smartly: a bald man is as bothered when his hair is plucked as a man with a full head. The same applies to rich and poor, you may be sure; in either case the money is glued on and cannot be torn away without a twinge, so that both suffer alike. It is less distressing, as I have said, and easier not to acquire money than to lose it, and you will therefore notice that people upon whom Fortune never has smiled are more cheerful than those she has deserted. Diogenes saw this, being the intelligent man he was, and refused to have anything which could be taken from him. Give this kind of security any invidious name you like—poverty, neediness, pauperism; I shall not count a man happy if you find me another who has nothing to lose. Unless I am wrong, it is a kingly prerogative to be the only man not susceptible to injury in an environment of moneygrubbers, cheats, robbers, and thieves.

If a man questions Diogenes' happiness, he can also question the status of the immortal gods and doubt that their existence is happy because they have no landed estates or parks or income-producing ranches abroad or large investments in the money market. Aren't you ashamed, you who gape at riches? Just look at the heavens: you will see that the gods are penniless; they give everything and have nothing. Do you think the man who strips himself of Fortune's accessories a pauper or peer of the gods? Would you call Demetrius happier than his master Pompey because he was not ashamed of being the richer man? He should have counted himself rich with two helpers and a roomier cell, but the roster of his slaves was reported to him daily, as his army's roster is to a general. But when Diogenes' only slave ran away he did not think it worth while to bring him back when the slave was pointed out to him. "Disgraceful," said he. "Manes can live without Diogenes; cannot Diogenes live without Manes?" I think what he meant was: "Fortune, mind your own business; there's no longer anything you have an interest in in Diogenes' premises. My slave has run away; it is I who have got off free." A household of slaves requires dressing and feeding; a crowd of ravenous creatures have to have their bellies filled, clothing has to be bought, thieving hands have to be watched, and the service we get is rendered with resentment and curses. How much happier is he whose only obligation is to a man he can easily refuse—himself! But since we do not have Diogenes' strength, we ought at least curtail our property and reduce our exposure to the assaults of Fortune. In war a physique which can be squeezed into armor is more serviceable than one which overflows, when a man's size exposes him to wounds in all directions. In money matters the best measure is not to descend to poverty nor yet to be too far removed from it.

[9] And with this measure we shall be content if we have learned to be content with thrift, without which no amount of wealth can satisfy and with which any amount suffices, especially since a remedy is available: even poverty can transform itself into wealth by applying thrift. We must habituate ourselves to reject ostentation and value things by their utility, not by their trappings. The function of victuals is to subdue hunger; of drink to quench thirst; of the sexual urge, its essential discharge. We must learn to lean on our own members, to conform our dress and food not to the latest style but to the modes our ancestors recommend. We must learn to strengthen self-restraint, curb luxury, temper ambition, moderate anger, view poverty calmly, cultivate frugality (though many are ashamed of it), use readily available remedies for natural desires, keep restive aspirations and a mind intent upon the future under lock and key, and make it our business to get our riches from ourselves rather than from Fortune.

It is never possible to erect defenses against the diversity and malignity of events strong enough to prevent a great spread of sail from being blasted by gales. We must compress our affairs into a narrow compass, to frustrate missiles; that is why exile and other disasters have sometimes proved salutary and have cured serious maladies with slight inconveniences. When a mind is deaf to instruction and cannot be cured by milder measures, is it not wholesome to apply poverty, disgrace, financial ruin, and to counter evil with evil? We must therefore learn the capacity to dine without a mob, to enslave ourselves to fewer slaves, to get clothes for the purpose they were invented for, to live less spaciously. The inside track is the one to take not only in foot races and horse races but also in the arena of life.

Even in literary pursuits, where expense is in the best of taste, it is justifiable only so long as it is kept within bounds. What point in countless books and libraries whose catalogue their owner cannot scan in a lifetime? The student is loaded down, not instructed, by the bulk; it is much better to give yourself to a few authors than to stray through many. Forty thousand books were burned at Alexandria. Admirers may praise the library as the noblest monument of royal wealth; Livy, for instance, called it the distinguished achievement of kingly refinement and benevolence. There was no refinement or benevolence about it, but only a studious luxury—and not even studious, for the books were collected not for study but for show, just as many people without a grade-school education use books not as appliances for study but as *objets d'art* for the dining room. Buy as many books as you need, but none for show. "But it is more respectable," you say, "to squander money on books than on Corinthian bronzes and on paintings." Anything carried to excess is wrong. Why make apologies for a man with a nose for bookcases of citrus and ivory who scavenges for unknown or rejected authors and sits yawning among his thousands of volumes and gets his pleasure from their bindings and labels? In houses most unstudious you can see the complete orators and historians in cases piled high as the ceiling; along with baths and steam rooms, a library has now become an essential appendage to a fine house. If it were an over-sharp zest for learning that led them astray I would, of course, indulge these men, but the fact is that the work of inspired writers, each under its portrait bust, are bought up for show, to decorate a wall.

[10] But you have stumbled, say, on some difficult sort of life, and all unwitting have been knotted by your public or private fortunes in a noose which you can neither untie nor break. Reflect that men newly shackled chafe at the ball and chain on their legs, but when they resolve to endure their fetters without fretting, necessity teaches fortitude and habit indifference. In any sort of life you will find amusements and recreations and diversions if you choose to count your evils insignificant rather than make them hateful. Nature has done better by us here than in any other department; knowing that man was born to sorrow she invented habit as an anodyne to calamity, thus reducing extreme hardship to the level of the ordinary. If adversity kept the force of its first shock permanently, no one could bear it.

We are all chained to Fortune. Some chains are golden and loose, some tight and of base metal; but what difference does it make? All of us are in custody, the binders as well as the bound—unless you suppose the left end of the chain is lighter. Some are chained by office, some by wealth; some are weighed down by high birth, some by low; some are subject to another's tyranny, some to their own; some are confined to one spot by banishment, some by a priesthood. All life is bondage. Man must therefore habituate himself to his condition, complain of it as little as possible, and grasp whatever good lies within his reach. No situation is so harsh that a dispassionate mind cannot find some consolation in it. If a man lays even a very small area out skillfully it will provide ample space for many uses, and even a foothold can be made livable by deft arrangement. Apply good sense to your problems; the hard can be softened, the narrow widened, and the heavy made lighter by the skillful bearer.

Our desires, moreover, must not be set wandering far afield; since they cannot be wholly confined, we may give them an airing in the immediate vicinity. What cannot be or can hardly be we should leave alone, and follow what is near at hand and in reach of hope, but in the knowledge that all alike are trivial; without, their aspects are diverse, but they are equally empty within. Nor should we envy men in higher place; what looks lofty is precipitous.

Those, again, whom an unkind lot has placed in an equivocal position will be safer if they eliminate the pride from a situation inherently proud and, so far as they can, reduce their fortune to the common level. Many, to be sure, must cling to the pinnacle from which they cannot descend without crashing. By their own testimony the greatest onus of their position is that they must be severe with others; they are not raised to their high post but nailed to it. They may balance on their perch more securely if they prepare safeguards for a successful descent by justice, gentleness, mercy, and generous and kindly administration. But the surest deliverance from these alternations of hope and despair is to fix a limit to our advancement; we should not leave the decision to Fortune, but ourselves come to a halt far this side the reaches suggested by precedent. The aspirations a man may entertain will keep the mind alert, but because they are limited they will not lead him into uncharted and ambiguous regions.

[11] This discourse of mine applies to the imperfect, the mediocre, the unsound, not to the sage. The sage does not need to walk timidly and grope his way. So sure is he of himself that he does not hesitate to confront Fortune and will never give ground to her. He has nothing to make him afraid of her, for he reckons not only his chattels and property and position but even his body and eyes and hand, all that a man cherishes in life, even his own personality,

as temporary holdings, and he lives as if he were on loan to himself, and is ready to return the whole sum cheerfully on demand. But the knowledge that he does not belong to himself does not cheapen him in his own sight; he performs all his duties as diligently and conscientiously as a devout and holy man guards property committed to his integrity. When the order to return the deposits comes he will not quarrel with Fortune but will say: "I am thankful for what I have held and enjoyed. My management of your property has paid you dividends, but as you order me to do so I give it back, and withdraw cheerfully and gratefully. If you still wish me to hold anything that belongs to you I will take care of it; otherwise I return and restore to you my silver, plate or coin, my house, and my household."

If Nature should reclaim what she had previously entrusted to us, we too shall say to her: "Take back the spirit, better than when you gave it me. I do not turn away or hang back. Here ready for you is what you gave me without my knowledge; I give it to you with good will; take it away." What hardship is there in returning whence you came? A man will live ill if he does not know how to die well. And so we must deflate the price of the commodity and class the breath of life with cheap goods. "We dislike gladiators," says Cicero, "if they go to every length to supplicate for their lives; we favor them if their swagger shows their contempt of life." The outcome for us, you must realize, is the same; fear of death is often the cause of death. Fortune, who organizes her own amusements, says: "Why should I reserve a worthless and timorous animal like you? You shall be hacked and mangled all the more because you do not know how to offer your throat. But you who do not cringe your neck or put your hands up to stop the blade but receive it boldly will live longer and die more expeditiously."

A man afraid of death will never play the part of a live man. But a man who understands that his very conception was conditional upon death will live according to the bond, and with the same ruggedness of spirit guarantee that nothing which befalls shall come as a surprise. By regarding future possibilities as certainties he softens the shock of disasters, which cannot disconcert men prepared and waiting; they bear heavily on thoughtless men whose view is limited to the agreeable. Death, captivity, ruin, fire, are actualities, and none of them is unforeseen; I always knew what a tempestuous crew Nature had shut me in with. Time and again has keening been heard in my neighborhood; time and again have torch and taper led funeral processions for the untimely dead past my door; often has the crash of a collapsed building thundered at my side; associates in forum and senate with whom I had been in friendly conversation have been carried away in the night, and the fellowship of joined hands has been severed: can I be surprised if dangers that have always hovered about me should at some time alight upon me? A great part of mankind never think of storms when they contemplate a voyage.

I don't mind citing a bad author if the line is good. Publilius had a more forceful genius than the tragic and comic poets when he left off his silly mimes and the fustian directed to the gallery, and said many things too robust for the buskin, let alone the sock. Among them is the line: "What can happen to somebody can happen to anybody." If a man locks this saying into his very marrow and remembers, when he looks at other people's troubles, of which there is a bountiful supply daily, that they have an open road to him also, he will equip himself long before he is attacked. It is too late to outfit a man for confronting danger after the danger has arrived. "I never imagined this would happen," one hears, or "Could you have believed such a thing could come about?" And why not? Where are the riches without poverty and hunger and beggary at their heels? What magistracy is there whose purple-bordered robe and augural staff and patrician ties are not attended by rags and the brand of infamy and a thousand stigmas and utter contempt? What royalty is there not on the brink of ruin and trampling and tyrant and executioner? Nor are the extremes separated by long intervals; between the throne and groveling at another's knee is but an hour. Know, then, that every station in life is subject to change, and whatever has befallen anybody can befall you as well.

You are rich: richer than Pompeius? But Pompeius had no bread or water when his old kinsman Caligula, a strange kind of host, opened Caesar's house to him so that he could close his own. He owned many rivers which rose and emptied within his own estates, and yet he had to beg drops of water. He perished of hunger and thirst in his kinsman's palace, and while he was starving the heir was arranging a state funeral for him. You have held high office: as high, as unlooked-for, and as autocratic as Sejanus'? In one day the senate gave him escort, and the people tore him limb from limb; of the man upon whom gods and men had showered every bounty nothing was left for the executioner to drag to the Tiber. You are a king: I will not refer you to Croesus, who saw his pyre kindled and quenched while he was still alive and was made to survive not only his reign but even his death, nor will I refer you to Jugurtha, whom Rome saw in chains the same year it had trembled before him. In our own days we have seen Ptolemy, king of Africa, and Mithridates, king of Armenia, in custody of Caligula's guards; the one was exiled (and assassinated), the other begged for an exile more honestly observed. With such kaleidoscopic shifts of rise and fall, unless you expect that what is possible may be actualized in your case, you will put yourself in the power of adversity; with foresight that power can be broken.

[12] Our next point is avoidance of labor for empty ends or out of empty motivation. That is to say, we must not covet what we cannot attain, or what, when we have attained it, will make us realize too late and shamefacedly

the vanity of our desires. In other words, labor should not be vain in the sense that it produces no result, nor should the result, if it produces any, be unworthy of the labor; whether the attainment is nil or embarrassing, the consequence is melancholy.

We must cut down on gadding about. So many men make the rounds of houses, theaters, and fora, thrust themselves into other people's affairs, and always give the impression of being busy. If you ask one of these men as he leaves home, "Where are you going? What do you have in mind?" he will answer, "Hercules! *I* don't know; I'll see some people, attend to something." They ramble about with no purpose, looking for some occupation, and do, not what they intended, but what they stumble upon. Their itinerary is thoughtless and purposeless, like ants crawling over bushes, impelled, for no reason, to go up and then down again. Many people lead an antlike existence; restless indolence would not be a bad name for it. Some of these wretches dashing as to a fire make a pitiful spectacle; they crash into people going the other way and go sprawling with their victims, and all this hurry is to pay a morning call on a man who will never return it, or attend the funeral of a man they do not know, or the trial of some litigious pettifogger, or the engagement reception of a much-married lady. They will attach themselves to somebody's litter and in places even lend the bearers a hand. Then, when they come home exhausted for nothing, they swear they do not know why they had left home or where they had been, but the next day they will retrace the same rounds.

Every exertion must have some rationale and some objective. Industry does not reduce men to nervousness; false ideas drive them to insanity. Even the latter are actuated by some hope; an attractive surface excites them, and their bemused minds cannot penetrate the emptiness within. That is how every single man who leaves home to swell the crowd is propelled through the streets by trifling and insubstantial causes. The man has nothing to absorb his energy, and when daylight drives him into the streets he is jostled at many front doors to no purpose, hands his name to a succession of butlers, is refused admittance by many, and finds after all that the most difficult man to find "at home" is himself. It is this abuse that gives rise to that most loathsome of vices, eavesdropping, prying into secrets public and private, acquiring quantities of information which it is not safe to report or to receive.

[13] Democritus was following this same train, I suppose, when he began: "A man who wishes to live in tranquillity must not engage in many activities, private or public." The reference, of course, is to useless activities, for if they are necessary a man ought to engage not merely in many but in innumerable activities, both private and public; it is when no sacred duty summons us that activity must be restricted. A man who engages in many activities often puts himself in the power of Fortune; it is safest never to tempt her too often but always to bear her in mind and take nothing for granted on her security. "I will sail if nothing happens," is the proper style, or "I shall become praetor if no obstacles arise," "This negotiation will prove satisfactory if nothing interferes." This is the basis for our assertion that nothing befalls the sage contrary to his expectations. We exempt him from the mistakes of mankind, not from their accidents. For him no more than for other men do all things turn out as he wished; they do turn out as he thought, and his first thought was that something might oppose his plans. The pang of disappointed wishes is necessarily less distressing to the mind if you have not promised it sure fulfillment.

[14] And we ought to make ourselves adaptable. We should not be partial to a rigid program but pass easily where chance has taken us without shrinking from change of plan or status, provided we do not fall into the vice of fickleness, which is an enemy to repose. Obstinacy is neces-

sarily anxious and unhappy because Fortune often forces it askew, but fickleness is a more serious fault because it never holds its posture. Each, inability to change and inability to persevere, is hostile to tranquillity. In any case, the mind must be recalled from externals and focus upon itself. It must confide in itself, find pleasure in itself, respect its own interests, withdraw as far as may be from what is foreign to it and devote itself to itself; it must not feel losses and must even construe adversity charitably.

Our master Zeno remarked, when he received word that all his possessions had gone to the bottom in a shipwreck, "Fortune bids me philosophize with a lighter pack." When a tyrant threatened the philosopher Theodorus with death and deprivation of sepulture, he said, "You are in position to please yourself; the two gills of blood are at your disposal. As for burial, what a fool you are to think it makes any difference to me whether I rot above ground or beneath it." Julius Canus was a man of the first quality, and the circumstance that he was born in our own age cannot dim our admiration of him. As he was taking his departure, after a long altercation with Caligula, that second Phalaris said to him, "Don't flatter yourself with any silly hope; I have ordered your execution." "Thank you, most excellent prince," was the reply. I am not sure of his meaning, for several explanations suggest themselves. Did he mean to sting him and make him realize the enormity of a cruelty which made death a kindness? Or was he taunting him with his chronic perversity?—men whose children were murdered and goods confiscated had to thank him. Or was it that he was grateful for his release? Whatever its meaning, the answer was magnificent. But someone may object: "Caligula might have reprieved him." Canus had no fear on that score; Caligula's integrity in orders of this kind was notorious! Can you believe he spent the ten days' interval before his execution without the slightest anxiety? The man's words, acts, composure are unbelievable. He was playing checkers when the centurion who was dragging a column of doomed men to their death ordered Canus called out to join them. At the summons he counted out his pieces and said to his companion, "Don't cheat after I die and say you won." Then he nodded to the centurion and said, "You are witness that I am one piece ahead." Do you think Canus was playing a game at that board? He was *making* game. His friends were sad at the prospect of losing such a man. "Why are you sad?" he said. "Your question is whether souls are immortal; I shall soon know." He actually carried his search for truth to the very end, and made his own death serve intellectual curiosity. His teacher of philosophy followed him on his last walk, and when they were not far from the mound on which daily sacrifice is offered to our Lord Caesar, asked him, "What are you thinking of now, Canus? Have you any ideas?" "I intend to observe whether the soul is aware that it is departing, in that most fleeting of moments," he said, and promised, if he made any discoveries, that he would make the round of his friends and inform them on the state of souls. There is tranquillity for you, in the midst of storm, there is a mind worthy of immortality, a mind that cites its own fate to prove truth, that continues its investigation of the soul as it is poised for the step that will carry it away, that continues to learn not merely up to the point of death but even from death itself! No one has persisted in philosophical inquiry longer. So great a man will not quickly be forsaken; we must make a point of speaking about him. I shall hand you down to posterity, noble heart, grievous segment of Caligula's carnage!

[15] But to get rid of the causes of personal sorrow gains us nothing, for sometimes hatred of the human race possesses us. When you reflect how rare simplicity is, how unknown innocence, how seldom faith is kept unless keeping it is good policy, when you recall the long calendar of successful crime, the profits and losses of lust, alike odious,

and ambition that no longer keeps to its proper confines but rises to eminence through skulduggery, then the mind is plunged into black night and darkness envelops us, as if the virtues were overthrown and we could no longer possess them or aspire to them. The trend of thought we ought to pursue, therefore, is to make the common failings of the crowd not odious but ridiculous, and emulate Democritus rather than Heraclitus. Heraclitus wept whenever he went out in public, and Democritus laughed: the one thought all our behavior pitiful, the other silly. We ought to take the lighter view of these things and cultivate tolerance; it is more civilized to laugh at life than to lament over it. Further, the man who laughs at the human race deserves more gratitude than the man who mourns over it, for he allows it hope of amelioration, whereas the foolish weeper despairs of the possibility of improvement. And in the larger view, the man who does not restrain laughter shows a nobler spirit than the man who does not restrain tears, for laughter involves slight emotional commitment and indicates that nothing in the appurtenances of life is important or serious or even pitiful.

Let a man take a look at the individual reasons for our joy and sadness and he will realize the truth of Bion's remark: "All the concerns of men are very like their beginnings, and their life is no purer or more austere than their conception; born of nothingness, to nothingness they return." Yet it is better to accept prevalent mores and human failings dispassionately, without bursting into either laughter or tears; for to be tormented by other people's troubles is misery, and to take pleasure in them sadism, so it is futile charity to assume a sad demeanor because someone is burying his son. In one's own troubles, too, the proper behavior is to allow grief its claims of nature, not of custom. Many people shed tears for display and keep dry eyes when there is no one looking on, because they think it unbecoming not to weep when everyone does. So deeply rooted is the vice of depending on public opinion that so simple a thing as grief is subject to counterfeiting.

[16] We come next to a topic which understandably saddens and perplexes us. When good men come to bad ends, when Socrates is made to die in prison, Rutilius to live in banishment, Pompey and Cicero to offer their necks to their own clients, and Cato, that walking epitome of virtue, to advertise, by falling upon his own sword, that he and the republic were done with, we are necessarily distressed at Fortune's inequitable requitals. What can a man hope for for himself when he sees that the best men fare worst? What is there to say? See how each of them bore his lot: if they were brave, aspire to their courage; if their death was unmanly and disreputable there is no loss. Either they deserve your admiration of their courage, or they do not deserve regret for their poltroonery. It is perverse indeed for the exemplary deaths of the great to make other men timid.

Let us be instant in speaking the praises of the man who deserves praise and let us cry, "The braver, the happier! You have escaped accident, envy, disease; you have emerged from custody. It was not that the gods deemed you worthy of ill fortune: they deemed you worthy not to be subject to Fortune at all. It is the man who shrinks back at the hour of death and looks longingly back on life who requires the application of force. I shall weep for none that is cheerful and for none that is tearful; the one has himself wiped my tears away, and the tears of the other prove him unworthy of mine. Shall I weep for Hercules because he is burned alive, or for Regulus because he is pierced by so many nails, or for Cato because he tore his wounds open? All these men found a means to immortality at a paltry cost in time, and their deaths have made them deathless.

[17] Another very considerable source of anxiety is the practice of maintaining a careful pose and never revealing your natural self to anyone. The life of many people is a

fiction, polished up for exhibition. But to be constantly on guard for fear of being caught out of an assumed character is a torment. And we are never fully at ease if we think we are being assayed every time we are looked at. Many things come up to strip us of the sham, and even if our acting is flawless it is neither agreeable nor safe to lead a life under a mask. But what pleasure there is in unglazed and untrimmed simplicity which does not screen its character! Yet this life in which every detail is open to everyone is liable to contempt, for there are people who disdain anything within reach. But virtue can stand scrutiny without being cheapened, and it is better to be scorned for simplicity than tormented by permanent hypocrisy. Still, we should observe due measure; there is a great difference between simple living and slovenly living.

It is important to withdraw into one's self. Association with a different sort of people unsettles ideas made orderly, reawakens passions, and aggravates mental cankers not yet thoroughly healed. But the two ought to be combined and alternated, some solitude, some society. Solitude will give us an appetite for people, society for ourselves, and the one is a cure for the other. Solitude will allay loathing of the crowd, and the crowd the ennui of solitude.

The intellect must not be kept at consistent tension, but diverted by pastimes. Socrates was not ashamed to play with little boys, Cato took wine to relax his mind when it was fatigued with official responsibilities, and Scipio's soldierly and triumph-crowned person trod the paces of the dance, not demeaning his virility by the modern sinuous mincing which is more voluptuous than a soft woman's, but as the heroes of old footed it in robust measures at their sports and festivals, without impairing their dignity even in enemy eyes. The mind must have relaxation, and will rise stronger and keener after recreation. Just as fertile fields must not be forced (without fallow periods their richness is soon exhausted), so incessant labor will crush the mind's *élan.* A little respite and relaxation restores the mind's energy, but unrelieved mental exertion begets dullness and languor.

Sport and amusement would not exert so strong an attraction if the pleasure they gave were not inherently natural, but frequent resort to them will rob the mind of all weight and energy; sleep, too, is a necessary recreation, but if you keep it up day and night it is tantamount to death. There is a great difference between slackening and letting go. Our founding fathers established holidays upon which men must foregather for jollity on the ground that such respites are an essential ingredient for labor, and, as I have remarked, some important people gave themselves vacations on specified days every month, and some divided each day into hours of leisure and of occupation. I recall that the distinguished orator Asinius Pollio belonged to this school. No business could keep him after four o'clock, and he would not even read letters after that hour for fear they might bring some new responsibility; in his two free hours he laid aside the whole day's weariness. Some break off in the middle of the day and keep some lighter task for the afternoon hours. Our ancestors also prohibited the introduction of new business in the senate after four o'clock. The army divides the night into watches, and men newly returned from active duty are exempt the night through. We must be kind to the mind and from time to time give it the leisure which is its sustenance and strength.

We ought to take outdoor walks, to refresh and raise our spirits by deep breathing in the open air. Sometimes energy will be refreshed by a carriage drive, a journey, a change of scene, good company, and a more generous wine. Upon occasion we should go as far as intoxication, half-seas over, not total immersion. Drink washes cares away, stirs the mind from its lowest depths, and is a specific for sadness as for certain maladies. Bacchus, who invented wine, is surnamed Liber, not because of the license wine gives the tongue, but because it liberates the mind from its bondage to care and emancipates it and animates it and gives it greater boldness for any enterprise. But in liberty moderation is wholesome, and so it is in wine. Solon and Arcesilas are believed to have been addicts, and Cato has been charged with drunkenness. But the man who makes such an indictment will find himself proving that the charge is respectable rather than that Cato was disreputable. We ought not indulge too often, for fear the mind contract a bad habit, yet it is right to draw it toward elation and release and to banish dull sobriety for a little. Whether we agree with the Greek poet that "sometimes it is jolly to be mad," or with Plato that "it is vain for the sober man to knock at poesy's door," or with Aristotle that "every great genius has an admixture of madness," in any case only a mind that is excited is capable of great and transcendant utterance. When it has spurned the trite and the commonplace and has been impelled aloft by the demonic urge, then and only then can it sing a strain too grand for mortal lips. So long as it is under its own sway the mind cannot attain the sublime, cannot reach the treasure which reposes upon a pinnacle. It must tear itself from the trodden path, palpitate with frenzy, take the bit in its teeth and run away with its rider to reach the height it would fear to climb in its own strength.

I hand you, my dearest Serenus, these prescriptions for preserving tranquillity, for recovering it, and for resisting the failings which surreptitiously vitiate it. But note well: none of them is potent enough to protect so frail a boon unless devoted and unremitting care encompasses it to prevent backsliding.

CONSOLATION TO HELVIA

In 41 B.C., at the beginning of Claudius' reign, Seneca was condemned on a charge of adultery with Julia Livilla, a sister of Caligula and Agrippina, and sentenced to exile in Corsica. He wrote this piece to his mother, probably in the second year of his seven-year banishment. This Consolation is doubtless the most carefully elaborated specimen of the genus we have. The arrangement of parts, the development of the argument, the rhetorical devices, and the examples are all carefully studied and highly polished. But the high polish cannot disguise the essential sincerity of the piece or the genuine affection and concern Seneca felt for his mother. It may strike the reader as odd that Seneca should assume that his mother felt his temporary loss more keenly than she had the death, two years before, of her devoted husband, especially when she had two other dutiful sons and a number of grandchildren, and he himself admits that a consolation addressed to the bereaved by the departed is unexampled. Nevertheless, the touching tenderness which this letter exhibits shows that there must have been a special bond between Seneca and his mother. The argument is twofold. Helvia's grief must be for him or for herself. He requires no sympathy because to a Stoic the deprivations exile entails are things indifferent and even advantageous; and Helvia's proven fortitude, supported by application to study, will enable her to bear her deprivation serenely.

[1] Repeatedly, dearest mother, I have felt impelled to write and comfort you, but as often I have refrained. A number of considerations prompted me to venture the attempt. In the first place, it seemed I might banish my troubles if I could at least wipe your tears away, even if I could not stop their flow; secondly, I felt sure I could raise you to your feet if I could first stand upright myself; and lastly, I was afraid that the power of Fortune which I had myself vanquished might yet prostrate one near and dear to me. And so I tried as best I could to put my hand over my own sore and creep forward to bandage your wounds.

On the other hand, there were deterrent considerations. I knew I ought not treat your sore while it was still fresh and angry, for the remedy might further irritate and inflame it; in physical ailments, too, nothing is more harmful than too hasty treatment. And so I waited until the violence of your affliction should break of its own accord and until the assuagement of time should enable it to be fingered and probed and submit to treatment. Moreover, though I leafed through treatises on the restraint and tempering of sorrow written by outstanding authorities, I found no case of a man who offered his dear ones condolence while he was himself the object of their grief. Where I had no precedent, therefore, I hesitated, for fear my effort might prove an exacerbation rather than a consolation. A man raising his head from the very pyre would surely need a novel vocabulary and forms of discourse not drawn from the commonplace vernacular. But the intensity of a grief which surpasses every precedent must necessarily choke off choice diction, for it suffocates bare utterance. Yet be that as it may, I shall make the attempt, not out of confidence in my eloquence, but because functioning as a comforter may bring me the most effective comfort. You never deny me anything and so will not prove unwilling, I hope, to let me set a limit to your yearning, even though sorrow is always stubborn.

[2] See how much I presume on your indulgence. I make no question that my power over you will be greater than your grief's, though to the wretched no power has precedence over grief's. But I shall not clash with your grief straightway; first I will take its side and heap rich fuel upon it to arouse it. I will expose and tear open the wounds which have already cicatrized. Someone may object: "What kind of consolation is this, to recall afflictions now obliterated and to parade a whole series of sorrows to a mind scarcely able to endure one?" But the objector should reflect that maladies grown so malignant that they outpace their usual remedies can frequently be treated by contraries. So I shall bring to bear upon your spirit its every grief and sorrow; my course of treatment will not be gentle but will involve cautery and surgery. What shall I accomplish? A spirit with such a history of grief will be ashamed to show distress at a single wound in a body covered with scars. Tears and incessant sighs are for dainty spirits unmanned by long prosperity; at the slightest stirring of discomfort they are prostrated. But people who have passed all their years in affliction should bear even the heaviest blows with unflagging fortitude. This is the one benefit of constant misfortune; eventually it hardens those whom it persistently afflicts.

No respite from its blows has Fortune allowed you. The very day of your birth was not immune: you lost your mother as soon as you were born, indeed in the process of birth, and entered life, as it were, a foundling. You grew up under a stepmother, whom, to be sure, your obedience and affection, as great as any daughter could show, converted into a mother perforce; still, even a good stepmother costs dear. My kindliest of uncles, a fine and gallant gentleman, you lost just when you were expecting his arrival. Nor would Fortune alleviate her cruelty by spacing her blows: within the month you buried your beloved husband, the father of your three sons. The sad tidings were brought to you when you were already in mourning, when your sons were all abroad, as if your afflictions had purposely been concentrated in a span when your grief would have no solace to ease it. I pass over the many perils and the many anxieties which assailed you without surcease and which you endured. Just recently, into that bosom from which you had sent forth three grandchildren, you received the bones of three grandchildren. Within twenty days of your burying my son, who died in your arms and amid your kisses, you heard that I had been snatched from you. This was the crowning touch, to mourn for the living.

[3] Of all the wounds that have gashed your frame this last, I confess, is the deepest; it has not merely scratched the surface skin but has cloven your very breast and vitals. But green recruits cry out at the slightest wound and cringe from the leech's treatment more than from the sword, whereas veterans, even when they are pierced through, patiently and without groaning allow their wounds to be drained as if their bodies were detached; just so ought you submit to treatment at this conjuncture. Away with lamentations and wailing and the noisy agitation expected of bereaved women; you have wasted all those sorrows if they have not taught you to endure misery. My treatment has not seemed timid, has it? None of your afflictions have I glossed over; I have stacked them all before you in a pile.

[4] I did so resolutely because I determined to conquer your grief, not cheat it. And conquer it I shall, I believe, if I demonstrate, in the first place, that there is nothing in my present situation which would justify my being called unhappy or making my kin unhappy; and secondly, if I then turn to you and prove that your lot, which depends wholly upon mine, is not a heavy one.

My first step shall be to declare what your affection is on edge to hear, that I am not in distress. I shall demonstrate, if I can, that the circumstances which you suppose crush me are not in fact intolerable. And if you find this incredible I shall at least felicitate myself on being happy under conditions calculated to make people unhappy. There is no reason for you to heed what others say about my mood; to obviate your confusion and uncertainty I myself declare to you that I am not unhappy. And to give you greater assurance I add that I cannot even be made unhappy.

[5] The terms under which we are born would be favorable if we did not play them false. Nature intended that no great equipment should be necessary for happiness; each of us is in position to make himself happy. Externals have little weight and exert only slight pressure in one direction or the other. The sage is neither elated by prosperity nor depressed by adversity. His endeavor always is to rely mainly on himself and to seek his whole satisfaction from within himself. Does it follow that I claim to be a sage? Not in the least; if I could make that claim, I should not only be denying that I am unhappy but vaunting myself the happiest of men, one who had attained nighness to god. But I have put myself in the hands of the sages, which is enough to allay all unhappiness in my present state; not yet in position to bring up my own reserves, I have taken refuge in the camp of others, of those, to wit, who guard themselves and their partisans with ease. It is they who have bidden me keep steadfast watch, as on a sentry post, and to forestall Fortune's every sally or attack in force long before it occurs. Her assault is formidable only when it comes as a surprise; it is sustained with ease if one is always on the alert for it. Even an enemy onset confounds only those it takes unexpectedly; those who are prepared for war before it strikes, ready marshaled and armed, can easily parry the initial charge, which is the most violent.

Never have I trusted Fortune, even when she seemed

to be at peace; all her generous bounties—money, office, influence—I deposited where she could ask them back without
disturbing me. Myself I kept detached and remote from
those bounties, and so Fortune has merely taken them
away, not wrested them from me. No one is crushed by
adverse Fortune who has not first been beguiled by her
smile. Only those who become enamored of her gifts as if
they were their own forever, and expect deference because
of them, are prostrated by grief when the deceitful and
ephemeral baubles abandon empty and childish minds ignorant of every abiding satisfaction.

But the man who is not inflated by prosperity does not
collapse under adversity. The man of tested constancy keeps
a spirit impregnable to either condition; in the midst of
felicity he knows his own power to meet adversity. I have
therefore never believed that any true good inhered in the
things men commonly pray for; I have found them empty
and daubed with specious and cheating colors, with no inner content to match their outward show. And in my present state, which is called evil, I find none of the fearfulness
and deprivation which vulgar opinion threatened. The conventional attitude gives the word exile a harsh sound in our
ears, and it strikes the listener as something gloomy and
accursed. So have the people decreed, but the decrees of
the people are in large measure repealed by the sages.

[6] We may, then, disregard the verdict of the majority,
who are gullible and carried away by specious appearances, and see what exile really is. Exile is a change of
place. Not to appear to diminish its implications or ignore
its most undesirable attribute, I will grant that certain inconveniences are attached to this change of place—poverty,
disgrace, contempt. These factors I shall cope with in the
sequel; for the present, I wish first of all to examine what
distress the mere change of place entails.

"To be deprived of one's country is intolerable." Do but
look at this throng which the enormous capital can scarcely

house: the greater part of that crowd is deprived of country. They have poured in from their towns and municipalities, from the whole wide world. Some ambition has brought, some the obligations of public office, some are on official missions, some luxury has attracted in search of a convenient and abundant field for malefaction, some are impelled by a zeal for scholarship, some by the public shows; some have been drawn by friendship, some by the ample field for displaying its quality which is offered to diligence; some have brought their beauty to sell and some their eloquence; virtues and vices alike fetch a high price in the city, and every species of humanity has congregated there. Have them all summoned by name and ask each of them, "Where are you from?" You will find that the greater part have left their own homes to come to the city, which is very large and very handsome, to be sure, but not their own. Then move on from the capital, in which everyone may be said to have a share, and make the circuit through other cities: in every one a large percentage of the population is foreign. Move on from the towns whose agreeable climate and convenient situation have been a great attraction; scrutinize deserts and craggy islands—Sciathus and Seriphus, Gyarus and Cossura: you will find no Siberia where people do not tarry of their own will. No place so bare and precipitous as this rock is imaginable, none so starveling in resources, so uncouth in population, so repulsive in terrain, so extreme in climate. And yet more foreigners reside here than natives. Mere change of place is therefore so far from being a disability that even such a place as this has lured people from their own country.

In some writers I find the statement that the itch to change one's climate and to move from place to place is part of man's natural constitution, for the mind he is endowed with is fickle and restive. It never stays content, but spreads abroad and scatters its fancies the world over, in places known or unknown; it is a vagabond, impatient of repose and happiest with novelties. Nor will you find this strange if you look into its primal source. Man's mind was not compacted of earthy and ponderous matter, but descended from the lofty heavenly spirit. But the nature of the celestial is always mobile; it is elusive and moves with great velocity. Consider the planets that illuminate the world: none of them stands still. The sun glides on incessantly and moves from place to place, and though it revolves with the universe, its own motion is nevertheless contrary to the world's. It courses through all the signs of the zodiac without halting; it is constantly on the move, constantly migrating from one place to another. All the planets are always revolving, always in transition, they pass from one position to another in accordance with the destined law of nature, and when, in a fixed span of years, they have completed their orbits, they again traverse the path they had traveled. How absurd then to think that the human mind, which is compounded of the same ingredients as is the divine, should be irked by travel and transposition, when the nature of god finds delight in perpetual and rapid change or even depends upon such change for its existence.

[7] Turn now from celestial to human phenomena, and you will see that whole tribes and nations have changed their abode. What is the meaning of Greek cities in the heart of barbarian country? Why the Macedonian idiom among Indians and Persians? Scythia and that whole expanse of savage and uncivilized peoples boast of Achaean cities planted on the shores of the Black Sea; neither the bitter and endless winters nor the character of the natives, which matches their climate's savagery, have deterred immigrants from settling there. There is a whole Athenian population in Asia Minor, and Miletus has poured forth enough people in one direction and another to populate seventy-five cities. The whole coast of Italy which is washed by the Lower Sea became a Greater Greece. Asia

claims the Tuscans for her own; Tyrians have settled
Africa; and Carthaginians, Spain. Greeks have penetrated
Gaul; and Gauls, Greece. The Pyrenees have not barred
the influx of Germans. Man the wanderer has made his
way through pathless and unfamiliar regions. And men
drag along their children and wives and their doddering
parents. Some, exhausted by their aimless wandering, hit
upon a spot to settle not out of deliberate choice but wearily
grasped what was nearest hand. Some asserted their claim
on a foreign land by right of arms. Whole tribes in search
of the unknown were swallowed by the sea. Some settled
where complete destitution stranded them.

The motives for leaving the old home and seeking a new
were not always the same. Some escaped enemy destruction when their cities fell and were forced into the lands of
others when they were stripped of their own. Some have
been cast out by internal revolution. The overcrowding of
excess population has sent some out to relieve the pressure.
Some have been driven out by plague or frequent earthquakes or some unbearable defect of ill-starred soil. Some
have been seduced by the overblown reputation of a fertile
region. One motive has impelled one man to move from
home and another another, but in any case it is clear that
none abides in the spot where he was born. The human
race is in perpetual motion; in this great world there is
change daily. The foundations of new cities are laid, new
names of nations arise, while earlier polities are annihilated
or transformed into appanages of stronger nations. But are
those exchanges of population anything else than whole-
sale exile? Need I drag you through the whole inventory?
Need I cite Antenor, founder of Padua, or Evander, who
established a realm of Arcadians on Tiber's shore? Need I
mention Diomedes and the others, victors and vanquished
alike, whom the Trojan War dispersed over lands not their
own? Verily, the Roman Empire reveres an exile as its
founder; his country was conquered and he was a refugee,

leading a salvaged remnant in search of some distant place, and destiny and fear of the conqueror brought him to Italy. But how many colonies did his people then establish in every province! Wherever the Roman conquers, there he settles. Settlers gladly put their names down for migrations of this kind, and old men leave their altars behind to follow the colonists across the sea.

The argument requires no long inventory, but I must add one instance which compels my attention. This very island has repeatedly changed its population. To omit its ancient history, which the passage of time has obscured, the Greeks from Phocis who now live in Marseilles settled in this island first. What made them leave it is doubtful: it may have been the harsh climate, or the dangerous proximity of powerful Italy, or the want of harbors; the savagery of the natives was clearly not the cause, for the Greeks then settled among what were then the fiercest and least civilized tribes of Gaul. Subsequently Ligurians crossed over to the island, and also Spaniards, as is plain from parallel usages. The Corsicans use the same head coverings and the same type of shoes as do the Cantabrians, and a number of their words are the same; intercourse with Greeks and Ligurians has altered their language as a whole from their ancestral idiom. Next, two colonies of Roman citizens were settled in Corsica, one by Marius and the other by Sulla—so many times has the population of this barren and thorny rock been changed! In a word, you will find scarcely any country which is still occupied by an indigenous population; everywhere the stock is mongrel and imported. One people has followed another, what one scorned another has coveted, one people has displaced another, only itself to be evicted in turn. Fate has decreed that no kind of fortune should abide in the same station permanently.

[8] To compensate for mere change of place—disregarding other inconveniences involved in exile—Varro, the most scholarly of the Romans, held the fact that we enjoy the

same order of nature wherever we go a sufficient resource. Marcus Brutus thought the fact that exiles could carry their virtues with them a sufficient compensation. Taken severally, a man might judge these palliatives inadequate consolation for an exile, but he must confess that in combination they can be very effective. What we have lost is but a trifle, but wherever we stir the two resources which are the fairest of all attend us—nature, which is universal, and virtue, which is our own. Such was the design, believe me, of whatever force fashioned the univèrse, whether an omnipotent god, or impersonal Reason as artificer of vast creations, or divine Spirit permeating all things great and small with uniform tension, or Fate with its immutable nexus of interrelated causes—the design, I say, was that none but the paltriest of a man's possessions should fall under the sway of another. Whatever is excellent in man lies outside man's power; it can neither be given nor taken away. This world, than which Nature has wrought nothing greater or handsomer, and the human mind, its most magnificent portion, which contemplates the world and admires it, are our own forever, and will abide with us as long as we ourselves endure.

Briskly, therefore, and with head held high, let us stride with dauntless step wherever circumstances carry us, let us traverse any lands whatever. Within the world there can be no exile, for nothing within the world is alien to man. From any spot whatever eyes can be raised to heaven equally well: the interval between the divine and the human is everywhere constant. So long as my eyes are not barred that spectacle with which they are never sated, therefore, so long as I may contemplate sun and moon, so long as I may dwell upon other planets, so long as I may study their risings and settings and speculate upon the realms of their rapid or slower pace, behold the numberless stars gleaming in the night, some fixed, some not sweeping in a wide orbit but circling their own track, some suddenly bursting forth, some dazzling our vision with an effusion of fire as if they were falling, or flying by with a long train of brilliant light—so long as I can commune with these and mingle with heavenly bodies as far as a mortal may, so long as I may keep my mind always directed to the contemplation of kindred stuff on high, what matter to me what ground I tread?

[9] "But," you object, "this land bears no trees for fruit or shade, it is not watered by large or navigable streams, it produces nothing that other nations desire but is scarcely fertile enough to support its inhabitants; no costly stone is quarried here, and there are no veins of gold or silver to mine." Petty is the mind that takes pleasure in things of the earth; it should be directed away from them to the supernal beauties which are everywhere in view and everywhere equally resplendent.

This, too, must be borne in mind: things earthy, because they are meretricious and beguile the gullible, stand in the light of true goods. The farther men extend their porticos, the higher they raise their towers, the more spacious they build their villas, the deeper they dig their underground summer casinos, the more massive the gables of their banqueting halls, the more there will be to hide heaven from their sight. Circumstances have marooned you in a region where the most sumptuous lodging is a hut: it is a puny spirit, surely, and a vulgar kind of consolation that will tolerate this lot only by recalling the Hut of Romulus. Say rather: "That lowly cottage can, I suppose, shelter the virtues? Soon it shall be handsomer than any temple when justice shall be conspicuous there, and temperance, and wisdom, and righteousness, and right reason in discharging duties correctly, and the knowledge of god and man. No place is strait if it can contain such an assembly of cardinal virtues, no exile is onerous when a man can walk in such a company."

Brutus remarks, in the treatise *On Virtue* he composed,

that he saw Marcellus in exile at Mytilene and found him living as happily as human nature allows and more devoted to liberal studies than ever before. He adds that when he was on the point of returning to Rome without him he felt that he was himself going into exile rather than leaving Marcellus exiled in Mytilene. How much happier was Marcellus winning Brutus' applause as exile than the state's applause as consul! What a man he must have been to make a visitor feel he was going into exile because he was parting from an exile! What a man he must have been to compel the admiration of a man whom even Cato had to admire! Brutus likewise tells us that Julius Caesar sailed past Mytilene because he could not bear to see a great man marred. The senate did indeed procure his recall by public supplication, and in so anxious and sorrowful a mood that they all appeared to be of Brutus' mind that day and to be petitioning not on behalf of Marcellus but on their own behalf, as if it were themselves that would be exiled if they were deprived of him. But far higher was the pinnacle he reached on the day Brutus could not bear to leave him, Caesar to look upon him. Happily, the testimony of both men favored him: Brutus grieved to return without Marcellus and Caesar blushed.

Can you doubt that the illustrious Marcellus, that towering hero, often encouraged himself to bear his exile with equanimity in terms like these? "The loss of your country is not a misfortune: you are sufficiently steeped in philosophy to know that the wise man is at home everywhere. Besides, was not the very man who exiled you without his country for ten years on end? It was to enlarge the empire, it is true, but he was without his country nevertheless. And now, look you, he is being dragged to Africa, which is teeming with threats of resurgent war; he is being dragged to Spain, which is renewing the strength of the shattered and prostrate opposition; he is being dragged to perfidious Egypt; he is being pulled, in a word, to every quarter of the globe, which is intently watching its opportunity as the empire is shaken. Which crisis will he meet first? To what quarter will he first turn? His own victory drives him from land to land. Let the nations revere and worship him: enough for you the admiration of Brutus."

[10] Marcellus bore his exile like a man, then, and his change of place, though it entailed poverty, changed his mind not a whit. That poverty is no disaster is understood by everyone who has not yet succumbed to the madness of greed and luxury which turns everything topsy-turvy. How little a man requires to maintain himself! And how can a man who has any merit at all fail to have that little? In my own case, I know that I have lost not wealth but distractions. The wants of the body are a bagatelle: it wishes cold kept off and food to quench hunger and thirst. If we crave extras it is vice we work for, not need. There is no necessity to ransack the depths of every sea, to burden the belly with the carnage of breathing creatures, to tear shellfish from the uncharted shores of remote seas—gods and goddesses damn the rogues whose luxury has over-leaped the bounds of an empire already invidiously wide! They want game from beyond the Phasis to furnish their ostentatious kitchens, and show no reluctance to import fowl from the Parthians, from whom Rome has not yet taken vengeance. Items familiar or strange are brought to-gether from all quarters to tempt their finicky palates; things a stomach debauched by dainties can scarcely re-tain they fetch from the ends of the ocean. They vomit to eat and eat to vomit and do not deign to digest the viands for which they have scoured the world. If a man despises these things, how can poverty hurt him? And if a man craves them, then poverty is to his advantage, for he is cured in spite of himself. Though a man will not swallow medicine even under compulsion, in this case, at least, his want of power is like a want of desire.

Caligula—I think Nature's purpose in fashioning him was

to demonstrate what the height of vice is capable of when combined with the height of power—dined one day at the cost of half a million dollars, and though everyone contributed his ingenuity he barely contrived to turn the tribute of three provinces into a single dinner. How unhappy the people whose appetite is roused only by costly food! And it is not special savor or sweetness of taste that makes food costly, but its rarity and the difficulty of procuring it. Otherwise, if men would choose to return to sanity, what need of so many trades that cater to the belly? Why import? Why ravage the forests? Why ransack the seas? Food is accessible at every step, nature has made it available everywhere, but these people pass it by as though they were blind and roam every land and cross the sea and whet their hunger at great cost when they could allay it for a trifle. One is moved to protest: "Why do you launch your ships? Why do you equip armies against both beasts and men? Why do you scurry about in such busy excitement? Why do you heap riches on riches? Will you not reflect how small your bodies are? Is it not madness, is it not the wildest lunacy to crave so much when you can hold so little? Increase your rating as you will, expand your holdings, still you can never enlarge the volume of your belly. Though your business has prospered, though your campaigns have proved a bonanza, when your tracking in all quarters has poured viands in, you will have no place to stow your luxuries. Why so acquisitive?

Our ancestors, whose virtue supports our vices to this day, were miserable, forsooth, because they got their food with their own hands, because their bed was the earth, because their ceilings did not yet glitter with gold, because their temples were not yet resplendent with jewels. The oaths they swore by gods of clay in those days they kept scrupulously: to keep faith, those who invoked them went back to the enemy, though doomed to die. Our great dictator (Manius Curius), he who stirred the pot of turnips on his jack, as he listened to the Samnite ambassadors, with the same hand which had often routed the enemy and had deposited his triumphal laurels on the lap of Capitoline Jupiter, led a more wretched life, forsooth, than our late contemporary Apicius, who was professor of cookery in the city from which professors of philosophy were once expelled as corruptors of youth and who tainted the age with his doctrine. It is worth our while to see what became of Apicius. When he had squandered five million dollars on his kitchen, when he had guzzled numerous imperial bounties and the enormous revenue of the Capitol at each of his revels, he found himself heavily in debt, and for the first time, under pressure, he examined his accounts. He calculated that he would have half a million left, and in the conviction that life at half a million was the ultimate in starvation he ended his life by poison. What luxury when half a million makes a man a pauper! How absurd to suppose that it is the financial balance, not the mind's, that matters! A man actually dreaded half a million, and took poison to avoid what others pray for! For a man so deranged, his final potion was the most wholesome. It was poison he was eating and drinking when he not only enjoyed his enormous feasts but boasted of them, when he paraded his vices, when he advertised his wantonness to the community, when he incited the young—who are docile enough even without bad examples—to imitate his practices. Such is the fate of those who gauge riches not according to reason, which has definite limitations, but according to demoralized convention, whose caprices are beyond limitation or definition. For greed nothing is enough; Nature is satisfied with little. The exile's poverty entails no hardship, therefore, for no Siberia is so barren that it cannot amply support human life.

[11] "But," you object, "the exile is likely to miss his wardrobe and his house." If he wants these, too, only for use, neither shelter nor cover will fail him; it takes as little

to protect the body as to feed it. Nothing that Nature has made necessary for man has she made difficult. But if he desires garments of purple deep dyed, interwoven with gold and spangled in various tints and designs, it is not Nature's fault that he is poor but his own. Even if you restore all that he has lost you will waste your effort, for after he is restored he will fall farther short of his desires than as an exile he fell short of what he once had. If his desire is for sideboards displaying vessels of shining gold, for silver ennobled by the signature of old masters, for bronze made valuable by the quaint fad of a few collectors, for a horde of servants that would clutter the most spacious mansion, for mules forcibly crammed to make them fat, for marbles quarried in every country, even if he heaps these things up in piles they will never satisfy his insatiable appetite, any more than any quantity of water will satisfy a man whose craving is begotten not by lack of moisture but by a fever burning in his vitals; that is not thirst but distemper. This applies not only to money or food; every craving which springs from a fault rather than a need has the same character: however much you give, it will be only a stage in cupidity, not its fulfillment.

A man who keeps himself within the bounds of nature, therefore, will not feel poverty; but one who exceeds those bounds will be pursued by poverty even in the greatest opulence. For necessities even exile is sufficient, for superfluities not even kingdoms are. It is the mind which makes men rich; the mind accompanies us into exile, and when it has found adequate sustenance for the body even in the most desolate wilderness its own resources provide an abundance which it can enjoy. The mind has no more to do with money than have the immortal gods. All those objects revered by untutored intellects enslaved to their own bodies —marbles, gold, silver, polished round tables of great size— are earthy dross which an unflawed mind aware of its own nature cannot love, for it is itself light and unencumbered, ready to soar aloft as soon as it shall be released. In the meantime, so far as the curbs of the members and the heavy load of body which surrounds it allow, it contemplates things divine in swift and airy thought. Neither, therefore, can the mind be exiled, for it is free, kin to the gods, adequate to all space and all times, for thought ranges through all heaven and has access to all time, past and future. This trivial body, the prison and fetter of the soul, is tossed hither and yon; upon it tortures, brigandage, diseases, do their worst. But the mind itself is sacred and everlasting, and not subject to violence.

[12] Do not think that I am limited to philosophers' precepts in making light of poverty, which no one feels is a hardship unless he thinks it is. Consider, in the first place, that far the greater part of mankind are poor, and yet you will notice that they are in no way more worried or depressed than the rich; indeed, I rather think they are happier, for they have less to distract their minds. But let us pass from wealth that is allied to poverty and proceed to the really opulent. How many occasions there are when they fare like the poor! When they travel their baggage is curtailed, and when their journey requires speed their numerous retinue is dismissed. In military service they can keep only a fraction of their belongings, for camp discipline forbids superfluities. And not only do circumstances of time and place reduce them to the scanty footing of the poor, but they themselves choose certain days, when they are bored with their elegance, to dine on the ground and use earthenware, with no gold or silver at all. Lunatics!—the simplicity they sometimes crave they always dread. Ah, what a mental fog, what ignorance of truth blinds people who are harassed by fear of the poverty which they sometimes pretend for pleasure's sake!

I myself am ashamed to cite compensations for poverty when I look back to the models of long ago, for nowadays luxury has reached the point where an exile's travel allowance is more than the patrimony of leading citizens used to be. Everyone knows that Homer had only one servant, Plato three, and Zeno, with whom the austere and manly philosophy of the Stoics began, none. Could anyone suggest that those men led wretched lives without thereby showing himself the wretchedest of all? Menenius Agrippa, who reconciled patricians and plebeians in the public interest, was buried by public subscription. Atilius Regulus wrote the senate that his hired man had levanted, while he was chasing Carthaginians in Africa, and that his farm was neglected, and the senate voted that the care of Regulus' farm should be a public charge in his absence. Was it not worth being without a servant to have the Roman people his tenant? Scipio's daughters received their dowry from the treasury because their father had left them nothing. It was only fair, by Hercules, for the Roman people to pay Scipio tribute once, when he exacted permanent tribute from Carthage. Lucky husbands, to have the Roman people for surrogate fathers-in-law! Do you suppose that men whose actress daughters marry with a dowry of $50,000 are happier than Scipio, who had the senate for foster father and received a dowry in pounds of copper? Will anyone disdain poverty when its pedigree is so illustrious? Can an exile be indignant at any privation when Scipio was short a dowry, Regulus a hired man, Menenius a funeral? When the provision for all their requirements brought them greater honor *because* they had been in need? With advocates like these to plead its cause, poverty is not only secure but even attractive.

[13] This protest may be entered: "Why do you introduce that unnatural separation between factors which can be endured individually but cannot when combined? Change of place is tolerable if only the place is changed; poverty is tolerable if it does not entail ignominy, which in itself is enough to crush a man's spirit." To refute the man who would terrify me with evils in a crowd I must use such

language as this: "If you have the fortitude to combat any phase of fortune, it will suffice to combat all. Once virtue has inured your spirit, it will render it invulnerable on every side. If avarice, which is the deepest sore in the human mind, has given up the race, ambition will give you no trouble; if you look upon the end of your life not as a punishment but as a law of nature and have cast the fear of death from your heart, then no other fear will venture to enter it; if you believe sex was given man not for the sake of pleasure but to propagate the race, and have not been impinged upon by this hidden plague planted in our very vitals, then every other craving will leave you untouched. It is not disparate vices that virtue lays low but all together; the conquest is complete and final.

Do you suppose that any wise man who relies wholly upon himself and stands apart from the opinions of the mob can be swayed by ignominy? Worse than ignominy is an ignominious death. And yet Socrates entered the prison with the same expression he bore when he reduced the Thirty Tyrants to size singlehandedly and thereby cleansed the place of ignominy, for no place where Socrates was could seem a prison. Who is so blinded to the perception of truth as to believe that Marcus Cato's twofold defeat in his candidacy for the praetorship and the consulship involved ignominy? The ignominy was the praetorship's and the consulship's, on which Cato's candidacy conferred distinction. None can be despised by another unless he is first despised by himself. An abject and groveling mind may invite contumely; but a man who raises himself to confront raging misfortunes and overthrows evils by which others are crushed wears his very disasters as a halo, for our temperament is such that nothing so compels our admiration as a man who is steadfast in adversity.

When Aristides was being led to execution at Athens everyone that met him cast his eyes down and groaned, as if it were Justice herself, and not merely a just man, that was sentenced to death. Still there was one man so base as to spit in his face. Aristides might have been irked, knowing that no man with a clean mouth would be so brazen; but he wiped his face and said to the official accompanying him, with a smile: "Admonish that fellow not to open his mouth so offensively another time." This was putting insult upon insult itself. I know some people declare that nothing is worse than contempt and think death preferable. To these I would answer that exile, too, is often free from contempt. If a great man falls and keeps his greatness where he lies, he is no more scorned than are the ruins of sacred edifices trodden upon; the pious revere them as much as when they were standing.

[14] Since, my dearest mother, there is nothing in my situation to drive you to endless weeping, it must follow that your impulse to tears derives from your own situation. There are two possibilities. Either you are affected by the apparent loss of a protector, or you find my absence unendurable in itself. The first point I must touch on very lightly, for I know that your heart loves its own only for themselves. This is of concern to mothers who use their children's power with female willfulness, who are ambitious through their sons because women are ineligible for office, who spend and try to monopolize their sons' patrimony, who make demands upon their eloquence to accommodate others. But you have taken the greatest joy in your sons' advantages, and exploited them least; you have always set limits upon our generosity but none on your own. Though legally a minor, you made presents to your wealthy sons. You managed our estates as if you were working for your own, but were as abstemious as if they belonged to strangers. You made as sparing use of our influence as if you were using a stranger's property; the offices we held brought you nothing but the pleasure and the expense. Your affection never had utility in view, and hence you cannot be missing in the son that was taken from you what

you never thought belonged to you when he was safe at home.

[15] It is to the other point my consolation must address itself, the source of the genuine force of a mother's grief. "I have lost my dearest son's embrace. I cannot enjoy his presence, his conversation. When I saw him my face relaxed its sadness, to him I unburdened myself of all my cares: where is he? Where are the talks, of which I could never have enough? Where are the studies which I shared with a pleasure beyond my sex and an intimacy beyond our relationship? Where are the encounters? Where the boyish glee at sight of his mother?" To this you can add the actual scenes of our happy times together and the souvenirs of our association which must inevitably induce the sharpest pangs. This blow, too, Fortune added to her cruel measure: she willed that you leave Rome, secure and wholly unsuspecting, only two days before I was struck down. It is a good thing that we had been far apart from one another, good that my absence of several years had prepared you for this blow. Your return to Rome brought you no pleasure of your son, but lost you the habit of doing without him. If you had gone long before, you might have borne your lot more bravely, for the protracted separation would have eased your longing; if you had not gone back you would at least have gained one last advantage of seeing your son two days longer. But as it is, cruel Fate arranged that you should neither be on hand for my disaster nor have grown accustomed to my absence. But the harder the case is, the greater the courage you must summon up; you must fight with higher spirit, as with an enemy you have come to know and have often beaten. It is not from an unscathed body this new blood flows; you have been wounded in an old sore.

[16] You must not excuse yourself on the plea of your sex, which has a virtual license for immoderate tears, but even so not for endless weeping; that is why our ancestors

assigned widows a period of ten months to mourn their husbands, thus limiting women's stubborn grief by public enactment. They did not forbid mourning but set a limit to it. To give way to endless grief when you have lost a dear one is foolish indulgence, to show none is flinty hardness. The best compromise between affection and reason is to feel regret and suppress it. There is no reason for you to pattern yourself after certain women whose sorrow, once assumed, ended only with their death—you know some who put mourning on when they lost their sons, and never took it off again. Life demands more of you because you were more steadfast from the beginning; the excuse of sex cannot apply when there is no trace of womanish weakness.

Unchastity, the greatest plague of our age, has put the majority of womankind in a different category from yours; gems nor pearls have tempted you; its glitter has not persuaded you that wealth is man's greatest good. You were well brought up in an old-fashioned and strict household, and you have never been led astray by the imitation of worse women, which is a hazard even to good ones. You have never been ashamed of your children, as though their number taunted you with your years; you have never concealed your pregnancy as an unsightly parcel, as do other women whose sole claim for approval is their beauty, nor have you destroyed the expectation of progeny conceived within your womb. You have not defiled your face with paint and meretricious cosmetics; you never fancied sheer dresses that revealed as much on as off. Your unique jewel, your fairest beauty, which time cannot wither, your greatest glory, is your proven modesty. You cannot, therefore, hold your sex up as a justification for your grief, for your virtues set you apart from your sex: you must be as superior to a woman's tears as you are to her vices. But there are even women who will not suffer you to succumb to your wound but bid you rise relieved after quick discharge of your mourning obligations; you need but look to those

women whose conspicuous merit has ranged them with our
great heroes.

Fortune reduced Cornelia from twelve children to two;
if you gauge Cornelia's loss by quantity she lost ten, if by
quality she lost the Gracchi. Yet when her friends were
weeping around her and execrating her fate, she forbade
them to malign the Fortune which had given her the Gracchi for sons. That was a proper mother for the man who
could say in the assembly, "Can you revile my mother, who
gave me birth?" But to me the mother's utterance seems to
show far greater spirit; the son set a high value on the
pedigree of the Gracchi, the mother valued their deaths as
well.

Rutilia followed her son Cotta into exile and was so
warmly attached to him that she thought exile easier than
separation and never came home until she came home with
him. Upon his return he rose to high position, but when he
died his mother bore his loss as steadfastly as she had followed him, and no one saw her crying after she had buried
her son. In his exile she displayed courage, in his death
good sense; nothing deterred her from affectionate duty,
and nothing made her persist in useless and foolish mourning. It is with such women as these I would have you
counted. Because you have always emulated their lives,
you had best follow their example in restraining and suppressing sorrow.

[17] I know the emotions are not under our control, and
that none will come to heel, least of all one born of sorrow;
it is untamed and intractable to every remedy. Sometimes
we will to master it and swallow our sighs, but the tears
still flood the spurious expression we have carefully arranged. Sometimes we occupy our minds with theatrical
or gladiatorial shows, but during the very spectacles calculated to distract it the mind is ambushed by some souvenirs of its loss. It is better to conquer our sorrow, therefore, than to cheat it, for a grief beguiled and distracted

by pleasures or amusements rises again, and the respite refreshes its energy for savage attack. But a grief which has submitted to reason is appeased forever. I shall not, therefore, prescribe the remedies which I know many adopt, that you seek amusement in travel to remote or agreeable places, that you devote much time to a careful review of your accounts and management of your property, or that you constantly involve yourself in some new enterprise. The help these devices give is very short-lived; they are obstacles to grief, not cures. I would rather have it ended than beguiled.

And so I would lead you to the sure refuge of all who fly from Fortune—to liberal studies. They will heal your wound, they will eradicate your sadness. Even if you had never been conversant with them it would be useful to apply yourself to them now, but you have some acquaintance with all the liberal arts, though the old-fashioned strictness of my father did not allow you to master them. I could wish that my father, excellent man that he was, had not been so set on following the practice of his elders and had allowed you to acquire a thorough grounding in philosophic doctrine instead of only a smattering. Then you would not now have to shape your campaign against Fortune but merely to set it on foot. His reason for not indulging you in deeper study was that some women do not use literature for philosophic ends but trim themselves with it for luxury's sake. But thanks to your acquisitive intellect you imbibed a great deal for the time you spent; the foundations for the various disciplines have been laid. Return to them now; they will keep you safe, they will console you, they will cheer you. If they truly enter your mind, then nevermore will grief find entry, or anxiety, or the idle distress of futile affliction. To none of these will your heart be open; to other weaknesses it has of course long been shut. These studies are the surest safeguards, the only deliverance, from the power of Fortune.

[18] But because you need props to lean upon until you reach the haven philosophy holds out, I shall in the meantime point out the comforts you have. Think of my brothers; while they live you have no right to find fault with Fortune. Each of them presents his particular excellence for your delight. The one has attained high office by his diligence, the other has philosophically despised it. Find repose in the prestige of one son, in the quiet retirement of the other, in the filial piety of both. I know the inward sentiments of my brothers. The one cultivates his career to bring credit to you, the other has withdrawn to a quiet and untroubled life to have leisure for you. Fortune has luckily arranged your children's lives for your protection and pleasure; you can be shielded by the prestige of the one and enjoy the leisure of the other. They will vie in their dutifulness to you, and the loss of one son will be supplied by the devotion of the other two. I can confidently promise that you will be short of nothing except the number.

After them, think too of your grandsons. Think of Marcus, that engaging child at sight of whom all sadness must vanish. No distress can be so great, no new wound can so rage in anyone's heart, as not to be soothed away by his caresses. Are there any tears his gaiety would not quench? Is there any tense and anxious spirit his chatter would not relax? Whom would his frolics not invite to playfulness? What brooding mind intent upon its own thoughts will his prattle that never cloys not distract to itself? I pray the gods that he may survive us. May all the cruelty of Fate be exhausted with me and go no further! May all the grief debited to you as mother and as grandmother be transferred to my account! May the rest of our band flourish unharmed! I make no complaint of my childlessness and none of my present situation; let me only be an expiation so my family have no more sorrow.

Cherish Novatilla, who will soon give you great-grandchildren. I had so cared for her and become attached to her that, in losing me, she might seem to have been orphaned though her father is alive. Love her for my sake as well as your own. Fortune has lately robbed her of her mother; your affection can prevent her from feeling the loss though she mourn for her mother's death. Now is the time to organize her habits and shape her character; instruction leaves a sharper impression when it is stamped upon tender minds. Let her grow accustomed to your conversation, let her be molded according to your judgment; even if you furnish her nothing but a model you will have given her much. This sacred duty will serve to relieve you; only reason or an honorable occupation can divert a mind grieving for close kin from sorrow.

Among your great comforts I would mention your father, also, if he were not away. From your own affection you can judge what his is for you, and you will realize how much juster it is for you to keep yourself for him than spend yourself for me. Whenever grief assails you with inordinate force and bids you surrender, think of your father. You have given him many grandchildren and great-grandchildren, to be sure, and are not his sole prop, but the rounding out of his happy life depends upon you. As long as he is alive it is impious of you to complain of your life.

[19] Of your greatest source of comfort I have so far said nothing—your sister, whose loyal heart selflessly carries the burden of all your cares, whose motherly feeling embraces us all. You diluted your tears in hers, upon her bosom you breathed again. She is always sensitive to your feelings, but in my case it is not for you alone that she grieves. Her arms carried me to Rome, her conscientious and motherly nursing restored my health after long illness. She used all her influence for my quaestorship, and though she was too shy to raise her voice in conversation or greeting, for my sake her affection overcame her bashfulness. Neither her retired mode of life nor her country-bred modesty, so different from the aggressiveness of town ladies,

nor her placidity, nor her habits of seclusion and cultivation of leisure prevented her from going so far as to
campaign in my behalf. She, dearest mother, is the solace
in which you can recover your strength. Cleave to her as
tightly as you can, bind yourself to her with the closest
embrace. Mourners usually avoid their particular friends
and seek liberty for their grief. But do you share your every purpose with her: whether you prefer to nurse your
grief or lay it aside, you will find in her either an end of
your sorrow or a companion to share it. But if I am not
mistaken in the good sense of that paragon of women, she
will not allow you to be corroded by profitless mourning,
and will cite an experience of her own, of which I too was
a witness.

On a sea journey she lost her beloved husband, my
uncle, whom she had married as a girl; she bore up under
her grief and the horror of shipwreck, but she rose above
the storm, saved her husband's body from the wreck, and
brought it home. How many glorious deeds of womankind
lie unknown to fame! If her lot had fallen in the days of
old when outstanding merit received candid admiration,
how men of genius would have vied in celebrating a wife
who disregarded her sex' weakness, disregarded the perils
of the sea which make even the boldest quake, risked her
life to give her husband burial, and was too busy planning
his funeral to be concerned for her own. All poets have
sung the praises of Alcestis, who gave her life as ransom
for her husband's. But your sister did a greater thing when
she risked her life to find her husband a tomb; love is
greater when it faces equal danger for a lesser gain.

In view of this, it is not surprising that during the sixteen years her husband was governor of Egypt she was
never seen in public, never admitted a native to her house,
never asked her husband for a political favor, never allowed
anyone to ask her for one. And so that gossipy province,
which has such a genius for inventing scandals about its

governors that even those free of dereliction do not escape vilification, revered that lady as a paragon of uprightness. The Egyptians restrained the license of their tongues—a very difficult thing for a population given to gibes, however risky—and to this day they hope, though they never expect, to have another governor's lady like her. It would have spoken well for her if the province had given her its approbation for sixteen years; it is more remarkable that her presence went unnoticed. My purpose in mentioning these things is not to recount her praises—to treat them so summarily is to do them injustice—but to set before you the high-mindedness of a woman who yielded neither to ambition nor greed, the scourges inseparable from power, a woman whom imminent death did not deter, when her vessel was disabled and shipwreck stared her in the face, from clinging to her lifeless husband and seeking not how she might escape from the wreck but how she might carry his body to burial. You must show courage to match hers, must recall your mind from grief, and give no one occasion to think you are sorry you bore a son.

[20] But despite all that you can do your thoughts must inevitably recur to me at times, and you will think of me more often than of your other children, not because they are less dear, but because it is natural to put one's hand to the place that hurts. Let me tell you, then, how you must think of me. I am as happy and lively as in my best days. Indeed, these days are my best, for my mind is now free of preoccupations and has leisure for its own concerns; now it amuses itself with lighter studies and now, pressing keenly after truth, it rises to the contemplation of its own nature and the nature of the universe. First it investigates the continents and their position, then the laws which govern the sea which surrounds them with its alternate ebb and flow, and then it examines the stretch which lies between heaven and earth and teems with such tumultuous and terrifying phenomena as thunder and lightning and

gales and the precipitation of rain and snow and hail. Finally, when it has traversed the lower reaches, it bursts through to the realms above where it enjoys the fairest spectacle of things divine and, mindful of its eternity, moves freely among all that was and all that will be world without end.

ON CLEMENCY

When Stoics perceived that they could not revolutionize the world directly, they sought to give their doctrines the fullest measure of realization by guiding men who held political power; so Sphairos influenced the reforming Spartan kings Agis and Cleomenes, for example; and Blossius of Cumae, the Gracchi. The challenge was greater after Posidonius had identified the empire with the oikoumene; a conscientious Stoic would consider it his duty to seize the opportunity to influence the ruler of the empire. The On Clemency is, in effect, an admirable Mirror of Princes. It was addressed to Nero in his eighteenth year; its point of departure (as we are told in the opening of the fragmentary second book) was Nero's remark, when he was asked to sign a death warrant, "I wish I had never learned to write." The adulations of Nero which the reader finds cloying are merely etiquette; the actual arguments are firm and enlightened, and calculated to impress upon Nero the expediency as well as the virtue of regarding himself as a servant of humanity (as the Stoic Marcus Aurelius would do) rather than as its absolute master, as Caligula, for example, had done.

[1] I have resolved to write on mercy, Nero, my emperor. I would serve the function of a mirror and display you to yourself as one within reach of the greatest of pleasures.

The true fruit of right deeds is, to be sure, in the doing, and no reward outside themselves is worthy of the virtues; yet it is a satisfaction to stroll around and inspect a good conscience, and then to cast an eye upon this enormous multitude—fractious, restive, unruly, quick to turbulence, which would ruin themselves and others alike if they snapped the yoke—and having done so to commune with oneself: "Have I, of all mortals, been approved and elected to function as the gods' vicar on earth? I am arbiter of life and death for mankind; every individual's lot and condition is in my discretion. What Fortune chooses to allot to each mortal she proclaims through my lips; from my utterances peoples and cities conceive reasons for rejoicing; no region anywhere can flourish without my will and favor. These thousands of swords which my peace has muffled would be drawn at my nod; which nations shall be destroyed root and branch, which carried into exile, which receive and which lose liberty, what kings shall become slaves and whose heads shall be crowned with the insignia of royalty, what cities shall be destroyed and what cities arise—all this is in my jurisdiction. With power so vast, anger has not moved me to unjust punishment, nor has youthful impulse, nor have men's audacity and contumacy which have often wrenched patience from the most tranquil of hearts, nor yet the vainglory which parades power through terror, a baneful but common concomitant of high dominion. In my domain the sword is put away, nay, fastened down. I am niggardly of even the vilest blood: a man with nothing to commend him but the title of human being will find favor in my sight. Severity I keep hidden, mercy ever at hand. I keep watch over myself as if bound to render an account to the laws which I have summoned out of neglect and darkness to the light of day. One man's youth sways me, another's age; one man I have reprieved for his eminence, another for his insignificance; and when I found no other ground for pity I have shown charity to myself. This day, if the immortal gods should call for an accounting, I am ready to report the human race intact."

You can assert with confidence, Caesar, that everything which has been committed to your charge has been kept safe and that the commonwealth has suffered no loss through you, neither through force or fraud. The rarest of distinctions, one vouchsafed to no previous emperor, you have coveted—innocence. The effort has not been wasted: your unique goodness has not encountered a thankless or grudging reception. Men are grateful to you; no individual has ever been cherished by another as you are by the Roman people; you are their great and enduring blessing. But it is an enormous burden you have taken upon your shoulders. No one any longer speaks of the late Augustus or of the early reign of Tiberius or seeks a model for you to copy other than yourself: it is expected that your reign will match the sample you have shown. This would have been difficult if your goodness were an assumed pose and not innate. No one can long hide behind a mask; the pretense soon lapses into the true character. But where the basis is truth and where the roots are solidly planted, time itself fosters growth in size and quality.

The Roman people were in great hazard when it was uncertain what direction your noble gifts would take; now the public prayers are assured of fulfillment, for there can be no danger that you will suddenly forget your character. Excessive felicity, it is true, makes men greedy, and desires are never under such close rein as to halt when they have reached an objective. Great things are a rung to greater, and when men attain what they never hoped for they embrace hopes more extravagant. Nevertheless, your subjects all cannot but acknowledge that they are happy and that no increment can be made to their blessings except that they may endure. They are constrained to make this acknowledgment, which men are loath to make. Peace is deep and abundant, justice is firmly seated above all injustice,

in full view for all to see is the happiest of administrations
in which the only limitation upon the completest liberty
is the denial of license for self-destruction. But in particular,
an equal admiration of your clemency pervades great and
small. Of other blessings, the individual experiences or expects a greater or lesser portion in keeping with his lot, but
in your clemency all repose the same hopes. There is no
one so satisfied with his own innocence as not to be glad-
dened at the sight of clemency ready to condone human
failings.

[2] I know there are some who hold that clemency is
a prop for villains, since it has room only after crime and
is the sole virtue which has no function among innocent
men. But first of all, just as medicine functions among the
diseased but is esteemed among the sound, so do the innocent, too, respect clemency, though only punishable culprits invoke it. Secondly, this virtue has scope even in the
case of the guiltless because misfortune is sometimes a sub-
stitute for guilt. And it is not innocence alone that clemency
succors but also virtue, for our circumstances give rise to
cases where praiseworthy actions are liable to punishment.
Furthermore, a large portion of mankind might be restored
to innocence if punishment is remitted. Still, pardon should
not be general, for if the distinction between bad men and
good is abolished, chaos will follow and an eruption of vice.
We must therefore apply a moderation capable of distinguishing the curable from the hopeless. The clemency we
practice should neither be promiscuous and general nor yet
exclusive; to pardon everyone is as cruel as to pardon none.
We must keep measure, but since it is difficult to maintain
the exact proportion, any departure from the balance
should weigh on the kindlier scale.

[3] But it will be better to speak of these things in their
proper place. Now I shall divide the material as a whole
into three sections. The first will deal with remissions. The
second will exhibit the nature and disposition of clemency,

for since there are vices which resemble virtues they cannot be separated unless you take good note of the signs by which they can be distinguished. In the third place we shall ask how the mind is introduced to this virtue, how it gives it validity and by habit assimilates it.

That none of the other virtues is more becoming to a human, none being more humane, must be accepted as axiomatic not only by us (Stoics) who hold that man is a social animal born for the common good, but also by those (Epicureans) who subordinate man to pleasure and all of whose words and deeds aim at personal advantage. If quiet and repose is what the Epicurean seeks, he finds this virtue, which loves peace and eschews violence, suited to his constitution. But of all men clemency is most becoming to a king or prince. Mighty strength is comely and glorious only if its power is beneficent; it is a pestilential force which is powerful only for mischief. A ruler's greatness is stable and secure when all men know that he is *for* them as much as *above* them, when experience shows them his vigilant and unremitting solicitude for the welfare of one and all, at whose approach they do not disperse as though some malignant and noxious beast had sprung from its lair but vie in flocking forward as to a shining and beneficent planet. For him they are perfectly ready to fling themselves upon the daggers of assassins and to pave his way with their bodies if human carnage is his path to safety, his sleep they protect with night-long vigils, his person they defend by interposing their bodies round about him, and they expose themselves to dangers that assail him.

The accepted practice of peoples and cities of rendering their kings such protection and such affection, of sacrificing their persons and property whenever the safety of their ruler requires it, is not unreasonable; nor do men hold themselves cheap or suffer madness when many thousands accept wounds and ransom a single life, not infrequently the life of a sick old man, by many deaths. The whole body's service to the soul is analogous. The body is much bigger and showier, while the soul is impalpable and is hidden we know not where, yet hands, feet, and eyes do its business and the skin furnishes it protection; at its bidding we lie still or scurry restlessly about; when it gives command we scour the sea for gain, if it is an avaricious master, or if it is ambitious we unhesitatingly thrust our right arm into the flame or willingly plunge into the pit. Similarly, this enormous populace which is the shell for the soul of one man is regulated by his spirit and guided by his reason; if it were not propped by his intelligence it would bruise itself by its own strength and crumble to fragments.

[4] It is their own safety they are in love with, therefore, when men marshal ten legions in a single battle line for one man, when they charge to the fore and expose their breasts to wounds to keep their general's standard from turning tail. He is the link which holds the commonwealth together, he is the breath of life which the many thousands draw; by themselves, if the intelligence of the empire were withdrawn, they would be only a burden and a prey.

Their king safe, single-minded are all [the bees];
Their king lost, they shatter fealty.
(Vergil, *Georgics* 4.212)

The end of the Roman peace would bring such a disaster, it would ruin the prosperity of so mighty a people. But this people will be far from such danger so long as it will understand submission to the reins; for if ever it severs them or does not suffer them to be replaced if some accident shakes them off, then this unity, this mighty fabric of empire, will explode into many fragments. The end of the capital's obedience will be the end of its domination. It is not remarkable, therefore, that princes and kings and guardians of the public order by whatever title are more beloved than are private connections. If sensible men put public interest ahead of private, it follows that the personage upon whom the public weal turns is also dearer to them. Long ago Caesar so welded himself to the state that neither could be separated without the ruin of both, for the one needs power and the other a head.

[5] My discourse seems to have strayed quite a distance from its theme, but actually, I swear, it is hard on the track. For if, as we have concluded, you are the soul of your state and it your body, you will realize, I fancy, how essential mercy is: it is yourself you spare when you appear to be sparing another. Reprehensible subjects must be spared precisely like ineffective limbs, and if ever blood is to be let the hand must be prevented from cutting deeper than necessary. In all men, as I remarked, mercy is a natural quality, but it especially becomes monarchs, for in them it has greater scope for salvation and ampler opportunity to show its effect. How petty the mischief private cruelty can work! But when princes are savage it is war. The virtues are, to be sure, in concord with one another and none is better or more honorable than another, yet one may be more appropriate to certain individuals. Magnanimity becomes every human being, even the lowliest of the low, for what could be grander or sturdier than to beat misfortune back? Even so magnanimity has freer scope at a higher level and shows to better advantage on the judge's bench than among the groundlings.

Mercy will make whatever house she enters happy and serene, but she is more admirable in the palace in the degree that she is rarer. What could be more memorable than that the man whose wrath nothing can block, to whose harsher sentences the doomed themselves give assent, whom no one will overrule, nay, if his anger flares hot no one will even supplicate—what could be more memorable than that this man should lay a hand upon himself and put his power to better and calmer use, and should reflect, "To kill contrary to law is in any man's power, to save only in mine"? For a high fortune a high spirit is appropriate, and if the spirit does not rise to the fortune's level and stand above it, it will drag the fortune to the ground also. Now the distinguishing marks of a high spirit are composure and serenity and a lofty disregard of insult and injury. To fume with anger is a womanish thing, and beasts (but not the nobler sort) bite and worry the prostrate. Elephants and lions pass by those they have struck down, relentlessness is a trait of ignoble animals. Savage and inexorable anger is not becoming to a king, for then he loses his superiority; anger reduces him to his victim's level. But if he grants life, if he grants their dignities to persons in jeopardy who have deserved to lose them, he does what none but a sovereign could do. Life may be taken even from a superior; it can be given only to an inferior. To save life is the prerogative of high estate, which is never so much to be revered as when it is privileged to emulate the power of the gods, by whose beneficence we are brought into the world, good and bad alike. Adopting the spirit of the gods, therefore, the prince should regard some of his subjects with pleasure because they are useful and good, some he should leave to fill out the number; he should be glad of some, and tolerate the others.

[6] Think of this city: the throng that streams through its broad boulevards is continuous and if the traffic is blocked there is a crush as when a rushing torrent is dammed; three spacious theaters fill up simultaneously; it consumes the produce of all the world's tilth. How deserted and desolate it would be if only those a strict judge would acquit were left! How many a prosecutor would be liable by the very laws they enforce! How rare an accuser would be free of guilt! I rather think no one is more obdurate in granting pardon than a man who repeatedly should have begged it for himself. We have all sinned, some grievously, some less so, some of set intent and some by chance impulse or by the misleading of others' wickedness; some have not been steadfast in good resolutions and have lost inno-

cence reluctantly and after a struggle. Not only have we been derelict but we shall continue to be so to the end of our time. And even if a man has purged his soul so thoroughly that nothing can now upset or deceive him, yet it is by sinning that he has reached that innocence.

[7] Since I have mentioned the gods I might propose that the ideal to which a prince might best mold himself is to deal with his subjects as he would wish the gods to deal with him. Is it expedient to have deities who are inexorable in the face of sins and derelictions? Is it expedient to have them intransigent to the point of ruination? What king would then be safe? Whose blasted limbs would the soothsayers not have to collect? But if the placable and equable deities do not instantly blast the derelictions of the mighty with their thunderbolts, how much more equable is it for a human given charge over humans to exercise his authority in a mild spirit and to ponder whether the state of the world is fairer and better pleasing to the eyes on a clear and serene day or when all is aquake with repeated crashes of thunder, and lightnings flash from this quarter and that! Yet a quiet and deliberate reign has precisely the same aspect as a serene and shining sky. A cruel regime is turbulent and befogged in darkness; while fear is general and men shudder at any sudden sound not even the author of the confusion is unaffected. It is easy to pardon private citizens who assert their claims tenaciously: they can be injured, and wrong gives rise to resentment; besides, they are afraid of being despised, for not to return blow for blow is interpreted as weakness rather than mercy. But where vengeance is easy the man who overlooks it secures unqualified praise for gentleness. Men in humbler station have greater freedom to use force, to go to law, to quarrel, to indulge their anger. Where rivals are well matched blows fall light; but for a king even a raised voice and intemperate language are a degradation of majesty.

[8] You suppose it is a disability for kings to be deprived

of free speech, which the humblest citizens enjoy. "That is servitude," you say, "not sovereignty." Have you not found out that the sovereignty is ours and yours the servitude? The situation of men in the crowd is different. If they do not range above the level they are unnoticed; they must struggle long for their virtues to show, and their vices are sheltered in darkness. But your deeds and words are caught up by rumor, and no one must have greater care for his reputation than the man sure to have a large one whatever his deserts may be. How many things are taboo for you but not, thanks to you, for us! I can stroll alone in any quarter of the city without fear, though no one attends me and I have no sword at my side or at home; but in the peace you have created you must live armed. You cannot stray from your eminence; it besets you, and its grand pomp follows you wherever you step down. Inability to descend is the bondage of supreme greatness; it is a disability you share with the gods. They too are bound to heaven and are no more free to step down; you are fettered to your pinnacle. Few are aware of our movements; we can come forward or step back or change our dress without public notice; you can no more hide than the sun. A brilliant light plays about you, and all eyes are focused on it. Do you suppose you walk out of your door? You dawn like the sun. You cannot speak without nations the world over hearing your voice; you cannot be angry without setting the world atremble, because you can strike no one without making all about him quake. Lightning's stroke imperils few but frightens all; so chastisement by a mighty power terrifies more widely than it hurts, and with good reason, for where power is absolute men think not of what it has done but of what it might do. There is another consideration. Patience under injuries received lays private persons open to further injury, but gentleness enhances the security of kings, because while frequent punishment does crush the hatred of a few, it provokes the hatred of all. The will to harsh measures must therefore subside before harsh measures do; otherwise a king's sternness will multiply enemies by destroying them, just as the lopped branches of trees shoot out many twigs, and many species of vegetation grow thicker when they are cut back. Parents and children, relatives and friends, step into the place of individuals who are put to death.

[9] How true this is I would remind you by an example from your own family. The late Augustus was a mild ruler, if we begin our evaluation with the beginning of his reign, but when he shared power (in the triumvirate) he did have recourse to the sword. When he was at your present age, just past his eighteenth year, he had already plunged daggers in the bosom of friends, he had already conspired against the consul Mark Antony, he had already been associated with proscriptions. But when he had passed his fortieth year and was sojourning in Gaul, information reached him that Lucius Cinna, who was a stupid man, was conspiring against him. He was told where, when, and how the attack was to be made; one of the accomplices was the informant.

Augustus resolved to exercise his rights and ordered a council of his friends convoked. He tossed about at night harried by the thought that it was a young aristocrat, quite decent but for this one offense, and a grandson of the great Pompey, who was to be condemned. The man to whom Mark Antony read out the edict of proscription as they dined could not now bring himself to kill one man. Amid repeated groans he uttered disjointed phrases that were at variance with one another: "What to do? Shall I suffer my assassin to stroll about at his ease while I am wracked?' Shall he not pay for his crime? This head of mine which so many civil wars could not lay low, which survived so many battles of armies and navies, now that peace has been won by land and sea Cinna has determined not to cut down but to sacrifice" (it had been decided to attack Augustus

at the altar). But after an interval of silence he used a
louder and angrier tone upon himself than he had against
Cinna: "Why live on if so many would have you dead?
What end to executions, what end to blood? My head is
the target for which young aristocrats whet their blades.
What price life if so many must perish that I may not?"

Finally his wife Livia interrupted and said: "Will you
hear a woman's advice? Follow the practice of doctors who,
when the usual remedies are not effective, reverse the treatment. So far severity has done no good: Salvidienus was
followed by Lepidus, Lepidus by Murena, Murena by
Caepio, Caepio by Egnatius, to say nothing of others whose
monstrous audacity I am ashamed to speak of. Now try
how mercy will succeed. Pardon Lucius Cinna. He has been
detected and can no longer harm you; he can advance your
reputation." Augustus was glad to find an advocate. He
thanked his wife, countermanded the invitation to a council
he had sent his friends, and had Cinna fetched alone. He
ordered another chair placed for Cinna and dismissed everyone else from the chamber.

"First I must ask you," he said, "not to interrupt what I
have to say and not to make protestations while I am speaking; you shall be given time to speak freely. When I found
you in my enemy's camp, Cinna, not a recruit but born to
that party, I saved you and allowed you to retain your
patrimony undiminished. Today you are so rich and prosperous that the victors envy the vanquished. When you
asked for a priesthood I gave it to you, passing over many
candidates whose fathers had fought at my side. And after
I have done these things for you, you have decided to kill
me." At this point Cinna exclaimed that such madness was
farthest from his intentions, and Augustus said: "You are
not keeping the pledge; it was agreed that you would not
interrupt. I say that you are preparing to kill me." He pro-
ceeded to cite the place, the accomplices, the day, the plan
of action, and the individual entrusted with the weapon.

When he saw that Cinna's eyes were fixed on the ground, silent now not because of the agreement but because of his bad conscience, he said: "What is your object? To be emperor yourself? The Roman people are in a bad way, by Hercules, if I am the only obstacle to your ruling them. Why, you cannot manage your own household; lately a freedman's influence defeated you in private litigation, and can you find nothing easier than to take steps against Caesar? Tell me, if I am the only impediment to your expectations, will Paulus and Fabius Maximus and the Cossi and Servilii, that numerous band whose nobility rests not on their lineage but who add distinction to their pedigree —will they tolerate you?"

I do not wish to take most of this volume up with quoting his remarks *in extenso*. (It is known that he talked more than two hours, to stretch out the penance, which was all he meant to require.) He concluded by saying: "Cinna, again I give you your life; before it was to an enemy, and now to a conspirator and assassin. From this day forward let us begin to be friends. Let us compete to see which shows better faith, I in giving you your life, or you in owing it to me." Afterwards he bestowed the consulship upon him unsolicited, complaining that he had not shown the courage to be an active candidate. Thereafter Augustus found Cinna devoted and loyal, and was named his sole heir.

[10] Your great-great-grandfather spared the vanquished; if he had not, whom would he have had to rule over? Sallustius and the Cocceii and the Deillii and that whole inner circle he recruited from the camp of his adversaries; it was to his clemency that he owed men like Domitius, Messala, Asinius, Cicero—the whole flower of the state. How long he suffered even Lepidus to linger! For many years he put up with Lepidus' retaining the insignia of rule, and allowed the supreme pontificate to be transferred to himself only after Lepidus died, for he wished the office to be called an honor, not a prize of war. It was this

clemency that carried him through to safety and security, it was this clemency that made him welcome and beloved though the Romans were not used to the yoke when he laid his hand upon them, it is this clemency which to this day assures him a reputation which even living rulers can scarcely match. We believe him a god, and not because we are bidden to. We confess that he was a good emperor and appropriately entitled father of his country for no other reason than because he did not requite with cruelty even personal affronts, which irk rulers even more than actual injuries, because he smiled at pasquinades aimed against him, because punishment seemed to pain him more than the culprits, because he not only refrained from executing the men condemned for adultery with his daughter but banished them for their safety and gave them safe conducts. To give not only life but even protection when you know there will be many to show indignation on your behalf and shed another's blood to oblige you—that is truly to pardon.

[11] Such was Augustus in his old age or verging upon it; in his youth he was hasty, his temper flared, and he did many things upon which he looked back with regret. No one will venture to compare the late Augustus with your own gentleness, even matching your youthful years with his more than ripe old age. Granted that he was restrained and merciful, but it was after Actium's sea had been stained with Roman blood, after his own and others' fleets had been shattered off Sicily, after the holocaust at Perugia and the proscriptions. I do not call exhausted cruelty clemency. The true clemency, Caesar, is that which you practice, which does not spring from remorse for savagery, which bears no taint and has never shed a compatriot's blood. Combined with unlimited power, this is the truest temperance of soul and all-embracing love of the human race as of oneself, when a man is not corrupted by lust or waywardness or the precedents of former rulers into trying how far he can go in excesses against his countrymen, but rather when he

blunts the edge of his sovereignty. You have offered us, Caesar, a state unbloodied, and your noble boast that you have not shed a drop of human blood anywhere in the world is the more notable and wonderful because no one has been given the sword's mandate at an earlier age.

Clemency therefore assures not only higher honor but higher safety; it is at once sovereignty's ornament and surest preservation. Why is it that kings have reached old age and handed their realms on to children and grandchildren while the dominion of tyrants is as brief as it is execrable? What difference is there between tyrant and king, their symbols and prerogatives being the same, except that the wrath of tyrants is capricious whereas the wrath of kings is grounded in cause and necessity?

[12] "What does this imply? Is it not the practice of kings, too, to put men to death upon occasion?" Only when public interest dictates; a tyrant's cruelty is willful. It is in conduct that a tyrant differs from a king, not in title. The elder Dionysius may rightly be given precedence over many kings for his merits, whereas Lucius Sulla may be styled tyrant without qualification, for he put a period to slaughter only when he had no more enemies to kill. He did abdicate his dictatorship and return to civilian status, but what tyrant ever drank human blood as greedily as he? He ordered seven thousand Roman citizens butchered, and when, as he presided over the senate in the adjoining temple of Bellona, the piercing shrieks of so many thousands being massacred frightened the senators, he said, "Let us attend to our business, my lords; it is only a handful of subversives who are being executed at my order." And it was no figure of speech; to Sulla they seemed a handful.

But of Sulla more later, when we come to consider the proper mode of expressing our indignation toward enemies, especially our own countrymen who have defected from our common polity and gone over to a hostile opposition. But for the present I revert to my previous remark, that it is clemency which constitutes the great distinction between king and tyrant. The one like the other may be fenced about with arms, but the one keeps his armament to use for building a strong peace, the other for suppressing great hatred by great terror; nor can the latter look with confidence to the very hands to which he has entrusted himself. Conflicting motives drive him to conflicting measures; since he is hated because he is feared, he chooses to be feared because he is hated, and applies the execrable phrase which has toppled many from their heights: "Let them hate provided they fear." He does not realize what frenzy may seethe up when hatred passes its measure. Fear tempered restrains passions, but when it is unremitting and acute and a goad to extremism it rouses spiritless men to audacity and impels them to leave nothing untried. A string hung with feathers may keep wild animals corralled, but if a mounted hunter begins shooting from behind they will trample their fear and try to dash through the very device they shied at. Valor forged by desperation is sharpest. Fear should leave a residue of security and hold out a larger prospect of hope than of menace; otherwise, if the docile man is in equal jeopardy with the activist, he will gaily rush into danger, indifferent to preserving a life no longer his.

[13] An even-tempered and passionless king can trust his guards. He uses them for the common safety, and the soldiers can see that their assignment is the public security; they are therefore proud and willing to perform arduous duties in protecting their country's parent. But the harsh and bloody ruler inevitably chafes his own henchmen. A man cannot have good and faithful servants when he uses them like rack and wheel as instruments of torture and death, when he throws human beings to them as he might to beasts. No prisoner at the bar is so harried and apprehensive as he; he is afraid of men and gods who are witnesses to and may punish his crimes, but is so far committed to his course that he cannot change.

Among cruelty's other handicaps perhaps the worst is this: a man must keep to the same road, with never an exit for return to better ways; crimes need more crimes to protect them. What can be unhappier than a man under compulsion to be bad? How pitiable!—at least to himself; it would be impious for others to pity a man who used his power for murder and rapine, who filled the world, at home and abroad, with suspicion, who resorted to arms because he feared arms, who did not trust the loyalty of his friends or the dutifulness of his children, who, when he surveys his deeds past and future and bares his conscience filled with crimes and tortures, must often fear death and oftener wish it, for he is more odious to himself than to his vassals.

On the other hand, a man whose solicitude is all-embracing, who gives greater heed to one part of the commonwealth and less to another but fosters every part as a member of himself, who is inclined to the milder course even when it is expedient to punish, who shows how reluctant he is to use harsh remedies, whose spirit is free of hostility and cruelty, who wields even-tempered and salutary power because he wishes his rule to satisfy his subjects, who counts himself abundantly happy if he can make his own prosperity a public asset, who is affable in conversation and easy of access, whose amiable expression wins the affection of his people, who is sympathetic to reasonable requests and not impatient with unreasonable—such a man is loved and defended and cherished by the whole state. Men speak no differently of him in private than they do in public. They are now eager to rear families; the sterility once imposed by the bad state of the nation is banished. A man can be sure his children will be grateful to him for letting them see so blessed an age. Such a prince his own beneficence renders safe and he needs no guards; the arms he keeps are only for ornament.

[14] What is the duty of such a prince? The duty of good parents: they reprove their children sometimes gently,

sometimes with threats, and occasionally they even admonish them with blows. Would any father in his right mind disinherit a son for a first offense? Only when serious and repeated derelictions have exhausted his patience, only when he fears greater mischief than he has condemned, does he have recourse to so grave a decision; first he tries various means to reclaim a character still tottering but now in a worse posture. When the case is hopeless he tries the extreme measure; no one reaches the limit of demanding execution until he has exhausted every remedy. This is how a father must behave, and so must a prince, whom we are not merely flattering when we style him "Father of his Country." Other titles have been bestowed *honoris causa;* we have called men "the Great," "the Fortunate," "the August," and we have heaped all the epithets we could upon ambitious lordliness, attributing these various qualities to it. But the appellation "Father of his Country" we have bestowed so that its bearer should understand that what he holds is the power of a father, who is most forbearing on behalf of his children and subordinates his interests to theirs. Slow indeed would a father be to cut off his own members; when he had cut them off he would wish to put them back, and in the process of cutting he would groan and hesitate much and long. A man who is quick to condemn is not far from being glad to condemn, and a man who punishes excessively is not far from punishing unjustly.

[15] Within my memory, the crowd in the forum used their writing styluses to stab a Roman knight named Tricho because he had flogged his son to death; the authority of Augustus Caesar was barely able to rescue him from the angry clutches of fathers and sons. But Tarius' conduct won universal admiration. His son was detected and convicted of a plot upon his life, but Tarius was content with exiling the parricide, and to the luxuries of Marseilles at that, and continued the same allowance he had given him when he

was innocent. The result was that in a city where every villain has someone to take his side no one doubted that the son was guilty, for the father who could not hate him had found him so.

This same case provides a comparison of a good prince with a good father. When Tarius was about to hold a consultation upon his son he invited Caesar Augustus to the council. Augustus came to a citizen's house, took his seat, and participated in a householder's deliberations. He did not say, "Let the man come to my house," for if he had, the proceedings would have been Caesar's, not the father's. When the case had been heard and the arguments thrashed out—what the young man said in his defense and the evidence brought against him—Caesar asked that each assessor write his sentence down, so that they should not all follow Caesar's verdict. Then, before the ballots were unfolded, Augustus took an oath that he would not become legatee of Tarius, who was very rich. "It was petty of him," it might be objected, "to be afraid of giving the impression that he would promote his own prospects of inheriting by condemning the son." I disagree; any of *us* should have enough confidence in his own good conscience to disregard calumny, but princes must have regard for what people say. Augustus swore that he would not be legatee, which meant that Tarius lost two heirs on the same day, but Caesar redeemed the integrity of his vote. After he had made it clear (as a prince must always take pains to do) that his severity was disinterested, he voted in favor of banishing the son to whatever exile his father chose. His sentence was not sack and snakes or the dungeon, because his mind was on the party whose assessor he was, not on the party at the bar of judgment. He declared that a father should be satisfied with punishment of the mildest degree in the case of a young son who had been led astray to attempt a crime, and whose timid bungling was very close to innocence. In such a case the son should be banished from the capital and his father's sight. [16] How well he deserved to be a father's assessor at a council! How well he deserved to be written down co-heir with children that were guiltless!

A king should reckon no one so cheap that he is indifferent to his death; he is part of his charge, notwithstanding. We can find a paradigm for greater sovereignties from lesser. There is more than one species of power: the prince rules his subjects, the father his children, the teacher his pupils, the colonel or captain his soldiers. Would a man not show himself the worst of fathers if he chastised his children with constant beatings for trivial offenses? And which is a worthier teacher of the humanities, a man who flays his pupils if their memory is wobbly or if their eyes are not agile enough and they halt in their reading, or a man who prefers to emend and teach by admonition and invoking a sense of shame? Take a martinet of a colonel or captain: he will promote desertion and make the offense seem venial. It cannot be right, surely, for a human to be subjected to harsher and crueler rule than dumb beasts, and yet the man trained to break horses does not terrify his animals by constant beating. Unless you soothe a horse with a caressing touch he will become timid and vicious. The same procedure is followed by the hunter, both when he teaches puppies to follow a trail and when he uses dogs so trained to rout the game out and run it down. He does not keep threatening them, for that would dull their high spirit, and their thoroughbred quality would be spoiled by hangdog timidity; nor yet does he give them license to roam and range. You may add the example of the driver of slow-footed beasts; though these are born for abuse and misery, yet excessive cruelty may drive them to refuse the yoke.

[17] No animal is more temperamental and none requires more skillful handling than man; none needs greater indulgence. To give play to passion in the case of pack animals and dogs makes us blush; what could be stupider then than for man to be subjected to man under terms as

vile? Diseases we treat without getting angry at them, and this is a disease of the mind; it requires gentle treatment and a doctor who is not gruff with the patient. Despair of a cure is the mark of a poor physician, and the same applies in cases of mental infection. The man charged with the general well-being should not be quick to abandon hope and pronounce the symptoms fatal. He should wrestle with vices and put up resistance; some invalids he should reproach with their distemper, some he should beguile with mild treatment, because the cure will be more efficacious if the remedy is unnoticed. The prince should be concerned not only with healing a wound but with cicatrizing it decently. Cruel punishment brings a king no glory, for everyone knows he can inflict it; but he wins very great glory if he restricts his own power, if he saves many from the wrath of others and sacrifices none to his own wrath.

[18] To exercise moderation in ruling slaves is praiseworthy. Even in the case of a chattel, the guiding thought must be not how much he can be abused with impunity but how much is allowable by the nature of justice and goodness, which bids us be considerate even of captives and slaves bought for a price. With much greater justice it enjoins us not to abuse free men of decent and respectable family as if they were chattels, but to treat them as persons who have not advanced so far as you and who are put into your care not as servants but as wards. Slaves may take asylum at statues; though power over slaves is absolute, there are things which the common law of animate creation forbids us to inflict on human beings. People hated Vedius Pollio even more than his slaves did; he fattened lampreys on human blood, and ordered trivial offenders thrown into his fishpond, which was nothing better than a snake pit. The fellow deserved a thousand deaths, whether he threw slaves to the lampreys to devour because he was going to eat the eels, or whether he kept the lampreys for the sole purpose of so feeding them.

Cruel masters have fingers pointed at them throughout the city and everyone hates and detests them; kings have a wider stage for their injustices, and their infamy and odium are handed down to the ages. How much better never to have been born than to be numbered among those born for public mischief!

[19] No one can imagine a quality more becoming a king than mercy, however and by whatever title he succeeded to his office. We shall of course acknowledge that the quality is more impressive and more magnificent in the degree that his power is greater; power need not be harmful if it is adapted to the law of nature. It was Nature that devised the institution of kingship, as we may learn from bees and other creatures. The ruler of the bees has the most spacious chamber, in a central and secure location. Moreover he is exempt from labor, but keeps the others to their tasks. Upon the loss of the ruler the swarm disperses. They tolerate no more than one, and they discover the best by combat. Besides, the ruler is outstanding in appearance; he differs from his fellows in stature and comeliness. But his most remarkable distinction is this: bees are touchy; they are very pugnacious for their size, and leave their stings where they wound. But the ruler has no sting; Nature did not wish him to be cruel or to seek revenge that would cost so dear, and so she deprived him of his weapon and left his anger unarmed.

This is a significant paradigm for kings, for it is Nature's habit to practice on a miniature scale and to provide tiny models for momentous issues. It should shame us not to pattern our conduct after minuscule creatures, for man's mind ought to be better governed in the degree that he is capable of more intense harm. How fine it would be if the same law applied to man, if his anger were broken along with his weapon, and he could harm only once, and not wreak his hatred through the agency of others! His fury would subside quickly if he could satisfy it only at his own cost and give rein to his violence only at peril of death. Even as it is, such a man's course is not safe. He must fear in the same degree that he wishes to be feared, he must watch everyone's movements, and even when he is not being hunted he must believe that he is the object of attack and can have no moment free of apprehension. Would anyone consent to lead such a life when he can be harmless to all, and for that very reason safe, when he can make salutary use of his lawful power to the happiness of all? It is a mistake to think that the king is safe when nothing is safe from the king; one bargains for security with security. There is no need to rear lofty citadels, escarp steep hills, cut mountainsides to a sheer drop, fence himself in with multiple walls and towers; clemency will guarantee a king's safety even in an open plain. The love of his countrymen is his one impregnable fortress.

What could be more glorious than a life for whose well-being all offer prayer and all pronounce vows, with none to prod them? When an indisposition rouses men's fears, not their hopes? When nothing is so precious to an individual that he would not willingly exchange it for the health of his chief? Surely a man so fortunate owes it to himself to stay alive; the ever-present proofs of his goodness declare, not that the state belongs to him, but that he belongs to the state. Who would dare heap a stumbling block for such a king? Who would not elect to keep even accident away from a man under whom justice, peace, decency, security, and dignity flourish, under whom the state prospers and abounds in fullness of all good things? Men gaze upon their ruler with just such veneration and adoration as we should upon the immortal gods if they gave us the power of looking upon them. Actually, is he not nearest the gods when he comports himself in accordance with the nature of the gods and is beneficent and generous and potent for good? This should be your goal, this your pattern, to be held greatest only if you are at the same time best.

[20] Generally, a prince punishes for one of two reasons: to avenge himself or someone else. First I shall discuss the first alternative, where he is involved personally, for it is more difficult to be moderate where punishment answers a hurt than when it serves as deterrent. In this connection it is irrelevant to admonish him not to be gullible, to penetrate to the truth, to favor innocence, and to understand clearly that defendant and judge are equally concerned with the issue, for all this has to do not with mercy but with justice. The point I now urge is that, though he has been manifestly injured, he should keep his temper in hand and remit punishment, if he can do so safely, and if not, to moderate it and show himself more charitable in condoning injuries to himself than injuries to others. Not the man who is liberal with other people's property is generous, but the man who deprives himself of what he gives to another; similarly, I will not call the man who is easygoing when somebody else is hurt merciful, but the man who does not flare up when his own withers are wrung, who understands that patience under injury when power is unlimited is a mark of magnanimity, and that nothing is more glorious than a prince who does not avenge an injury.

[21] Generally, vengeance effects one of two purposes: it either compensates the person injured or ensures him for the future. A prince's estate is too high to require compensation, and his power too great for him to seek a reputation for strength by hurting another. This applies where he has been affronted and attacked by inferiors; in the case of his sometime peers he is sufficiently avenged by seeing them below him. A slave or a snake or an arrow can kill a king, but none can save unless he is greater than what he saves. A man who can give life and take it away should therefore be high-minded in using this great gift of the gods. Particularly where he has obtained this sovereignty over persons he knows once occupied his own high level, has he satisfied his vengeance and paid out all that true punish-

ment requires; for the man obliged for his life has in fact lost it, and when he is cast down from on high to the feet of his enemy and awaits another's decision upon his life and realm, he lives only to the glory of his preserver and contributes more to his fame unhurt than if he had been put out of the way. He is permanent evidence of another's merits; the spectacle of a triumph is soon done with. But if it has been possible and safe to leave him in possession of his kingship and restore him to the throne whence he fell, then the luster of a sovereign content to take nothing but glory from a vanquished king will increase enormously. This is tantamount to triumphing over his own victory and demonstrating that he has found among the vanquished nothing worthy of the victor. With his countrymen, the unknown and the humble, the ruler should deal more moderately because there is less advantage in prostrating them. Some you should spare gladly, some you would disdain to take vengeance on and recoil as you would from an insect that dirties the hand that crushes it. But in the case of persons who will be the talk of the town whether they are reprieved or punished, the opportunity for a notable clemency should be utilized.

[22] We must now proceed to the injuries done to others, in the punishment of which the law has three objects in view, which the prince, too, should pursue: (1) to reform the man punished; (2) to improve other men by his example; (3) to assure greater security to the rest of the population by putting bad men out of the way. For purposes of reform a lesser punishment is more effective; a man will live more heedfully if he retains something worth saving. No one spares a reputation he has lost; to leave no room for punishment is a species of immunity. As regards the morality of the state, a sparing use of punishment is a better corrective; where sinners are numerous sin becomes commonplace. A stigma is less onerous when its effect is minimized by widespread application, and constant

use deprives severity of its remedial force. A prince establishes good morality in his state and eliminates vice if he is patient with it, not as if he encouraged it, but as if he approached the task of castigating it reluctantly and with deep pain. A ruler's clemency in itself makes men ashamed of wrongdoing, and punishment seems more grievous if it is inflicted by a kindly man.

[23] You will observe, furthermore, that sins frequently punished are sins frequently committed. Within five years your father sewed more men into the sack than are recorded to have been sewn in all history. Children did not venture on the ultimate enormity [of parricide] when the law did not envisage such a crime. Very wisely those lofty souls who understood human nature so well preferred to ignore the crime as a thing incredible and surpassing all limits of audacity rather than show that it could be committed by legislating a penalty for it. Parricide thus began when a law was passed about it; the penalty pointed the way to the crime. Filial piety reached its nadir when the sack was a commoner sight than the cross. In a state where men are seldom punished innocence becomes the rule and is encouraged as a public good. If a state think itself innocent, it will be; it will be more indignant with those who transgress the accepted level of sobriety when it sees that they are few. It is dangerous, believe me, to show a community that the wicked are preponderant.

[24] A motion was once made in the senate to distinguish slaves from free men by dress; but then it was discovered how dangerous it might be if our slaves began to count us. You must understand that we would incur a similar danger if no one was pardoned; it would quickly become apparent how much the worse element in the state was in the majority. For a prince many executions are as discreditable as many funerals are for a doctor; one who governs less strictly is better obeyed. The human mind is naturally contumacious, it is refractory and strives against

opposition; it follows more readily than it is led. And just as spirited thoroughbreds are better ridden with a loose rein, so clemency begets a spontaneous and unprodded innocence. Such innocence the state thinks worth preserving for its own interest; this is the path of greater progress.

[25] The vice of cruelty is not innate to man and is unworthy man's kindly temper; it is a bestial kind of madness to delight in blood and wounds, to cast off humanity and be transformed into a creature of the forest. I ask you, Alexander, what difference does it make whether you throw Lysimachus to a lion or mangle him with your own teeth? The mouth is yours, the fierceness yours. How you would have liked to have claws and a maw that could gape wide enough to devour men! We do not insist that the hand which is the inexorable destruction of your intimates should bring healing to anyone, or that your fierce temper, the insatiable bane of nations, should be satisfied short of slaughter and massacre: we will call it mercy if you choose some human executioner to butcher a friend.

This is the reason why cruelty is most abominable: first it exceeds ordinary limits, and then human limits; it finds exquisite modes of execution, retains talent to devise instruments for diversifying and prolonging pain, and takes pleasure in human suffering. The diseased mind of our notorious tyrant reached the ultimate of madness when cruelty became a pleasure and murder a delight. Hard on the heels of such a man follow repugnance and loathing, poison and the sword. He is assailed by perils as numerous as the men he imperils; sometimes a private plot corners him, sometimes a general insurrection. An insignificant or individual disaster does not stir whole cities; but when it begins to rage abroad and menace all comers, weapons begin to prick it from every side. Little snakes go unnoticed and society does not hunt them down; but when one exceeds the ordinary measure and grows into a monster, when it infects springs with its venom, scorches with its breath, and crushes everything in its path, artillery is brought to bear against it. Petty evils may cheat and elude us, but we march out to meet great ones. A solitary invalid does not upset even his own household, but when a rapid succession of fatalities shows that plague is abroad there is a general outcry and men flee the city and shake their fists at the very gods. If a fire breaks out under a single roof, the family and neighbors douse it with water, but a wide conflagration which has fed on many houses can be smothered only by the ruin of a whole quarter.

[26] The cruelty of private citizens even slaves have taken it upon themselves to avenge, where the indubitable penalty is crucifixion. The cruelty of tyrants whole races and nations, people touched by the evil and people threatened by it, have taken steps to extirpate. Sometimes their own guards have risen against them and brought to bear upon the tyrant the perfidy and disloyalty and savagery which they learned from him. What can anyone expect from a man he has taught to be evil? Wickedness does not stay docile long and sin only as it is bidden.

But imagine that cruelty is safe: what is its kingdom like? Like the shape of stormed cities, like the awful show of general terror. Everything is gloomy, panicky, confused; men fear even their pleasures. It is not safe to go to a dinner party, for even the tipsy must watch their tongues; it is not safe to go to the shows, for they are the hunting grounds of informers. Though they are most lavishly mounted, with regal opulence and a cast of stars, how can a man enjoy shows in jail?

To kill, to rage, to take pleasure in clanking chains and lopped heads, to shed streams of blood at every turn, to terrify and scatter people at a look—good heavens, what a bane! Would life be any different if lions and bears ruled over us, if serpents and every noxious beast were given power over us? Those same beasts, irrational though they are and outlawed by us for their ferocity, nevertheless spare their own kind; among wild creatures likeness is a safeguard. But the tyrant's fury does not abstain even from kin; it treats strangers and familiars alike, and increases in intensity with use. From the slaughter of individuals it creeps on to the destruction of nations, and thinks firing houses and plowing over ancient cities is a sign of power. To order one death or a second, it believes, is to belittle its lordliness; unless a whole gang of wretches stands to the stroke it thinks its cruelty is reduced to the ranks.

Happiness is vouchsafing safety to many, calling back to life from the brink of death, deserving a civic crown for clemency. No decoration is fairer or worthier a prince's eminence than the crown awarded "for saving the lives of fellow citizens"—not trophies torn from the vanquished, not chariots bloodied with barbarian gore, not spoils won in war. To save men in crowds and in the exercise of duty is a godlike power; to kill in multitudes and without discrimination is the power of fire and ruin.

Books Two and Three, except for the opening sections of Book Two, are lost. The surviving fragment adds little to Book One and is here omitted.

LETTERS

Several collections of correspondence have come down from antiquity. Cicero's are indubitably genuine, but subsequently edited for publication. Pliny's were genuine letters, but written with an eye to publication. In others, as for example those of Alciphron and perhaps Sidonius, the letter is merely a literary form. Many critics have thought that Seneca's letters belong to the same category, yet there is no reason to suppose that they are not real, but written with a view to publication and with personal matters suppressed. At one point, indeed (Letter 21), Seneca promises Lucilius immortality on the strength of his being the addressee. There is no logical consistency in the sequence, but it is possible to establish certain groups according to Seneca's current reading or place of residence. The first twenty-nine, for example, seem to follow the model of Epicurus' letters to Idomeneus and each closes with an Epicurean nugget. Another group is dated from the resort region on the Campanian shore. The letters were written in A.D. 63 and 64, at the end of Seneca's life. They are more personal than even the Consolations, less formal than Seneca's other writings, and readers have always found them the most appealing. It should be remarked that a selection equally attractive and informing could be made without repeating a single piece here included. The formal salutation prefaced to each letter, "Seneca to Lucilius greeting," is here omitted.

3. FRIENDSHIP

It was your friend, as you write him down, that brought me your letter, and then you warn me not to discuss your affairs with him freely because you yourself avoid doing so. In the same letter, then, you assert that the man is your friend and say that he is not. If you give that quite specific word its popular usage and call a man "friend" as we call all candidates for office "gentlemen," or greet men whose names slip us when we meet them as "my dear sir," we shall let it pass. But if you think a man you do not trust as fully as yourself is a friend, you are grievously mistaken and do not understand the meaning of true friendship.

Deliberate upon all questions with your friend, but first deliberate about him. After friendship there must be full trust, but before it, discretion. If you reverse Theophrastus' precept and assay the man you have loved instead of loving the man you have assayed, you put the cart before the horse and confuse the rules of social behavior. Think long whether a man should be admitted to your friendship, and when you have decided he should be, admit him with all your heart and speak with him as freely as with yourself. You should, of course, so live that you have no confidences you could not divulge even to an enemy; but because custom has made certain passages in a man's life secret, share your reflections and your anxieties with a friend. If you believe he is loyal you will make him so. Some people's fear of being deceived has taught men to deceive them; their suspicions give a license to injury. Why should I watch my words in the presence of my friend? Why should I not consider myself alone in his presence?

Some people give casual acquaintances full accounts of

what ought to be confided only to friends and unload whatever is on their minds into any ears at all. Some, on the other hand, shrink from the privity of their dearest friends; they would not even trust themselves, if that were possible, but suppress their every confidence deep within them. Neither course is correct. Trusting everyone and trusting no one are both wrong, though I might say the one wrong is an excess of frankness and the other an excess of security.

Another reprehensible pair is the man who is never at ease and the man who is always at ease. Bustle is not briskness but the agitation of a turbulent mind. And disdaining all activity as a nuisance is not ease but enervation and inertia. Keep in mind the remark I read in Pomponius: "Some people have withdrawn to darkness so deep that they think anything in the light is dim." The two attitudes should temper one another: the easygoing man should act, the active man take it easy. Consult Nature: she will tell you that she created both day and night. Farewell.

5 . MODERATION

Your assiduity and your single-minded concentration on daily improvement give me satisfaction and joy; I urge, nay beg, you to persevere in your course. But I admonish you not to behave like those whose aim is notoriety rather than progress; do not make your dress or mode of life conspicuous. Rough clothing, an unshorn head, an untrimmed beard, militant scorn of silverware, a pallet spread on the ground, and all other perverse media of self-advertisement you must shun. The mere title of philosophy, however modestly worn, is invidious enough; what if we should begin to except ourselves from the ordinary uses of mankind? Within we may be different in every point, but our front should conform to society. The toga need not be exquisitely laundered, but it should not be dirty. We need not possess silver encrusted with designs in solid gold, but let us not equate the absence of gold and silver with frugality. Our endeavor must be to make our way of life better than the crowd's, not contrary to it; else we shall turn from us and repel the people we wish to improve. The result would be that they would refuse to imitate anything in our program for fear they would have to imitate everything in it.

Philosophy's first promise is a sense of participation, of belonging to mankind, being a member of society. Unlikeness will alienate us from our promise. We must be careful that our efforts to awaken admiration are not ludicrous or odious. Our principle, you remember, is "life according to nature"; but it is against Nature to torment one's body, to loathe neatness easily come by, to make a point of squalor, to use victuals that are not only cheap but loathsome and repulsive. To desire dainties is a mark of luxury; it is just as much a mark of lunacy to avoid ordinary food that is not expensive. It is frugality that philosophy asks, not affliction, and frugality need not be slovenly. This I hold is the correct mode: life should be steered between good mores and public mores; men should respect our way of life, but they should find it recognizable.

"What is the upshot? Shall we do as others do? Will there be no distinction between us and them?" A very great distinction. Anyone who looks closely will realize that we are unlike the crowd. Anyone who enters our home will admire us rather than our furniture. It is a great man who uses earthenware as if it were silver; he is no less great who uses silver as if it were earthenware.

But I proceed to hand you your regular share of my day's profit. I find in Hecaton that curtailing desire serves as a specific against fears; "You will cease to fear," says he, "if you cease to hope." You may ask, "How can things so different go hand in hand?" The truth is, my dear Lucilius, that though they seem to differ they are in fact attached; one chain joins the prisoner and his guard, and these two, different as they are, walk in step in the same way. Fear keeps pace with hope. Nor do I find it surprising that they keep company, for each belongs to a mind in suspense, a mind hanging on what the future might bring. The cause in both cases is failure to adjust ourselves to the present and a tendency to project our mental processes far into the future. Foresight, which is mankind's greatest advantage, is thus turned to disadvantage. Beasts avoid the dangers which confront them, and when they have avoided them they stand at ease; we are tormented alike by the future and the past. Our superiority brings us much distress; memory recalls the torment of fear, foresight anticipates it. No one confines his misery to the present. Farewell.

What should you put down as a thing especially to be avoided? I say a crowd; it is not yet safe for you to trust yourself to one. At least, I confess my own infirmity: I never bring back the same character I took with me. Some balance I have achieved is upset, some bogy I have banished comes back. What happens to invalids who are so debilitated by long illness that they cannot be brought outdoors without harmful effects happens to us also; it is our souls that are undergoing treatment for a chronic disease. Contact with the crowd is deleterious; inevitably vice will be made attractive or imprinted on us or smeared upon us without our being aware of it. In every case, the larger the crowd with which we mingle the greater the danger.

But nothing is so injurious to character as lounging at the shows. Pleasure paves an easy way for vice to creep in. What, specifically, do I mean? I come home more greedy, more self-seeking, more pleasure-loving, yes, even more cruel and more inhuman because I have been among humans. I happened on the noon interlude at the arena, expecting some clever burlesque, some relaxation to give the spectators a respite from human gore. The show was the reverse. The fighting that had gone before was charity by contrast. Now there was no nonsense about it; it was pure murder. The men have nothing to protect them; the whole body is exposed and every stroke tells. Many spectators prefer this to the usual matches and to the champion bouts. Why shouldn't they? There is no helmet or shield to parry the steel. Why armor? Why skill? Such things delay the kill. In the forenoon men are thrown to lions and bears; at noon, to the spectators. They order those who have made a kill to be thrown to others who will kill them, the victor is kept for fresh slaughter. The conclusion of every fight is death; no quarter is given. And this goes on while the stands are empty. "But the fellow was a highwayman; he killed a man!" So what? Because he killed a man he deserves this fate, but what did you do, poor man, to deserve having to look on? "Cut him, drive him up with knout and firebrand! Why is he so timid about meeting the blade? Why are his strokes so hesitant? Why is he so reluctant to die? Scourge him to face up to the slashing! Make them trade blows, bared breast to bared breast!" Then comes the intermission: "Let's have a little throat-cutting; we must have some action."

Listen, can't you even understand that bad examples backfire on the doer? Thank the immortal gods that your pupil in cruelty is one who cannot learn. But a tender soul which is not yet tenacious of the right must be kept away from the crowd; it is so easy to go over to the majority. A Socrates, a Cato, a Laelius might have had their character shaken by a crowd unlike themselves; even when we have done our best to regularize our personality, none of us can withstand the assault of vices supported by such a host of vassals. A single example of luxury or avarice works great mischief. A comrade who is squeamish gradually enervates us and makes us soft; a neighbor who is rich pricks up our covetousness; a companion who is malicious rubs some of his rust off upon us, however frank and ingenuous we may be. Then what do you suppose happens to character when an assault is made upon it with total mobilization? Inevitably you either imitate or loathe. But both alternatives must be avoided. Neither become like the bad because they are many, nor hostile to the many because they are different. Retire into yourself, so far as you can. Associate with people who may improve you, admit people whom you can improve. The process is mutual; men learn as they teach. There is no reason why ambition to advertise your talents should lure you to the public platform to give popular readings or discourses. I should agree to your doing so if your wares suited such customers, but none of them can understand you. A solitary individual or two may come your way, but even him you will have to educate and train to understand you. "Then why did I learn all this?" Never fear that you have wasted your effort; you learned for yourself.

What I have learned today I shall not keep to myself but share with you. Three excellent sayings expressing a virtually identical sentiment have come my way; one will pay my shot for this letter, and you may credit me with the other two as advance payment. Democritus says: "To me an individual is as good as a crowd, and a crowd as good as an individual." The saying of the second man (whoever he was; his identity is under dispute) is also good. When he was asked the object of applying himself so assiduously to an art which would reach so very few people, he said: "For me a few are enough, one is enough, none is enough." The third is a notable saying of Epicurus'. Writing to one of his fellow researchers, he said: "This is not for the many but for you; we are a sufficient audience for each other." These sentiments, my dear Lucilius, must be laid up in your heart, so that you may scorn the satisfaction which comes from popular approval. The many admire you, but have you grounds for self-satisfaction if you are the kind of man the many understand? Your merits should face inwards. Farewell.

Wherever I turn I see proof of my age. I went to my country place and complained of the maintenance of the dilapidated buildings. My superintendent said the trouble was not remissness on his part; he had done everything, but the house was old. That house had taken shape under my own hands; what is to become of me if stones that are my contemporaries are disintegrating? I was peeved with the man and seized the first opening for venting my spleen. "Obviously," said I, "these plane trees have been neglected. They have no foliage. See how knotty and shrunken the branches are, how woebegone and slatternly the trunks! This would never have happened if anyone had hoed around the roots and watered them." He swore by my tutelary deity that he had attended to all these tasks and had in no way been derelict; the trees were simply superannuated. *Entre nous,* it was I that planted those trees, and I had seen their first leaves. Turning to the entry, I said: "Who is that decrepit wreck? His position by the doorway is right enough; he'll soon be carried out feet first. Where did you find him? What's the point of playing undertaker for some stranger's corpse?" "Don't you recognize me?" the man said. "I am Felicio; you used to bring me toy soldiers for the holidays. I am Philositus the superintendent's son; I was your special pet." "The fellow is clean out of his mind—he's turned into a little boy and my pet! But it could be, at that; his teeth are going at a great rate."

I am indebted to my country place for bringing my age home to me wherever I turned. We should welcome old age and love it; it is full of pleasure if you know how to use it. Fruit tastes best when its season is ending; a boy

is handsomest at boyhood's close; and it is the last drink
which brings the toper delight, the one that submerges him
and polishes off his jag. Every pleasure saves its most agreeable scene for the finale. Age is most agreeable on its downward arc—not when the drop is sheer. But in my judgment,
even the man standing on the cornice tile has his own
pleasures, or perhaps not wanting any is a surrogate for
pleasure. How sweet it is to have outworn desires and left
them behind! "But it is a bore," you say, "to have death
before your eyes." In the first place, old and young alike
should have death before their eyes; we are not summoned
in the order of our birth registration. In the second place,
no one is so old that he cannot legitimately hope for one
day more, and one day is a stage of life.

Life as a whole consists of parts, with larger circles cir-
cumscribed about smaller. One circle encompasses and
cinches the rest; it extends from our first day to our last.
Another includes the years of young manhood. Another
embraces all of childhood in its periphery. Then there is
another series where the year encompasses all time units
whose aggregate comprises life. The months are included
in a smaller circle. The smallest of all is the day's, but even
this goes from beginning to end, from sunrise to sunset.
That is why Heraclitus (whose style gave him his surname
"Dark") said, "One day is equal to all." This has been variously understood. One opinion holds the equality is in the
number of hours, which is right enough, for all days are
equally composed of twenty-four hours, and if the daylight
hours are shorter the night hours are longer. Another holds
that one day is equal to all in similitude, because even a
very long span exhibits no phenomenon which you cannot
find in a single day—light and dark; and if you continue
to eternity you will find these alternations more numerous
but not different or at different intervals. Every day must
therefore be ordered as if it were the last in the series, as
if it filled our measure and closed our life.

Pacuvius, who lived in Syria long enough to acquire squatter's rights, used to give himself a mourning dinner, with wine and the usual funeral meats, and then he was carried from the dining room to the bedroom to the clapping of eunuchs who chanted, "His life has been lived! His life has been lived!" Pacuvius gave himself a funeral every single day. What he did out of perverted motives we should do out of good, and as we retire to our beds we should say, cheerfully and contentedly, "I have lived; I have finished the course Fortune set me" (*Aeneid* 4.653). If god adds the morrow we shall accept it gladly. The man who can look to the morrow without anxiety is the happiest and has the firmest hold on himself. The man who says, "My life has been lived," receives a windfall with each new day.

It is time to seal my letter. "What," you say, "will it not bring me some little windfall?" Never fear, it does bring something—not something: a great deal, for nothing could be nobler than this saying which I commit to this letter for delivery to you: "It is bad to live under constraint, but nothing can constrain a man to live under constraint." Nothing at all; many short and easy roads to freedom are open on every side. We should thank god that no man can be chained to life; we are in position to trample the very constraints. "It was Epicurus that said that," you object. "What business have you with what belongs to somebody else?" Whatever is true is mine. I will persist in deluging you with Epicurus, so that people who swear fealty to a school and regard not the value but the source of dicta may realize that the best things are common property. Farewell.

The month is December, and the whole city is in a sweat. Public luxury is given license, everywhere there is the noisy bustle of elaborate preparation—as if there were any difference between the Saturnalia and a business day. The saying that "December was once a month but now it's a year" (and I think its author hit the mark) proves that there is no difference.

If you were here, I would enjoy sounding out your opinion on the proper attitude: whether we should make no change in our everyday program or, not to give an impression of being at variance with public mores, put on a gay dinner and lay the toga aside. (It used to be that we laid the toga aside only in times of civil dissension when the state was in a crisis; now we do it for pleasure's sake, to celebrate a holiday.) If I know my man, in the role of referee you would have us be neither wholly like the liberty-capped crowd nor wholly unlike. But perhaps this is the very season for being stern with the soul and making it abstain from pleasure just when the crowd is all pleasure bent; a man gives himself the surest proof of his steadfastness if he neither goes nor allows himself to be led to agreeable pastimes which involve self-indulgence. It shows more austerity to stay dry and sober when the crowd is puking drunk, but more control not to make oneself an exception, not to be markedly different nor yet one of the crowd, but to do as others do, only not in the same way. It is possible to observe a holiday without self-indulgence.

The notion of testing the steadfastness of your soul is so engaging that I shall give you a prescription from the precepts of our great teachers. Set aside a number of days during which you will be content with plain and scanty food and with coarse and crude dress, and say to yourself, "Is this what frightened me?" It is in time of security that the soul should school itself to hardship, and while Fortune is benign it should gather strength to meet her harshness. In the midst of peace the soldier charges, he throws up a rampart when there is no enemy, he wearies himself with superfluous exertions, in order to make himself adequate to necessary exertions. If you don't want a man to panic in action you must train him beforehand. This is the program of the school which approaches actual want in its monthly imitation of poverty; the object is to be unflinching in the face of a situation they have often rehearsed.

Don't imagine I mean meals like Timon's or the rigged paupers' cells or luxury's other devices for beguiling the ennui of wealth; the pallet must be real, and the poncho, and the bread hard and dirty. Put up with this for three or four days and sometimes longer, to make it a real test, not a game. Then, Lucilius, believe me, you will be overjoyed when you fill up on two cents and realize that security is not beholden to Fortune; the essentials she supplies even when she is angry.

But there is no reason to credit yourself with a remarkable achievement. You will be doing what many thousands of slaves, many thousands of poor men do. But on this you can compliment yourself: your behavior is not under duress, and it will be as easy for you to maintain it permanently as to try it occasionally. We must train on the punching bag; poverty must become our familiar so that Fortune may not catch us unprepared. We can be rich with easier mind if we are convinced that poverty is not a disaster.

That doctor of pleasure Epicurus kept certain days on which he appeased his hunger on short commons, with the object of ascertaining whether this was a diminution of full and complete pleasure, how great the diminution was, and whether it was worth supplying at the cost of great exertion. At least that is what he says in his letter to Polyaenus, dated in the archonship of Charinus. Indeed, he boasts that his food came to less than a nickel, while Metrodorus, who had not progressed so far, required a whole nickel. Do you suppose such diet is adequate? It even gives pleasure, and not the fickle and fleeting sort which always needs renewal but a pleasure sound and sure. Water and porridge and a crust of barley bread are not the jolliest fare, but it is a very great pleasure to be able to derive pleasure from such things and to have established a regimen which no malignancy of Fortune can spirit away. Prison fare is more generous, the executioner is not so stingy with food for culprits awaiting capital punishment. What loftiness of spirit to descend voluntarily to a level which a man sentenced to death is spared! That is taking the offensive against the darts of Fortune!

Begin then, my dear Lucilius, to follow this practice: appoint certain days on which you will abandon your routine and become intimate with scarcity; begin to establish relations with poverty. "Venture, friend, to scorn wealth; make yourself worthy a god" (*Aeneid* 8.364 f.). Only a man who scorns wealth is worthy a god. I do not interdict the possession of wealth, but my aim is for you to possess it fearlessly, and this attitude you can achieve only if you are convinced that you can live happily even without wealth, if you look upon it always as on the point of vanishing.

But I must now begin to seal my letter. "First hand over what you owe," say you; I give you an order on Epicurus, who will pay cash: "Immoderate anger begets madness." You should know how true this is, for you have had both a slave and an enemy. The emotion flares up against characters of all kinds; it is born of love as well as hate, and in serious occupations as well as games and sport. It is not the weightiness of the cause but the quality of the soul it visits that makes the difference, just as it makes no difference how big a fire is but where it catches. Even a big fire does not find lodgment in solid beams, but dry and inflammable material will nurse even a spark into a great blaze. That is how madness is the upshot of great anger, my dear Lucilius, and hence anger is to be avoided not for the sake of moderation but for the sake of sanity. Farewell.

Do you think you are the only one this has happened to? Do you find it uniquely extraordinary that such extensive travel and such a variety of scene have not shaken off your melancholy and heaviness of spirit? It is your soul you need to change, not the climate. Though you cross the vast deep, though, as Vergil says, you "leave lands and cities receding in your wake" (*Aeneid* 3.72), your failings will follow, whatever your destination. This is what Socrates said to a man who made the same complaint: "Why do you wonder that travel abroad does no good, when you carry yourself along? What drove you from home still sticks close." How can strange lands help you? Or acquaintance with new cities and regions? Tossing about hither and yon is futile. If you ask why escape is not feasible, you are escaping *with* yourself. You must lay down the weight on your soul; until you do, no place will satisfy. Imagine that your present state is like the Sibyl's whom Vergil represents as goaded to frenzy and filled with a spirit not her own: "The priestess is possessed and seeks to shake the mighty god from her bosom" (*Aeneid* 6.78 f.). You march here and you march there to shake the oppressive weight off, but the very motion exacerbates it, like freight on a ship; when it is battened down it rides easily, but if its shifting disrupts the ship's balance it will keel the ship over at the point where it settles. Any action you take has an adverse effect, the very movement is injurious; it is a sick man you are shaking up.

But once you have rid yourself of that incubus any change of place becomes agreeable. Though you are banished to the ends of the earth, though you are marooned in a corner of Barbary, your domicile will be hospitable whatever its character. The quality of the sojourner is of more consequence than the place of his sojourn, and therefore we ought not indenture our minds to any locality. Life must proceed in the conviction that "I am not born for a single cranny; this whole universe is my fatherland." If you saw the truth of this, you would not be surprised that the variety of new places you visit out of boredom with the old do you no good. Whichever you struck first would have satisfied you if you had believed you were at home in all. As it is, you are not traveling but straying and being hounded; you change one place for another when the thing you are looking for, the good life, is available everywhere.

Could any spot be as turbulent as the forum? Even there it is possible to live quietly if need be. If I were given the option, I would run far away from the sight and even the proximity of the forum. Just as unwholesome localities are trying even to the soundest constitution, so some places are not salutary for even the good mind which is not yet perfect but gaining strength. I do not hold with those who choose a strenuous life and go straight into the boisterous waves for a high-spirited bout with obstacles. The sage will tolerate such an existence but not choose it; he will prefer to be at peace rather than at war. It profits a man little to have jettisoned his failings if he must wrestle with other people's. "Thirty tyrants surrounded Socrates," you say, "but could not break his spirit." What difference how many masters there are? Slavery is unitary, and the man who despises it is free amid whatever mob of masters.

It is time to stop, but I must first pay my tariff. "The beginning of salvation is the knowledge of sin." Epicurus said this, and I think it excellent. A man who is not aware he is sinning does not wish to be amended; you must catch yourself at fault before you can correct yourself. Some people boast of their failings; do you suppose a man who counts his vices as virtues can take thought for remedying them?

So far as you can, then, be your own prosecutor, investigate yourself, function first as accuser, then as judge, and only in the end as advocate. And sometimes you must overrule the advocate. Farewell.

You request that I append to these letters, as I did to my earlier ones, selected sayings of our outstanding teachers. Those men were not concerned with gems; the texture of their work is all virile. You may recognize unevenness in a work when attention is attracted by what rises above the level. One tree is not noteworthy if the whole forest rises to the same height. Poetry is replete with such lines and so is history, and so I would not have you think those sentiments peculiar to Epicurus; they are in the public domain, and we Stoics in particular acknowledge them. They are more noticeable in Epicurus because they are infrequent, because they are unexpected, and because it is surprising to find virile utterances in a man who professes softness. That is how the majority judge him; for me Epicurus is virile though he did wear long sleeves. Courage and perseverance and readiness for war occurs among Persians as well as among men girt for action.

There is no point in your demanding excerpts and memorable dicta; the sort of thing which is excerpted in others forms the continuous text of our writers. We do not have advertising specialties to lure customers, who find, when they enter the shop, that all the goods are in the display window. We allow them to take samples wherever they like. Suppose we wanted to label individual apothegms in the stock: whom would we assign them to? Zeno? Cleanthes? Chrysippus? Panaetius? Posidonius? We are not subjects of a monarch; every individual asserts his freedom. Among the Epicureans anything that Hermarchus or Metrodorus said is attributed to their one authority. Anything anyone in that fellowship says is credited to the commander-in-chief. We could not, I insist, even if we tried, choose from such a crowd of peers. Wherever you turn, your eye will light on something which might stand out if the whole context were not on an equally high level.

Don't expect, then, that you can sample the masterpieces of great minds by way of summaries; you must examine the whole, work over the whole. Their structure is a totality fitted together according to the outlines of their special genius, and if any member is removed the whole may collapse. I have no objection to your examining the disparate members provided you consider them as parts of the totality. An admired ankle or arm does not make a woman beautiful; a beautiful woman is one whose total appearance silences praise of her parts.

But if you insist, I shall not be parsimonious but deal passages out with an open hand; there is a great mass of them lying at random. They need only be taken up, not picked out; they do not come intermittently but flow in a stream. They form a continuous weft, with no blanks between. Doubtless they have much to offer the uninitiate who listen from without; brief maxims set off like a line of poetry take hold more easily. That is why we give boys apothegms, what the Greeks call *chriai*, to learn by heart, because the childish mind, which cannot comprehend more, is able to grasp them. But for a man advanced in study to hunt such gems is disgraceful; he is using a handful of clichés for a prop and leaning on his memory; by now he should stand on his own feet. He should be producing bons mots, not remembering them. It is disgraceful for an old man or one in sight of old age to be wise by book. "Zeno said this." What do *you* say? "This Cleanthes said." What do *you* say? How long will you be a subaltern? Take command and say things which will be handed down to posterity. Produce something of your own. All those men who never create but lurk as interpreters under the shadow of another are lacking, I believe, in independence of spirit.

They never venture to do the things they have long rehearsed. They exercise their memories on what is not their own. But to remember is one thing, to know another. Remembering is merely overseeing a thing deposited in the memory; knowing is making the thing your own, not depending on the model, not always looking over your shoulder at the teacher. "Zeno said this, Cleanthes that"—is there any difference between you and a book? How long will you learn? Begin to teach! One man objects, "Why should I listen to lectures when I can read?" Another replies, "The living voice adds a great deal." It does indeed, but not a voice which merely serves for another's words and functions as a clerk.

There is another consideration. First, people who have not rid themselves of leading-strings follow their predecessors where all the world has ceased to follow them, and second, they follow them in matters still under investigation. But if we rest content with solutions offered, the real solution will never be found. Moreover, a man who follows another not only finds nothing, he is not even looking. What is the upshot? Shall I not walk in the steps of my predecessors? I shall indeed use the old path, but if I find a shorter and easier way I shall make a new path. The men who made the old paths are not our suzerains but our pioneers. Truth is open to all; it has not been pre-empted. Much of it is left for future generations. Farewell.

41. GOD IN MAN

It is a fine and salutary course if, as you write, you are persevering in your pursuit of a good mentality; it is stupid to pray for it when you can obtain it by your own efforts. We do not need to lift our hands to heaven or beg the sexton for nearer access to the idol's ear, as if he could hear us more clearly; god is near you, with you, inside you. Yes, Lucilius, there is a holy spirit abiding within us who observes our good deeds and bad and watches over us. He treats us according as we treat him. No man is good without god. Could any man rise above Fortune without his help? It is he that imparts grand and upstanding counsel. In every man "indwells a god, what god we know not" (*Aeneid* 8.352).

Have you ever come upon a grove thick with venerable trees which tower above the ordinary height and by their layers of intertwined branches dim the light of heaven? The height of the forest, its quiet seclusion, the marvel of thick and unbroken shade in untrammeled space, will impart a conviction of deity. A cavern formed by deep erosion of rocks holds a mountain above it, a spacious void produced not by man's handiwork but by natural causes: your soul will be stirred by religious awe. We venerate the sources of great rivers; we build altars where ample streams suddenly burst from the unseen; we worship hot geysers; and we consecrate lakes for their opaque waters and unplumbed depths. If you see a man undaunted in danger, untouched by passion, happy in adversity, calm in the raging storm, viewing mankind from a higher level and the gods from their own, will you not be moved by veneration? Will you not say: "This is too grand and lofty to be of a quality with the little body that contains it; the power that has informed that man is divine"?

A soul which is of superior stature and well governed, which deflates the imposing by passing it by and laughs at all our fears and prayers, *is* impelled by a celestial force. So great a thing cannot stand without a buttress of divinity. Its larger portion therefore abides at its source. Just as the rays of the sun do indeed warm the earth but remain at the source of their radiation, so a great and holy soul is lowered to earth to give us a nearer knowledge of the divine; but though it is in intercourse with us, it cleaves to its source; it is tied to it, it looks toward it, it seeks to rejoin it, and its concern with our affairs is superior and detached.

And what is this soul? It shines with no good but its own. Could anything be stupider than to praise a man for what is not his own? Or madder than to admire what may be forthwith transferred to another? Golden reins do not make a horse better. A lion with gilded mane, worked over and worn down to submit to grooming, enters the arena quite a different animal from the untrimmed lion with spirit unbroken. Bold in attack, as nature meant him to be, handsome because unkempt—the terror he inspires is the essence of his attraction—he has the edge over that bedizened and spiritless creature.

No one ought to preen himself on what is not essentially his. We praise a vine if it loads its tendrils with fruit, if its weight pulls the very props that support it down to the ground. Would any man prefer the famous vine which had golden grapes and golden leaves hanging from it? In a vine the peculiar virtue is fertility, and in a man, too, we should praise what is peculiarly his own. He has a handsome troop of slaves, a fine house, broad acres, large investments; but none of these things is *in* him, they are *around* him. Praise what cannot be given or taken away, what is peculiarly the man's. What is this, you ask? It is soul, and reason perfected in the soul. For man is a rational animal, and his good is realized if he implements the potentiality for which nature gave him being. And what does reason demand of him? A very easy thing: to live according to his nature. But general derangement makes this difficult; we shove one another into vice. And how can people be recalled to safety when there is a crowd pushing them and nobody to hold them back? Farewell.

47. SLAVES

Your attitude to your slaves is one of familiarity, as I learn
from people who have been in your company. I am pleased;
it is what one expects of your good sense and cultivation.
"They are slaves"—no, men. "They are slaves"—no, com-
rades. "They are slaves"—no, humble friends. "They are
slaves"—no, fellow slaves, if you remember that Fortune
holds equal sway over both.

That is why I laugh at people who think it degrading
for a man to dine with his slave. Why, except that conventional exclusiveness has decreed that a master must be
surrounded at his dinner by a squad of slaves standing at
attention? The master eats more than he can hold; his inordinate greed loads his distended belly, which has un-
learned the belly's function, and the digestion of all this
food requires more ado than its ingestion. But the unhappy
slaves may not move their lips for so much as a word. Any
murmur is checked by a rod; not even involuntary sounds
—a cough, a sneeze, a choke—are exempted from the lash.
If a word breaks the silence the penalty is severe. Hungry
and mute, they stand through the whole night.

In consequence, when they cannot speak in the master's
presence, they speak *about* him. Yet when slaves spoke not
only in the master's presence but *with* him, when their lips
were not sewn tight, they were ready to put their necks
out for their master, to turn any danger that threatened
him upon their own heads; they spoke at dinners, but under
torture their lips were sealed. But afterward the arrogance
of masters gave currency to the proverb, "So many slaves,
so many enemies." We do not acquire them as enemies,
we make them such. Other cruel and inhuman treatment

I pass over: we abuse them as one does pack animals, not even as one abuses men. When we recline at table one slave wipes up the hawking, another crouches to take up the leavings of the drunks. One carves the costly game, separating the portions by deft sweeps of a practiced hand —unhappy man, to live solely for the purpose of carving fowl neatly, unless the man who teaches the trade for pleasure's sake is more wretched than the man who learns it for necessity's! Another, who serves the wine, is got up like a woman and must wrestle with his age; he can never escape boyhood but is dragged back to it. His figure may now be a soldier's, but his hairs are rubbed away or plucked out by the roots to make him smooth, and he must divide his sleepless night between his master's drunkenness and his lust; in the bedroom he is a man, in the dining room a boy. Another has the assignment of keeping book on the guests; he stands there, poor fellow, and watches to see whose adulation and whose intemperance of gullet or tongue will get him an invitation for the following day. Add the caterers with their refined *expertise* of the master's palate; they know what flavors will titillate him, what table decorations will please his fancy, what novelty might restore his appetite when he feels nauseous, what his surfeit will scorn, what tidbit he would crave on a particular day. With slaves like these the master cannot bear to dine; he would count it an affront to his dignity to come to table with his own slave. Heaven forbid!

But how many of those slaves are in fact his masters! I have seen Callistus' master a suitor outside Callistus' door and have seen him shut out while others were admitted— the master who tagged him for sale and sent him to market with a job-lot of chattels. But the slave included in this preliminary batch on which the auctioneer tried out his voice paid tit for tat. He crossed Callistus' name from the roster in turn and judged him unfit to enter his house. His

master sold Callistus, but how much did Callistus cost his
master!

Remember, if you please, that the man you call slave
sprang from the same seed, enjoys the same daylight,
breathes like you, lives like you, dies like you. You can
as easily conceive him a free man as he can conceive you
a slave. In the Marian disasters many men of noble birth
who had entered military service as the preliminary to a
senatorial career were declassed by Fortune and reduced
to being shepherds or cottagers; now despise a man for
his condition when you may find yourself in the same even
as you despise it!

I do not wish to take up the large topic of the treatment of slaves, where we show ourselves proud, cruel, and
insulting in the highest degree. The essence of my teaching is this: Treat your inferior as you would wish your superior to treat you. Whenever the thought of your wide
power over your slave strikes you, be struck, too, by the
thought of your master's equally wide power over you. "But
I have no master!" you object. All in good time; you may
have one. Remember how old Hecuba was when she became a slave, or Croesus, or Darius' mother, or Plato, or
Diogenes.

Treat your slave with compassion, even with courtesy;
admit him to your conversation, your planning, your society. Here the genteel will protest loudly and unanimously:
"Nothing could be more degrading or disgusting!" But
these same people I shall catch kissing the hands of other
people's slaves. Can't you see how our ancestors stripped
the title of master of all invidiousness and the title of slave
of all contumely? The master they called "paterfamilias"
and the slaves "family"; this usage still obtains in the mimes.
They instituted a festival at which masters dined with their
slaves—not, of course, the only day they could do so. They
allowed slaves to hold office in the household and to act

as judges; the household they regarded as a miniature republic.

"What is the upshot? Am I to bring all slaves to my table?" No more than all free men. But if you imagine I would exclude some because their work is dirty, that muleteer, for example, or that cowhand, you are mistaken. I value them not by their jobs but by their character; a man gives himself his own character, accident allots his job. Have some dine with you because they are deserving, some to make them deserving. If their sordid contacts have left a taint, association with respectable people will shake it off. There is no reason to go to the forum or senate house in search of a friend, my dear Lucilius; if you pay careful heed you will find one at home. Without an artisan good material often lies unused; try it and you will find out.

A man is a fool if he looks only at the saddle and bridle and not at the horse itself when he is going to buy one; he is a greater fool if he values a man by his clothing and condition, which only swathes us like clothing. "He is a slave!" But perhaps a free man in spirit. "He is a slave!" Shall that count against him? Show me a man who is not; one is a slave to lust, another to greed, another to ambition, all to fear. I can show you a consular who is slave to a crone, a millionaire who is slave to a housemaid; I can point to young aristocrats indentured to pantomimes. Voluntary slavery is the meanest of all.

Those squeamish types should not deter you, therefore, from camaraderie with your slaves and make you proudly superior. Slaves ought to respect rather than fear you. Here someone will protest that I am now rallying slaves to the cap of liberty and toppling masters from their elevation by saying, "Slaves ought to respect rather than fear a master." "That is what he said: slaves ought to respect him, like his clients or those who pay him formal calls." The protester forgets that what is enough for a god is not too little for a master. If a man is respected he is also loved, and love cannot blend with fear.

Your own attitude is consequently as right as can be, in my judgment; you do not choose to have your slaves fear you, you use words to castigate them. A lash is to admonish dumb beasts. What offends need not wound. It is our daintiness that drives us to distraction, so that anything that does not meet our caprice provokes our wrath. We assume regal lordliness. Kings forget their own strength and others' weakness and fly into a white-hot fury as if they had really been injured, when their exalted position guarantees them complete immunity to any possibility of injury. Nor are they unaware of their immunity; by complaining, they solicit an opening for inflicting harm. They profess they have been injured in order to work injury.

I do not wish to detain you longer; you need no exhortation. Among its other traits good character approves its decisions and abides by them. Wickedness is fickle and changes frequently, not for something better but for something different. Farewell.

Yesterday I shared with sickness; it claimed the forenoon and yielded the afternoon to me. First I tested my spirit with reading. Then when it passed this test I ventured upon larger demands, or rather gave it larger scope. I set to writing, and indeed with more than my customary concentration, for I was wrestling with a difficult subject where I refused to give in, until friends interceded and applied force to restrain me, like an invalid overdoing. Conversation supplanted composition. I now bring you the case under litigation; you have been designated arbiter. The assignment is more troublesome than you imagine, for the dispute is threefold.

As you know, we Stoics hold that there are two factors in nature which give rise to all things, cause and matter. Matter lies inert, susceptible to any use but yielding none if no one sets it in motion. Cause, which is to say reason, shapes matter and turns it where it will, to produce various objects. For any object raw material and a maker are requisite; one is matter, the other cause.

Every art is an imitation of nature. Apply the general principle I have stated to man's handiwork. A statue is the product of matter, which is susceptible to the artificer, and the artificer, who gives the matter its form. Here the material is bronze, the cause the craftsman. The same applies to everything; the material is one factor, the maker the other. The Stoics maintain that there is only one cause, the maker. Aristotle holds that "cause" has three connotations. "The first cause," he says, "is the matter itself, without which nothing can be produced. The second is the craftsman. The third is the form which is imposed on an indi-

vidual product, as on a statue." Form is what Aristotle calls
idos. "There is, in addition, a fourth cause," Aristotle adds,
"the purpose of the work as a whole." I shall explain.
① Bronze is the first cause of the statue, for it could never
have been made if there were no material out of which it
② could be cast and modeled. The second cause is the craftsman, for the bronze could not have been given the statue's
③ figure without expert hands to shape it. The third cause is
form; the Doryphoros or Diadumenos would not have received their names unless their particular form had been
④ imposed upon them. The fourth cause is the purpose of the
work, for without one the statue would not have been
made. What is this purpose? It is what motivated the artist, the object he pursued in making the statue. It might
have been money, if he made it for sale, or glory, if he was
bent on reputation, or religion, if he was preparing an offering for a temple. Purpose too, then, is a cause; or do you
think a factor without which a thing could not have been
produced is not to be reckoned among its causes?

To these Plato adds a fifth, the pattern, for which his
name is "idea"; this is the thing the artist kept his eye on
when he made the object he planned. It makes no difference whether he had an objective pattern to which he could
actually turn his eyes or whether the pattern was within
himself, a conception he himself had placed there. Such
patterns of all things god has within himself; his mind encompasses the measures and numbers of absolutely everything which is to be acted upon. He is filled with
the forms—eternal, unchanging, incorruptible—which Plato
terms "ideas." Men may perish, therefore, but humanity,
which is the pattern to which man is molded, persists, and
though men suffer and die, the pattern is not subject to
change. According to Plato, then, there are five causes:
material, agent, form, pattern, purpose. Their product
comes last. In the case of the statue, which was our point
of departure, the material is the bronze, the agent the art-

ist, the form is the figure given the material, the pattern
the model the maker imitated, the purpose the object the
maker had in view, and the product of all these the statue
itself. The universe, as Plato asserts, possesses all these
factors. The agent is god, the material matter, the form the
contours and order of the visible universe, the pattern, of
course, that according to which god created his mighty and
magnificent work. Its purpose is his object in creating it.
You ask what god's purpose may be? Goodness. So, at
least, Plato says: "What was god's cause for creating the
universe? He is good, and none that is good grudges anything good. His creation is therefore the best possible." Pronounce your sentence then, arbiter, and declare which
formulation seems truest—not which *is* truest, for that is as
far beyond us as truth itself.

The crowd of causes posited by Aristotle and Plato includes either too many or too few. If they regard as cause
any factor whose absence would make the product impossible, they have named too few. They should reckon time
among the causes, for nothing can be made without time.
They should reckon place, for if there was no place for a
thing to be made in, it could not be made. They should
reckon motion, without which nothing comes into being or
perishes. There is no art without motion, there is no change
without motion. But the cause we are seeking is the primal
and general cause. It must be simple, for matter too is simple. If we ask what this cause is, it is surely Creative Reason, which is to say, god. Those you listed are not a congeries of disparate causes but all depend on one, to wit, the
creative cause. Do you hold that form is a cause? It is what
the artist imposes upon his work, a part of the cause but
not the cause. Neither is pattern a cause, but rather the
cause's necessary instrument, as necessary to the artist as
his chisel or rasp, without which his work cannot proceed.
But these are neither parts of art nor causes of it. "The
artist's purpose, what motivates him to create an object,"

it may be objected, "is its cause." Even if it is, it is not the
efficient but an accessory cause, of which there are an infinite number; our investigation concerns the general cause.
The position that the whole universe, which is a perfected
work, is a cause, is not consistent with Aristotle's and
Plato's customary acumen, for there is a wide difference
between a work and the cause of the work.

Either pronounce sentence or take the easier course in
such cases with a *non liquet* and an order to recapitulate.
"Why," say you, "do you choose to waste time on questions
which do not banish passions or master concupiscence?" It
is as a valid means for pacifying the mind that I deal with
these problems and discuss them; first I scrutinize myself,
and then the universe. Not even now am I wasting time,
as you suppose. All these questions, provided they are not
minced and fragmented into futile hair-splitting, uplift the
soul and make it light when it is weighed down by a heavy
load and eager to return whence it sprang. For body is a
weight upon the soul and its punishment; under its pressure
the soul is squeezed and trussed until philosophy comes to
its support by prescribing contemplation of nature as a refreshment and directs it away from the earthy to the divine. This is the soul's liberation, this its enlargement; in
the process it obtains release from the custody which constrains it and recovers its heavenly energy. Craftsmen engaged in fine work which strains and wearies the eyes go
out into the open, if their light has been grudging and precarious, and refresh their vision with the free daylight in
some spot devoted to the people's leisure; so the soul imprisoned in this dark and gloomy domicile seeks the open
air as often as it can and finds refreshment in the contemplation of nature.

The wise man and the devotee of wisdom is indeed attached to his body, but in his better part he is elsewhere;
his thoughts are directed to lofty matters. He is bound, as
it were, by a military oath, and regards his life span as his

term of enlistment. He is disciplined neither to love life nor hate it; he puts up with mortality, though he knows there is a fuller kind of existence. Will you forbid me examination of nature, will you distrain me from the whole and restrict me to a part? May I not inquire into the beginnings of all things, who shaped them, who sorted out matter that was heaped in an indiscriminate mass? May I not ask who the artificer of this universe is, what system reduced its huge bulk to law and order, or who gathered together what was scattered, sorted out what was confused, or distinguished the aspects of what lay inert in undifferentiated ugliness? What is the source of such outpouring of light? Is it fire or something brighter than fire? Should I not study such questions? Should I be ignorant of the region whence I descended? Am I to see all this once, or undergo repeated births? Where am I to go from here? What abode awaits my soul when it is released from the bondage of humanity? Do you forbid me to be concerned with heaven, which is to say, do you bid me live with head downcast? I am too big, I was born for a bigger destiny, than to be a chattel of my body, which in my own view is nothing else than a chain to fetter my freedom. My body I oppose to Fortune; upon it she may spend her force, but I will allow no wound to penetrate through it to myself. My body is the part of me that is subject to injury, my soul dwells in this vulnerable domicile. Never shall this flesh drive me to fear, never to assume a posture unworthy of a good man; never shall I lie out of consideration for this paltry body. When it seems right I shall sever my partnership with it, and even now, while the attachment holds, we are not equal partners; the soul can claim complete jurisdiction. Contempt of body is unqualified freedom.

To come back to our subject, the contemplation of which I was just now speaking will contribute greatly to this freedom. All things consist of matter and god. God modulates matter, which is poured about him and follows him as

*cf Letter 41, p.188 above
also 198*

guide and leader. The creative element, that is, god, is more powerful and more precious than matter, which is acted upon by god. The place god holds in the universe the soul holds in man. What is matter in the universe is body in us; the worse should therefore serve the better. We should be steadfast in the face of accident. We should not be apprehensive of injuries or wounds or chains or poverty. What is death? Either end or transition. I do not fear ceasing to be, for it is the same as not having begun to be; nor am I afraid of transition, for no alternative state can be so limiting. Farewell.

I have been looking over your home town of Pompeii, where I had not been for a long time, and it gave me a vista of my youth. The things I did there as a young man I thought I could still do, and had in fact done only a little while ago. We have sailed past life, Lucilius, and as Vergil says of the sea (*Aeneid* 3.72), "lands and cities recede," so in this flight of time we lose sight first of our boyhood, then of our adolescence, then of the interval between youth and old age which occupies the marches of both, and then of the best years of old age itself. Last of all, the common end of human kind hoves into view. We think it a reef, fools that we are; actually it is a haven, sometimes to be welcomed, never to be refused, and if a man makes this harbor in his early years he ought no more complain than a traveler who makes a quick passage. One voyager, as you know, is bemused and detained by sluggish winds and grows sick and tired of creeping through the calm; another is carried to his destination speedily by a steady blow.

Fancy that our course is the same. Some life brings speedily to the bourn they were bound to reach even if they tarried, others it torments and frets. Such a life, as you know, it is not always advisable to hold on to. Living is not the good, but living well. The wise man therefore lives as long as he should, not as long as he can. He will observe where he is to live, with whom, how, and what he is to do. He will always think of life in terms of quality, not quantity. If he encounters many vexations which disturb his tranquillity, he will release himself. He will do this not only in an extreme exigency, but as soon as he begins to suspect Fortune he will look about him carefully to determine whether he ought to have done. He will consider it of no importance whether he causes his end or merely accepts it, whether late or early. He does not shrink as before some great deprivation, for not much can be lost from a trickle. Dying early or late is of no relevance, dying well or ill is. To die well is to escape the danger of living ill.

That is why I regard the familiar Rhodian's dictum as most unmanly. A tyrant had thrown him into a dungeon where he was fed like some wild beast, and when someone urged him to starve himself, he said: "While there is life, there is hope." Even if this is true, life is not to be bought at all costs. However splendid a thing may be, however certain its acquisition, I will not come at it by acknowledging my lack of character. Should my motto be "Fortune is all-powerful over the living," when it can be "Fortune is powerless over one who knows how to die?"

Nevertheless, if certain death impends and he knows he is doomed to torture, a man will *not* do his executioner's work; he will do his own (by staying alive). It is folly to die for fear of dying. A man will come to kill you: wait for him. Why take the initiative? Why take on the discharge of someone else's cruel assignment? Is it because you envy the executioner his job or because you want to spare him? Socrates might have ended his life by fasting and have died of starvation rather than poison, yet he spent thirty days in jail awaiting death. His motive was nothing like "Anything can happen," or "While there's time, there's room for hope," but to conform to the laws and make the ultimate Socrates profitable to his friends. Could anything have been stupider than to despise death and be afraid of poison?

Scribonia was an austere woman. She was the aunt of young Drusus Libo, who was as stupid as he was noble and aspired to a higher station than anyone could hope for in his time or he himself at any time. When Libo was carried out of the senate in a litter, sick, he had a very small retinue, for all his connections deserted him—disloyally, for he was no longer a culprit but virtually a corpse. He held a consultation on whether he should compass his death or await it. Said Scribonia: "Why are you pleased to do another man's business?" She failed to convince him, and he laid hands upon himself. And with some justification, for if a man is sure to die in two or three days at his enemy's pleasure, then by living he is "doing another man's business."

So you cannot make a universally applicable pronouncement on the advisability of anticipating or awaiting death when an outside power has decreed it. There are many considerations to incline us to either view. If one death involves torture and the other is simple and easy, why not reach for the easier way? Just as I choose a ship to sail in or a house to live in, so I choose a death for my passage from life. Moreover, whereas a prolonged life is not necessarily better, a prolonged death is necessarily worse. Nowhere should we indulge the soul more than in dying. Let it go as it lists: if it craves the sword or the noose or some potion that constricts the veins, on with it, let it break the chain of its slavery. A man's life should satisfy other people as well, his death only himself, and whatever sort he likes is best. There is no sense in thinking: "X will say that I lacked fortitude, Y that I was too impulsive, Z that another kind of death would have shown higher spirit." Think rather: "What people say is irrelevant to the proposal in hand." Your sole object is to wrench free of Fortune with the greatest expedition; there will always be people to disapprove of what you have done.

You will find even professed philosophers who assert that a man may not do violence to his own life and pronounce it sinful for a man to be his own executioner; we must wait, they say, for the end Nature has decreed. The man who says this does not see that he has blocked his road to freedom. Eternal law has never been more generous than in affording us so many exits from life to one entry. Must I wait for the pangs of disease or the cruelty of man when I can stride through the midst of torment and shake my adversaries off? This is the one reason we cannot complain of life: it holds no one back. The situation of humanity is good in that no one is wretched except by his own fault. If you like, live; if you don't like, you can go back where you came from. Frequently you let blood to relieve headache. To lighten your body you have had incisions in your veins. There is no need of a gaping wound to cleave your chest; a scalpel opens the way out to the great emancipation, a prick makes you carefree.

What is it, then, which makes us stolid and slow to move? None of us thinks that he must one day move from his apartment; just so, attachment to a place and habit keeps old tenants from moving even when they are ill used. Do you want to be free despite your body? Live in it as if you were ready to move. Keep in mind that you will one day lose your quarters, and you will have greater fortitude for the necessary departure. But how can a man keep his own end in mind if there is no end to his craving? Yet it is most essential to keep our end in mind. Other exercises may prove futile. Train your soul against poverty, and you may stay rich. Arm yourself to scorn pain; your health may continue safe and sound and never put your virtue to the test. Teach yourself to bear the loss of loved ones bravely, and all of them will happily survive you. This one training *must* one day be put to use.

Do not imagine that only great men have had the toughness to break through the trammels of human bondage; do not suppose that it can only be done by a Cato, who used his hand to wrench loose the life his sword had not released. Men of the meanest condition have made a mighty effort to break through to deliverance, and when they were not allowed to die at their discretion or choose their instruments for dying they snatched up whatever was ready to hand, and by their own strength transformed implements naturally harmless into weapons. Lately a German in the beast-fighting barracks who was practicing for the morning show excused himself to relieve his bowels—the only function for which the guards would allow him privacy. Then he took the sponge-tipped stick used as a torchecul and rammed it down his throat and choked his breath till he suffocated. That was a way to insult death! Yes indeed, not very clean or very nice, but how stupid to be fastidious about dying! Stout fellow, the right man to let choose his own fate! How gallantly he would have used a sword, how coolly he would have leaped into the sea's abyss or down a sheer precipice! But though he was deprived of every resource, he contrived a scheme and a weapon to use—from which you can learn that there is nothing to keep a man from dying but the will. Every man can have his own opinion of that keen fellow's act, but on this all will agree: the dirtiest death is preferable to the daintiest slavery.

Since I have begun with vulgar exemplars I shall keep on. A man will demand more of himself if he sees that people he despises can despise death. The Catos, the Scipios, and the others we are used to reading about with wonder tower too high for our imitation; now I shall demonstrate that the virtue we are speaking of has as many exemplars in the beast-fighting barracks as among Civil War generals. Recently when a gladiator was being carted to the morning show under guard he simulated sleep and nodded his head far enough down to get it between the spokes, and kept his seat until the turning wheel broke his neck. The very tumbril that was carrying him to punishment he used to escape it.

Nothing stands in the way of a man who wants to break loose and get away. Nature's corral is an open space, and when pressure reaches the allowable point a man can look around for an easy exit. If a number of devices for claiming freedom are available, a man can exercise choice and consider what mode of liberation is best for him; but if opportunity is difficult, let him snatch the nearest means as the best, though it be unprecedented, though it be novel. If you have the courage to die you will have the ingenuity. You see how the lowliest chattel slaves are aroused, under the goads of suffering, and deceive the most attentive guards. It is a great man who not only orders his own death but contrives it.

I promised you more examples from the same exhibitions. In the second event of a sea-fight spectacle one of the barbarians sank the whole spear which he was to use against his opponents down his own throat. "Why," he cried, "have I not long ago escaped all this torment, all this mockery? Why? Why do I wait for death, with a weapon in my hand?" The show was the better worth looking at in the degree that men learned that it is more decent to die than to kill.

What is the upshot? Shall men whom long meditation and Mistress Reason, who teaches all things, have equipped to meet such contingencies not possess as much spirit as abandoned and lawless types? Reason teaches us that the approaches of fate are many but its end the same, and that it makes no difference where what must come begins. The same reason teaches you to die as you like if you may, but if not, as you can, and to use whatever comes your way for laying hands upon yourself. To live by violence is unfair, to die by violence is the fairest of all. Farewell.

You proclaim a state of hostility if you are not kept informed of my doings day by day. See how frank I can be with you: I will even confide to you that I have been listening to a philosopher. This is the fifth day I have been attending; the lecture begins at two o'clock. "Very timely!" say you. But it *is* timely; what could be stupider than refusing to learn because you have not learned for a long time? "Do you mean that I must behave like a dandified undergraduate?" If this is the only thing that ill becomes my time of life I am well off. This school admits men of any age. "Do we get on in years to trail after youngsters?" If I go to the theater at my age and ride to the circus and insist on seeing every bout to its end, shall I blush to go to a philosopher?

A man should keep learning as long as he is ignorant, as the proverb has it, as long as he lives. And the principle applies most of all to my own study. As long as he lives a man should learn how to live. But there is something I teach in the school. What, you ask, do I teach? That even an old man should learn. When I step into the school I feel ashamed of the human race. To go to Metronax' house I must pass the theater of the Neapolitans, as you know. The place is packed. The point at issue is whether a man is a good flautist. The Greek piper and the herald also have their following. But in the place where the issue is "What is a good man?", and how a good man is to be defined, and how a man learns to be good, the audience is sparse, and even the few people there, the majority thinks, are not occupied in any business worth doing; they are called feckless and lazy. I would welcome such mockery. The reproaches of the ignorant should be received with mind imperturbable; a man making his way toward an ideal must be contemptuous of contempt.

Get on with it, Lucilius; hurry, don't let what happened to me happen to you; don't wait to be an elderly undergraduate. There is greater need to hurry because you have not touched the subject for a long while and it is one you can scarcely master when you are old. "How far can I advance?" As far as you try. What are you waiting for? Wisdom is never a windfall. Money may come unsought, office may be bestowed, influence and prestige may be thrust upon you, but virtue is not an accident. Even knowing virtue is no light or offhand task, but it is worth the effort to acquire all that is good at a stroke. For there is only one good, to wit, the honorable; the objectives commonly esteemed are neither true nor stable. I shall tell you why the honorable is the sole good for you, for you maintain that my earlier letter did not pursue the proposition far enough and consider that I applauded rather than demonstrated it.

I shall compress what has been said on the subject. Everything is valued by its particular good. Yield and bouquet commend the vine, fleetness the stag. The question in regard to a pack animal is the strength of his back, for his sole use is to carry freight. In a dog keenness is the primary consideration if he is to track game, fleetness if he is to overtake it, boldness if he is to come to close quarters and attack it. In every case the function for which a thing is created and by which it is rated ought to be the best. What is best in man? Reason, which puts him ahead of the animals and next to the gods. Perfect reason is, then, his peculiar good; his other qualities are common to animals and vegetables. He is strong; so are lions. He is handsome; so are peacocks. He is fleet; so are horses. My point is not that he is surpassed in all these qualities, for I am not asking what is greatest in him but what is peculiar to him. He has body; so have trees. He has impulses and can move at will;

so can beasts and worms. He has a voice, but how much louder has a dog, shriller an eagle, deeper a bull, sweeter and of greater range a nightingale? What is peculiar to man? Reason. When this is right and perfected his measure of happiness is full. Hence, if an entity is praiseworthy and has attained the limit of its nature when it has perfected its peculiar good, and if man's peculiar good is reason, then if a man has perfected his reason he is praiseworthy and has attained the limit of his nature. This perfect reason is called virtue, and is equivalent to the honorable.

The sole good in man, therefore, is what is solely man's, for our question does not concern the good but the good of man. If nothing but reason is peculiarly man's, then reason is his sole good and balances all the rest. If a man is bad I presume he will be disapproved of, and if good, approved of. The gauge for approval or disapproval is his principal and unique quality. That this is a good there can be no doubt; you can doubt only whether it is the sole good. Now if a man possess all other qualities—health, wealth, long lineage, a crowded salon—but is confessedly bad, you will disapprove of him. Likewise, if a man possess none of the qualities I have listed but is without money, a throng of clients, nobility, a roster of grandparents and great-grandparents, but is confessedly good, you will approve of him. Consequently this is the one good of man, for the man who possesses it is praised though he lacks all else, and the man who lacks it is condemned and rejected despite his abundance of other qualities. What applies to man applies also to things. A ship is said to be good not when it is painted with costly colors or its beak coated with silver or gold or its mascot decorated with ivory reliefs, nor when it is loaded with state funds or regal treasure, but when it is stable and stanch and its seams tightly calked to keep the water out, and it is rugged enough to withstand the assaults of the sea, when it answers the rudder and is speedy and indifferent to the gale. You will call a sword good not when the baldric is gilt or the scabbard studded with gems but when its edge is sharp enough to slash and its point keen enough to pierce any protection. We do not ask how beautiful a rule is but how straight. Each thing is praised by reference to what is peculiar to it.

In man too, therefore, it is irrelevant to ask the extent of his plantations, the volume of his loans, the number of his clients, the costliness of the bed he lies on, or the transparency of the cups he drinks out of; the point is, how good is he? He is good if his reason is straightforward and upright and suited to the will of his nature. This is called virtue, this is the honorable, and man's unique good. For whereas reason perfects man, perfect reason makes him blessed; what makes a man blessed is his sole good. We maintain that what proceeds out of virtue and is involved in it, that is to say, all its works, are also good; but virtue itself is the sole good because there is no good without it. If every good is in the soul, then whatever stabilizes, raises, and enlarges the soul is good; but virtue does make the soul stronger, loftier, and more spacious. Other things which prick our concupiscence depress the soul and unhinge it, and while they appear to uplift it they are in fact inflating it and beguiling it with utter vanity. The only good, therefore, is what makes the soul better.

Every action of the whole of life is regulated by consideration of the honorable and the base. The rationale for acting or not acting is controlled by this consideration. I will tell you how this is. A good man will do what he thinks will be honorable for him to do even if it is laborious, he will do it even if it is damaging to him, he will do it even if it is dangerous. On the other hand, he will not do what is base even if it brings him money, even if it brings him pleasure, even if it brings him power. Nothing can deflect him from what is honorable, nothing tempt him to what is base. Hence, if he is bound to pursue the honorable course at all costs and to eschew the base at all costs and to look to these two principles in every act of his life, equating the good with the honorable and the bad with the base, if his virtue is wholly uncorrupted and maintains its bearings, then virtue is his sole good and it is impossible for any accident to make it otherwise. He has escaped the danger of change; folly may creep toward wisdom, but wisdom does not backslide to folly.

I have said, as you may recall, that irrational impulse has driven many a man to trample over things commonly cherished or dreaded. There are cases where a man has thrust his arm into the flames, has laughed in the face of his torturers, has shed no tear at the death of his children, has gone unfalteringly to his death. Love or anger or lust have thrown the gauntlet down. What a spurt of obstinacy flaring up under some stimulus can achieve, surely virtue, whose power is not impulsive or sudden but consistent and whose strength is enduring, can do. It follows that what the irrational can scorn occasionally and the wise regularly is neither good nor evil. The sole good is therefore virtue itself, which strides between this lot and that and despises both equally.

If you entertain the view that there is any good beside the honorable, then every virtue will be hamstrung. None can be maintained if it must look to something outside itself. If there is any such thing it must conflict with reason, from which the virtues derive, and with truth, which is impossible without reason. And any opinion in conflict with truth is false. A good man, you cannot but agree, has full piety toward the gods. Whatever happens to him he will bear with serenity because he knows it has happened by the divine law which governs the universe. That being the case, he will have one sole good, to wit, the honorable; this involves obedience to the gods, not flaring up at sudden contretemps or deploring one's lot, but accepting fate patiently and fulfilling its commands. If there is a good other than the honorable, we shall be hounded by greed for life and greed for life's comforts. This is boundless, undefined, and intolerable; the honorable is definable, and hence the sole good.

I have remarked that human life would be happier than the gods' if the things that the gods do not use, such as money and magistracies, were goods. Furthermore, if souls released from the body do indeed survive, the state that awaits them is happier than while they are involved with body. And if things of which we make bodily use are goods, then our souls will be worse off when they are released; but it is incredible that souls imprisoned and besieged are happier than souls liberated and given freedom of the universe. I also remarked that if what man has in common with dumb animals are goods, then animals could lead a happy life; but this is altogether impossible. For the sake of the honorable we must put up with anything, which we need not do if there were any good other than the honorable. I have dealt with these arguments more fully in an earlier letter; here I have compressed them and run through them summarily.

Such a view as this will never strike you as true unless you raise your soul and ask yourself whether, if an exigency demanded that you die for your country and ransom the safety of your fellow citizens by your own, you would put your neck out not only patiently but gladly. If you would do such a thing then there is no other good, for you relinquish all else to possess this alone. See what force the honorable has! You will die for your country when you know you ought, even if you must do so forthwith. Sometimes noble action wins great joy, momentary and brief though it be, and though no profit of his achievement will accrue to a man who has run his course and is released from human concerns, yet the very contemplation of what is to be is a delight; when the brave and righteous man contemplates what his death will buy, his country's liberty and the salvation of those for whom he is laying his life down, he attains the height of pleasure and rejoices in his own jeopardy. But even the man who is deprived of the joy which fingering his greatest and last achievement affords will leap to his death without hesitation, content that his action is right and dutiful. Confront him even now with many deterrents; say to him, "Your deed will speedily be forgotten, public opinion is ingrate," and he will answer, "Those things are extraneous to my job, which is all I have to think of. I know that it is honorable, and so I go wherever it leads and calls me."

This then is the only good, and it is perceived not only by the perfect soul but by the generous and well-endowed also; other goods are frivolous and transitory. That is why possession of them is attended by anxiety. Even if by Fortune's favor they are piled in a heap, they are a heavy incubus upon their owners; always they press down upon them and sometimes they crush them. None of that purple-clad group is happy, any more than the players whose roles bestow scepter and cape upon them; before their audience they strut buskined and expansive, but at the stage door they are unshod and return to their own figure. None raised to a higher pinnacle by riches or magistracies is great. Why then does he seem to be? Because you include his pedestal in the measurement. A dwarf is not big even if he stands on a mountain top, and a colossus retains his stature even if he stands in a well. This is the mistake which misleads us; we are imposed upon because we never estimate a man by what he is but add his trappings on. If you wish to arrive at a true estimate of a man and understand his quality, look at him naked. Make him lay aside his inheritance, his titles, Fortune's other specious trimmings; make him lay even his body aside and look at his soul to ascertain its quality and size and whether its greatness is its own or detachable.

If a man can look at flashing swords with eyes unswerving, if he knows that it is of no moment to him whether his

soul departs through mouth or throat, call him happy. Call
him happy if, when physical torture is decreed for him,
whether by some accident or by *force majeure,* if with
mind unperturbed he hears of chains and exile and the
empty terrors of mankind and says (*Aeneid* 6.103 ff.):

> "No new fashion of hardship, none unexpected
> Rises to confront me; all have I anticipated,
> All have I traversed in my mind—

Today it is you that confront me with this doom; I have
always confronted myself with it, and as a man am prepared for man's lot." The blow of an anticipated evil falls
soft. Fools, however, and those who trust Fortune find every "fashion new and unexpected." For the untaught a
large portion of the evil is its novelty. The proof is that men
bear with fortitude, when they have grown accustomed to
them, things they had thought very difficult. The sage ac-
customs himself to evils before they come, and what others
make easy by long toleration he makes easy by long cogita-
tion. Sometimes we hear the untaught say, "I knew this was
in store for me"; the sage knows that everything is in store
for him, and whatever happens he says, "I knew it." Farewell.

I write you this from the actual villa of Scipio Africanus.
I have just done reverence to the hero's spirit and to an
altar which I suspect is his tomb. His soul, I am convinced,
has returned to the heavens whence it came, not because
he commanded great armies—mad Cambyses did that, and
exploited his madness to good effect—but because of his
singular moderation and piety. This, I think, was more remarkable when he abandoned his country than when he
defended it; it was impossible that he continue in Rome
and Rome continue free. "I have no wish to make light
of our laws and constitution," he said. "All citizens must
have equal rights. Use the service I have done you, my
country, but without my presence. I have been the cause
of your liberty, and I shall be its proof. I depart if I have
grown too big to be good for you."

How could I not admire the high spirit which withdrew
him into voluntary exile and so disburdened the state? A
situation had come about where either liberty must injure
Scipio or Scipio liberty, and neither was admissible. So he
made way for the laws and betook himself to Liternum,
in the thought that his exile was as much a service to the
state as was Hannibal's.

I have looked at the villa built of squared blocks, the
wall enclosing a grove, towers buttressed on both sides as
a bulwark for the house, a cistern hidden among buildings
and shrubbery which might be adequate for an army, and
a cramped bath, quite unlighted, after the old fashion; our
ancestors thought a hot bath must be dark. It afforded me
great satisfaction to compare Scipio's habits with ours. In
this cranny the terror of Carthage, whom Rome had to

thank that the Gallic sack was not repeated, used to wash
down a body tired out by field chores. For he used to do
real work, and himself cultivated his acres, as was the regular practice in the old days. It was under this dingy ceiling
he stood, this very ordinary floor held his weight.

Who would tolerate such bathing nowadays? A man
thinks himself poor and slovenly if his walls are not shiny
with large and costly mirrors, if his Alexandrian marbles
are not figured with slabs from Numidia, if there is no bor-
der elaborately worked around the whole with a varied
pictorial pattern, if there is no room enclosed in glass, if
there is no Thasian marble—once a rare sight in an occasional temple—to line the pools into which we lower our
bodies when they have been reduced by a hard sweat,
when the spigots for discharging the water are not silver.
So far I have been speaking of ordinary establishments;
what shall I say when I come to the freedmen's baths?
What a quantity of statuary, what a quantity of columns
that hold nothing up but are planted as extravagant orna-
ments! What a quantity of water, arranged to produce a
series of crashing falls! We have become so dainty that
we will tread only on gems.

In this bath of Scipio's there are not windows but chinks
cut out of the masonry to admit light without weakening
the structure. Nowadays they call baths moth-dens if they
are not planned to get sun all day through spacious windows, unless they can bathe and tan simultaneously, unless they have a view of the countryside and the sea from
their tubs. So it is; bathhouses which drew admiring throngs
when they were dedicated are dismissed and relegated to
the category of the superannuated as soon as luxury has
devised some new gadget to bury itself under. Once baths
were few and had no elegant trimmings. Why trim out a
place meant for use, not luxury, where the admission is a
penny? There were no showers in those days, nor a continuous stream as from a hot spring, and they didn't think

it mattered how crystal the water to leave their dirt in was.

Good heavens, what a joy to step into that dimly lit bath, covered with an ordinary roof, in the knowledge that Cato as aedile, look you, or Fabius Maximus, or one of the Cornelii had tempered the water with his own hand! Even the noblest aediles, as part of their function, used to enter the resorts which catered to the populace and insist upon cleanliness and a moderate and healthy temperature, not the blazing heat newly introduced, so great indeed that a slave convicted of crime should be bathed alive! Now I think a man might as well say, "The bath is on fire," as, "The bath is warm."

Nowadays some people write Scipio down a yokel because he let no daylight into his sweat room, did not broil in a strong glare, or wait in his bath until he stewed. "Ah, a disaster of a man! He didn't know how to live. The water he bathed in was not filtered but often cloudy, and after heavy rains almost muddy." Baths like that did not bother Scipio; he had come to wash off sweat, not perfume. And what kind of remark do you suppose this will elicit? "I don't envy Scipio; a man who bathed that way was really living in exile." If you must know, he didn't bathe every day. Writers who have recorded the manners of our old Romans tell us that they washed their arms and legs every day—these, of course, they dirtied working—and took a whole bath once a week. "I can see they were very dirty," someone will say. "How do you suppose they smelled?" Of soldiery and exertion and manliness. Men are fouler now, after baths came to be trimmed out. When Horace chooses to describe an infamous fellow, notorious for his mincing foppishness, what does he say? "Buccillus smells of pastilles" (*Sermones* 1.2.27). Show me a Buccillus today: his smell would seem goatish, like the noisome Gargonius with whom Horace contrasts Buccillus. For today it is not enough to use perfume unless you apply it two or three times a day, to keep it from evaporating on the body. And why should a man preen himself on the scent as if it were his own?

If all this strikes you as too gloomy charge it up to Scipio's house, where I learned from Aegialus, who is a frugal householder and now owns the farm, that a tree can be transplanted even if it is quite old. We old fellows need to know this, for we all plant olive orchards for others to enjoy. [*Two pages which describe Aegialus' technique are here omitted.*]

You ask me to analyze the massive organism of philosophy and identify its several members; this is a useful project and indeed essential for the serious student of wisdom, for study of the parts induces an easier understanding of the whole. I could wish that philosophy could come into our purview as a totality, just as the firmament as a whole does; the spectacle would be very like the firmament's. All mankind would find it ravishing and abandon the things our ignorance of greatness makes us think great. But such a wish is beyond realization, and so we must examine philosophy as we analyze the mysteries of the firmament.

The sage's mind does indeed comprehend the whole mass, which it scans no less quickly than our vision surveys the sky; but we who must still penetrate the fog and whose vision is deficient even for nearby objects are not capable of comprehending the whole and find explanation of individual parts easier. I shall therefore accede to your request and divide philosophy into parts—but not into scraps, for dissection, not mincing, is the useful thing. Tiny fragments are as hard to grasp as huge gobbets. A population is divided into tribes, an army into companies; anything greatly expanded is easier to classify if it is separated into parts, but these, as I have said, should not be too many or too small. Excessive partition is as unsatisfactory as none at all; a mass reduced to powder is still undifferentiated.

First, then, if you agree, I shall explain the difference between wisdom and philosophy. Wisdom is the perfect good of the human mind; philosophy, love of wisdom and progress towards it. Philosophy's objective, wisdom has attained. The meaning of philosophy is clear from its derivation, which indicates love of wisdom (*phil-*, "love"; *sophia*, "wisdom"). One definition of wisdom is "knowledge of things divine and human"; another is "knowledge of things divine and human and their causes." To me the addition seems superfluous, because the causes of things divine and human are part of the divine. Philosophy, too, has been variously defined. Some have called it the study of virtue, some the study of mental improvement, and some have called it the striving for right reason. But that there is a distinction between philosophy and wisdom is virtually agreed. The subject and the object of the act of seeking cannot be identical. The difference between philosophy and wisdom is as great as that between avarice and wealth; one craves, the other is craved. The one is the result and prize; it is the goal, to which the other is en route. Wisdom is what the Greeks call *sophia*. The Romans once used this word, too, as they now use "philosophy." You can find proof of this in our primitive native drama and in the inscription on Dossennus' monument: "Pause, stranger, and read the wisdom (*sophia*) of Dossennus."

Certain Stoics, agreeing that philosophy is the study of virtue, and the seeker where virtue is the sought, have nevertheless thought that the two cannot be separated, on the grounds that philosophy cannot exist without virtue nor virtue without philosophy. Philosophy is the study of virtue, but virtue is its means, so that virtue cannot exist without study of itself nor the study without virtue itself. It is not like attempting to hit a target from a distance, where target and marksman are in different places, nor, like the roads which lead to a city, are the approaches of virtue outside itself; philosophy and virtue are an amalgam.

The greatest and most numerous authorities have declared that philosophy has three parts: moral, natural, and rational. The first regulates the soul, and the second scrutinizes nature. The third exacts precision in the use of terms, combinations, and arguments, to keep falsehood from usurping the place of truth. But there are authorities who make fewer divisions in philosophy and some who make more. Certain Peripatetics add a fourth division, called "civil" because it requires special exercises of its own and is concerned with different materials. Some have added a division they call "economics," the science of administering private property. Some have set sections off for various professions and careers. But all of these sections are subsumed under moral philosophy.

The Epicureans held that philosophy consists of two parts, natural and moral, and dispensed with rational philosophy. Then, when facts compelled them to define ambiguities and expose fallacies lurking under a cloak of truth, they introduced a section which they called "on arguments and rules," which they consider an adjunct of natural philosophy. The Cyrenaics dispensed with natural as with rational philosophy and were content with moral, but they, too, bring in what they dispensed with under a different title. They divide moral philosophy into five parts, viz.: (1) what to avoid and what to strive for; (2) emotions; (3) actions; (4) causes; (5) proofs. Causes actually belong to natural philosophy and proofs to rational. Ariston of Chios declared that natural and rational philosophy are not only superfluous but contradictory. Even the moral, which was the only philosophy he admitted, he curtailed, for he eliminated the section that contains admonitions on the ground that this was a pedagogue's, not a philosopher's business—as if the sage were anything else than the pedagogue of the human race!

We assume, then, that philosophy is tripartite and proceed first to analyze the moral part. This it has been agreed to divide into three sections, with the theoretic section first. This is most useful, for it assigns everything its proper place and assesses its individual value, and what is so necessary as fixing values? The second section has to do with impulses, and the third with actions. Your first task is to judge a thing's value, your second to assume a controlled and tempered impulse with reference to it, and your third to harmonize your action with your impulse, in order to achieve consistency in all these particulars. If there is a deficiency in one, the whole is confounded. What good is it to establish correct values if your impulse is excessive? Or what good is it to repress your impulse and control your concupiscence if, in the point of action, you disregard timing and do not know when, where, or how each act is to be performed? It is one thing to know the worth and cost of things, another to know their proper conjunctures, and still another to bridle impulses and walk, not rush, into action. Life is therefore at harmony with itself when action has not betrayed impulse and when impulse is regulated by the worth of the individual object, adjusting itself to feeble or vigorous according as the object merits effort.

The natural part of philosophy is split into two, organic and inorganic. Each is divided into its own grades, if I may use the word. The first concern of the organic section is its activity and its issue; its issue are the elements. The section on elements is unitary according to some, but according to others it is divided into matter, into cause, which is the source of all motion, and into the elements.

It remains for me to analyze rational philosophy. Every discourse is either continuous or cut up into questions and answers; the accepted term for the former is rhetoric and for the latter dialectic. Rhetoric is concerned with words, meanings, and arrangements. Dialectic is divided into two parts, terms and their significations, that is, the things which are said and the terms used to say them. Each is then subdivided into elaborate ramifications, but I shall put a period to my analysis and "touch only the high points" (*Aeneid* 1.342); otherwise, if I should choose to detail divisions of divisions, this would turn into a debater's handbook. I do not deter you from reading such things, good

Lucilius, provided only you put your reading into practice immediately.

Practice is what you must keep under rein: rouse what is growing faint in you, tighten what is relaxed, master what is stubborn, chide your and the public's appetites as far as you can, and when men say, "How long this same tune?" answer, "I ought to say, How long your same sins? Do you want my cure to stop before your disease does? But I shall talk all the more; because you object I shall persevere. Medicine is beginning to take effect when the distempered body twitches at a touch. What I say will benefit you even if you don't like it. Words that are not soothing must sometime reach you, and because you do not wish to listen to the truth individually hear it as an audience. How far will you extend the boundaries of your possessions? An estate that has held a population is too little for a single owner. How far will you stretch your tilth, you who are not content with ranches the size of provinces? Notable rivers have their courses through your private domains, great streams which serve as boundaries for great nations are yours from source to mouth. Even this is too little unless you gird the seas with your acreage, unless your overseer lords it across the Adriatic, the Ionian, the Aegean seas, unless the islands which are homes of great generals are trifling items in your inventory. Extend your ownership to your heart's desire, call what was once a kingdom your farm, add all you can to your holdings—they *must* be more than your neighbor's.

"And now I address you whose luxury takes as broad a scope as does the first group's avarice. To you I say, How long will you keep building tall country houses on every lake you can find? Keep covering every river bank with your mansions? Wherever veins of warm water shoot up, there new resorts of luxury are erected; wherever the seashore curves into a bay, there you will at once put foundations down; land will not satisfy you unless it is artificially made, and you will enclose the very sea. Though your tall roofs are splendidly conspicuous in various locales, whether perched on mountain tops to afford a broad view of land and sea or raised to mountainous height from the plain, numerous as your mansions may be and huge as they may be, you still have only one puny body each. What is the advantage of so many bedrooms? You lie in only one. A place is not yours if you are not there.

"Next I pass to you whose bottomless and insatiable gullet scours the seas on this side and the land on that, laboriously tracking some creatures down with hooks and some with nooses and some with various kinds of nets; none have peace unless you are surfeited. And what a tiny fraction of those viands which have required so many hands to procure can you nibble at with palate so jaded? What a tiny fraction of the game taken at such peril can the dyspeptic and nauseated nabob taste? How tiny a fraction of the shellfish brought such a distance will pass through your insatiate stomach? Unhappy men, can't you realize that your appetite is bigger than your belly?"

This is the sort of thing you should say to others, provided you hearken to what you say. Write it too, provided you read what you write and apply it all to practice and to allaying the mania of the passions. Study not to increase your knowledge but to improve it. Farewell.

Life, my dear Lucilius, is the gift of the immortal gods, and the good life the gift of philosophy; of this there can be no doubt. Consequently it should be equally clear that our debt to philosophy is as much greater than our debt to the gods as a good life is a handsomer gift than mere life, were it not that philosophy itself is a gift of the gods. Philosophic knowledge, indeed, they have given to no one, but the philosophic faculty to everyone. If they had made philosophic knowledge also a common attribute and we were all born wise, then wisdom would have forfeited its principal quality, which is that it is not fortuitous. What is precious and magnificent about it is that it does not merely happen to people but that the individual is himself responsible for it and cannot obtain it from others.

If philosophy came as a bounty would there be any reason to respect it? Its sole function is to discover truth concerning things divine and human. Religion is inseparable from it, as are piety and justice and the entire retinue of intertwined and cohesive virtues. Philosophy has taught us to worship the divine and to love the human; it has taught us that sovereignty belongs to the gods and fellowship to men. For a time this fellowship remained uncorrupted, until greed fragmented its unity and made even those it enriched poor, for when men came to wish to possess all things for their own they forfeited their possession of all things.

But the first mortals and their offspring were uncorrupted in their obedience to nature; they accepted the same individual as their leader and as their law, entrusting themselves to the judgment of the better man. It is the way of nature for the inferior to submit to the stronger. Even among dumb species the biggest or the fiercest rule. It is no runt bull that leads the herd but one whose size and muscles surpass the other males. Among elephants the tallest is the leader, and among men the best is accepted as the highest. Mind was therefore the criterion in choosing a ruler, and the fullest happiness was enjoyed by people where only the better could be the more powerful. It is safe to allow a man to do what he likes if he is convinced that he must do only what he should.

In that age described as golden, therefore, Posidonius holds that rule belonged to the wise. They exercised scrupulous self-control, protected the weak from the strong, urged or dissuaded, explained what was useful and what disadvantageous. Their foresight provided against dearth, their steadfastness averted danger, their benevolence enlarged and adorned their subjects. To govern was to serve, not to reign. None would explore the limits of his power against those who gave his power its inception, nor was there any mood or occasion for subversiveness, for the good ruler received willing obedience, and the severest threat a king could hold over intractable subjects was banishment from his realm.

When the infiltration of vice transformed monarchies into tyrannies a need was felt for laws, and these, too, were initially framed by the sages. Solon, who founded Athens upon equable law, was among the Seven Sages. If that same age would have produced Lycurgus, he would have been added to the sacred number as an eighth. The laws of Zaleucus and Charondas are admired; they learned jurisprudence, not in the forum or in the foyers of jurisconsults, but in the holy quiet of Pythagoras' retreat, and they gave their laws to Sicily (then in its heyday) and to the Greek part of Italy.

So far I agree with Posidonius, but I will not admit that the arts employed in daily life were invented by philosophy, nor will I claim for philosophy the reputation of a handicraftsman. "When men were scattered," says Posidonius, "and were sheltered in caves or hollowed-out cliffs or trunks of rotted trees, it was philosophy which taught them to build houses." I cannot believe that philosophy contrived these intricate structures rising floor upon floor and cities nudging cities any more than it did the fishponds enclosed to protect the gullet against the risk of storm, so that luxury should have safe havens in which to fatten assorted schools of fish, however fierce the raging sea. What say you? Philosophy taught men bolts and keys? They but put the seal on avarice. Did philosophy rear these towering tenements which imperil their tenants? To take cover as chance provided, to find some natural shelter without art and without trouble seemed too little. But believe me, the age before architects and builders was the happy one. It was burgeoning luxury that gave birth to the practice of dressing timbers square, of hewing beams to the line with steady hand, whereas "of old men split wood with wedges" (Vergil, *Georgics* 1.144). It was no roof for a banquet hall they were readying, nor did long trains of carts shake the streets as they hauled balks of pine or fir to hold ceilings coffered with heavy gilt. Their cottage was propped up by a forked pole at either end. Packed branches piled with leaves and set at a slope drained off the heaviest showers. Such was their shelter, but their life was secure. Thatch protected free men; under marble and gold dwells slavery.

I differ from Posidonius also when he holds that metalworking was excogitated by philosophers. We might then give the title of philosopher to the men through whom "invented then was the art of trapping beasts with nets, of deceiving with limed twig, of circling the forest with dogs" (Vergil, *Georgics* 1.139 f.). It was practical shrewdness, not philosophy, that contrived these things. Nor do I hold with Posidonius that it was philosophers who invented mines and smelting, when earth, heated by forest fires, ran with molten metal from surface veins; such inventions are made by practical workers. Nor does the question whether hammer or tongs came into use first seem as acute to me as it does to Posidonius. Each was the invention of an alert and sharp, but not of a great or lofty, mind, and so were other appliances which are worked at with body stooped and mind directed earthward.

The wise man was adaptable in his mode of living—of course he was, for even in these days he would wish to be as unencumbered as possible. How, I ask you, can you consistently admire both Diogenes and Daedalus? Which do you consider a sage, the man who thought up the saw, or the man who took his cup from his wallet and smashed it as soon as he saw a boy drinking water out of the hollow of his hand? "What a fool I was to keep unnecessary luggage," he scolded himself, and then curled up in his tub and went to sleep. And today which would you count the wiser, the man who invents a process for spraying saffron from hidden pipes to an enormous height, who fills or empties decorative pools with a sudden rush of water, who fits assorted ceiling coffers of dining halls so ingeniously that one pattern follows close upon another and the roof changes as often as the courses, or the man who demonstrates to himself and others that Nature makes no harsh and difficult demands upon us, that we can live without the marble-worker and engineer, that we can be clothed without the silk trade, that we can have the necessities we require if we are content with what earth carries on its surface? And if the human race would hearken to this sage it would realize that the cook is as superfluous as the soldier. The men whose physical needs were simple were sages or very like sages. Necessities require little care; it is luxury that costs labor. Follow Nature and you will not wish for artificers.

Nature did not will people to be harassed. Whatever she made exigent she supplied us with. "Cold is intolerable to a body unclothed." What of that? Cannot pelts of game and other animals provide abundant protection from cold? Do not many tribes shield their bodies with bark? Are not birds' feathers sewn together to serve as clothing? Does not a large segment of the Scythians to this day wear the hides of foxes and mice, which are pliant and keep the winds off? "But a thicker shelter is wanted to ward off the heat of the summer sun." And what of that? By the passage of time, erosion or some other process has hollowed out many cavelike recesses. What? Have not ordinary men woven reed mats together by hand and smeared them over with common mud and then roofed them over with stalks or other thatch so that the pitch carried the rains off, and so kept snug through the winter? What? Do not the peoples at the Syrtes shelter in dugouts; do not all peoples do so when the torrid sun leaves them no solid protection against heat except the arid earth itself?

Nature was not so grudging; when she gave other creatures an easy way of life she did not make it impossible for man to live without a host of appliances. None of these does she demand of us, none must we anxiously acquire in order to survive. At our birth things were in readiness for us; it is we who have made difficulties for ourselves by our disdain of what is easy. Housing, shelter, physical comfort, victuals, the things which have now been made into an enormous enterprise, were easily available gratis and could be obtained with slight effort. The limit was set by the need; it is we who have made those things costly and admired and the object of intense and ingenious pursuit. Nature suffices for her own requirements, but luxury has defected from Nature; daily it pricks itself on, and through the ages has waxed large, and its cunning promotes vice. At first luxury began to crave superfluities, and then abnormalities, and in the end enslaved soul to body and compelled its abject obedience to the body's lusts. All the occupations which keep the city at work, or keep it in an uproar, carry on the business of the body; once the body was supplied with its requirements, like a slave, but now everything is acquired for it, like a master. Hence the weavers' and cabinetmakers' shops, hence the savors of the chefs, hence the voluptuousness of the teachers of mincing postures and of wanton falsetto crooning. The natural measure which limited desires by essential requirements has retreated; to desire a mere sufficiency is now a mark of boorishness and wretchedness.

It is incredible, my dear Lucilius, how even great men are seduced from truth by the charm of eloquence. Look at Posidonius, in my judgment one of the most considerable contributors to philosophy, when he sets about a description of weaving. First some threads are twisted and some drawn from the soft and loose hank; the upright warp stretches the threads with hanging weights; the woof-thread inserted through the warp relaxes its tension at either edge of the web and the batten presses it down to join the cloth. Posidonius asserts that the art of weaving, too, was invented by the sages, forgetting that this ingenious craft was a later discovery. As Ovid (*Metamorphoses* 6.55 ff.) says:

> The web is fixed to the frame, the reed
> Separates the warp, and between its threads
> Pointed shuttles introduce the woof,
> And the broad comb battens it down.

If Posidonius could only have visited the looms of our age which manufacture textiles that conceal nothing, which are no help to the body, needless to say, but none even to modesty!

Posidonius then proceeds to farming and with equal eloquence tells how the ground is crisscrossed by the plow to loosen the soil and give roots easier play, then how the seed is sown and weeds plucked out by hand to prevent random growths from spoiling the crop. This too, says Posidonius, is the work of the sages—as if agriculturists were not to this day discovering many new devices for increasing productivity! Not content with these trades, he even sends the sage to the mill. By imitating nature, he tells us, the sage began to make bread. "The grain received into the mouth," he says, "is crushed by the hard teeth striking together, and the tongue brings back to these same teeth any grains that have fallen away; then it is kneaded together for easy passage down the slippery throat. When it reaches the stomach, that organ's regulated temperature digests it and only then is it assimilated into the body. Following this model someone placed one rough stone over another, like teeth, where the stationary set awaits the action of the other. The friction between the two stones crushes the grain, which is brought back again and again until repeated grinding reduces it to a powder. Then the inventor sprinkled his meal with water and by constant kneading mastered it and shaped it into a loaf. At first the loaf was baked in hot ashes or heated earthenware, and then gradually ovens were invented and other devices for making heat serviceable." It wanted but little for Posidonius to say that cobbling, too, was an invention of the sages.

It was reason indeed that devised these handicrafts, but not right reason. They are inventions not of the sage but of man, as are ships by which we cross rivers and seas, fitted with sails for catching the force of the wind and with rudders at the stern for directing the vessel's course this way or that. The model followed was the fish, which steers with its tail and turns its course this way or that by flexing it slightly. "It *was* the sage that invented these things," says Posidonius, "but they were not important enough for him to handle personally and so he gave them to his more mechanical assistants." No; those inventions were thought up by the same people who are concerned with them today. We know that certain inventions have been made within our own memory, as for example the use of windows which admit clear light through transparent panes, or vaulted baths with conduits let into the walls for diffusing heat which warms the upper and lower space alike. Need I mention the marbles with which our temples and mansions are resplendent, or the masses rounded and polished to support colonnades and roofs spacious enough for a whole population? And what of the stenographic symbols which can take down a speech however rapidly delivered and enable the hand to keep pace with the agility of the tongue? But these are inventions of low-grade slaves.

Wisdom's seat is higher; she does not train hands but is mistress of souls. Would you like to know what she has brought to light, what she has produced? Not the stylish posturings of the body or the musical scales of horn and pipes, in which breath, as it passes through or as it emerges, is modulated into sound. Not arms nor bastions nor the appurtenances of war does philosophy fashion: she fosters peace and summons the human race to concord. She is not, say I, the artisan of the appliances of our daily use; why attribute such trifles to her? In her you see the artificer of life. Other arts, to be sure, she holds under her sway, for where life is mastered so are life's perquisites also; but it is toward happiness that philosophy aims, to it she leads us, and its approaches she paves for us. She shows us what is evil and what only seems so, she strips our minds of vanity, she bestows solid greatness but suppresses that which is inflated and specious, she makes us understand the difference between real and puffed-out stature, she communicates knowledge of all nature and of her own. She reveals the nature and quality of the gods—the nether gods, the household deities, the protecting spirits—and the position, function, capacity, and desires of the everlasting souls in the second rank of divinity. Such is the doctrine of Wisdom's initiates; it unbars no local shrine but the temple of all the gods, the universe itself, whose true likeness and visage philosophy offers our mind's eye. For so vast a spectacle our corporal vision is too dull. Then Wisdom returns to the beginnings of things, to the eternal Reason which was infused into the whole, and to the force implanted in the seeds of all things which give all their proper form. Then Wisdom begins to inquire into the soul—its source, its location, its survival, its divisions. From the corporeal, finally, Wisdom turns to the incorporeal and scrutinizes truth and its manifestations and determines the modes for distinguishing ambiguities in life or speech, for in both the false is mingled with the true.

No, the sage did not withdraw from the mechanic arts, as Posidonius thinks, but never touched them at all. The sage would never have esteemed an invention worth making if it was not likely to merit permanent use; he would not have taken up what would have to be laid aside. "Anacharsis," says Posidonius, "invented the potter's wheel, which shapes earthenware by rotation." The potter's wheel is mentioned in Homer (*Iliad* 16.600 f.) and Posidonius prefers to consider the lines rather than his tale as spurious. My own position is that Anacharsis was not the author, and if he was, then it was indeed a sage who invented the wheel, but not in his capacity as sage, just as philosophers do many things not qua philosophers but qua men. Imagine a philosopher who is fleet-footed; he will outsprint his rivals not because he is a philosopher but because he is fast. I should like to show Posidonius a glass blower whose breath gives glass intricate shapes which a skillful hand could scarcely fashion! These things were invented after we ceased to discover wisdom.

"Democritus is reported to have invented the arch," says Posidonius, "in which stones leaning in a curve are bound together by a keystone." I would say this is wrong; there must have been bridges and gateways curved at the top before the time of Democritus. You fail to mention that this same Democritus also invented a method for softening ivory and for transforming a pebble into emerald by cooking—a method still in use for coloring stones found susceptible to the process. Though it was a sage who invented these methods, he did not do so qua sage; a sage does many things which we see done equally well or even more deftly and expertly by the most thoughtless of men.

What *did* the sage track down, you ask; what did he bring to light? First, truth and nature, which he followed, not as other creatures do, with eyes too dull for the divine. Then, the law of life, which he directed to universals, teaching men not merely to know the gods but to follow them and to receive chance happenings exactly as if they were commands. He has forbidden us to yield to baseless opinions and has weighed the value and character of each thing at its true estimate. He has condemned pleasures which involve regret and has praised goods whose satisfaction will be unalloyed. He has demonstrated that the man who has no need of happiness is the happiest, and the man who has power over himself most powerful.

I do not mean the philosophy which puts the citizen outside his country and the gods outside the universe and which has made a virtue of pleasure, but rather the philosophy which accounts nothing a good unless it be honorable, which cannot be softened by gifts of man or Fortune, of which the price is that it cannot be acquired at any price. I cannot believe that this philosophy existed in that untaught age when crafts were still unknown and use was the teacher of the useful arts.

There followed the blessed ages when Nature's bounty lay open to all to be used without distinction, before avarice and luxury severed mankind's unity, so that from partnership men scurried after individual rapine. Those were not wise men even if they behaved as wise men should. No other state of the human race deserves higher respect; if god should delegate the molding of earthly creatures and the formation of peoples' habits to some individual, he could find no more admirable condition than that reported of the age when (Vergil, *Georgics* 1.125 ff.)

No farmers harried the tilth; to mark out fields
And separate boundaries was not lawful. They shared
Pursuits, and earth itself produced more freely
When none demanded.

Could any race be more blessed than that? Men enjoyed
Nature in common, and she that begot them supplied them
all as guardian and assured them possession of shared resources. Might I not call that breed the richest of mortal
kind when no pauper could be found among them?

But avarice invaded this happy system, and in its desire
to withdraw property to subvert to its own uses it alienated
the whole and reduced itself to narrowly delimited instead
of undefined resources. It was avarice that introduced poverty; by craving much it lost all. Though it now strive to
repair its loss, though it add field to field, ejecting neighbors by fee or force, though it expand estates to the area
of provinces and call an extended tour of its estates possession, yet will no widening of boundaries bring us back
to the state from which we have fallen away.

When we have done all that we can we shall own a great
deal, but we did own the whole. The earth itself was more
fertile when it was not worked, and provided amply for
peoples who did not seize for themselves. Men took as great
pleasure in finding what Nature offered as in displaying it
to their neighbors. None could have excess or dearth; there
was fair division among people like-minded. Not yet did
the strong overpower the weak, not yet did the miser hide
what he found and so deprive another even of necessities;
each cared for his neighbor as for himself. Weapons lay
idle and hands untainted by human blood turned all their
pugnacity against wild beasts. Some thick grove sheltered
those men against the sun and a humble steading protected
them against the blasts of cold and rain; they lived under
the leaves and passed nights untroubled and free of sighs.
We, in our purple, are tossed with anxiety, which pricks

us with sharp goads; what soft slumber the hard earth afforded those men! No coffered fretwork hung over them,
but as they lay in the open the stars glided overhead and
the mighty spectacle of night's firmament moved apace in
silence in pursuit of its grand task. By day, as by night, the
vistas of this fairest mansion lay open to them. They could
freely gaze upon constellations as they declined from heaven's arch and upon others as they rose from the unseen.
How could roving among marvels so spaciously spangled
fail to give delight? But you tremble at every sound in your
houses and flee in dismay if there is any creak among your
wall paintings. Those men had no houses as big as cities.
The breezes blowing free through the open, the flitting
shade of rock or tree, pellucid springs and rills untamed
and unspoiled by channeling or piping but flowing at will,
meadows artlessly beautiful—such was the setting of the
rustic home dressed by a country hand. This was a house
in accordance with nature, and in it living was a pleasure,
with fear neither of the house nor for it. Today our houses
are a large portion of our dread.

But however exemplary and free of guile life was for
those people, they were not philosophers, for that title is
applicable only to the highest career. I would not deny that
there were men of lofty spirit who were, if I may so put
it, fresh from the gods. There can be no doubt that the
world brought forth better types before it grew effete. But
though they were endowed with fortitude and ready for
toil, their talents were not yet perfected in every respect.
For virtue is not Nature's gift; to become good is an art.
But those men did not root for gold and silver and translucent stones in earth's lowest dregs, and they were still merciful even to dumb animals—so far from man killing man,
not in anger or fear, but to provide a spectacle! Their clothing was not yet embroidered, nor was gold woven into
cloth; gold was not even mined.

What does this amount to? It was ignorance that kept

them innocent. There is a great difference between not willing to sin and not knowing how. They knew nothing of justice, of prudence, of temperance and courage. Their uncultivated life did possess qualities analogous to these virtues, but virtue can occur only in a soul trained and taught and raised to its height by assiduous exercise. For this, but not with it, were we born, and in even the best of men you will find, before they are educated, the raw material of virtue, not virtue itself. Farewell.

You and I are at one, I assume, in holding that externals are acquired for the sake of the body, the body is tended out of respect for the soul, and that the agencies of the soul which direct motion and sustenance are given us for the sake of the essential soul. The essential soul has an irrational factor and also a rational. The irrational serves the rational and is the one element which is not referred to something else but refers all things to itself. For the divine reason, too, is sovereign over all things and subordinate to none, and our reason possesses the same quality because it is derived from the divine.

If we are at one on this point, it follows that we shall be at one also on the proposition that the happy life depends solely on our reason being perfect. Only perfect reason keeps the soul from being submissive and stands firm against Fortune; it assures self-sufficiency in whatever situation. It is the one good which can never be impinged upon. A man is happy, I maintain, when no circumstance can reduce him; he keeps to the heights and uses no buttress but himself, for a man sustained by a bolster is liable to fall. If this is not so, then many factors outside ourselves will begin to have power over us. But who wishes Fortune to be paramount, or what prudent man preens himself on what is not his?

What is the happy life? Self-sufficiency and abiding tranquillity. This is the gift of greatness of soul, the gift of constancy which perseveres in a course judged right. How can these attitudes be attained? By surveying truth in its entirety, by safeguarding in every action order, measure, decorum, a will that is without malice and benign, focused

undeviatingly upon reason, at once amiable and admirable.
I shall summarize in a brief formula: The wise man's soul
should have the quality of a god's. What can a man desire
if he possesses everything that is honorable? If the dishonorable can contribute to the optimum state, then the
happy life will be comprised of elements other than honorable. And what could be meaner or stupider than to
weave the good of the rational soul out of irrational
strands?

Yet there are those who hold that the supreme good can
be augmented, because it is incomplete when Fortune
makes inroads upon it. Antipater, a major authority of this
school, says that he makes allowances, albeit very slight
ones, to externals. But you see how absurd it is not to be
content with daylight unless a tiny flame adds its illumina-
tion. What contribution can a spark make in bright sun-
light? If the honorable alone does not satisfy you, then you
must desiderate either the repose which the Greeks call
aokhlesia ("undisturbedness") or else pleasure. But the first
can be had in any case: when the mind is at liberty to
survey the universe and nothing distracts it from the contemplation of nature it is free of disturbance. The second,
pleasure, is the good of cattle; this is to add the irrational to
the rational, the dishonorable to the honorable. Physical
titillation contributes to pleasure; why do you boggle at
saying that a man is in a good state if his appetite is in a
good state? Would you count as a human being (I will not
say a true man) one whose supreme good consists of flavors
and colors and sounds? He should be crossed off the roster
of the noblest of all living species, which is second only to
the gods; an animal whose delight is in fodder should herd
with cattle.

The irrational part of the soul has two divisions: one
spirited, ambitious, headstrong, swayed by passion, and the
other passive, unforceful, devoted to pleasure. The former,
which is unbridled but yet of better quality and at least

more stalwart and virile, these philosophers have neglected, and have deemed the latter, nerveless and abject as it is, essential to the happy life. They have put reason under its orders and have made the supreme good of the noblest of creatures a thing spineless and ignoble, a monstrous hybrid, moreover, compounded of ill-assorted and badly joined members. As Vergil says in his description of Scylla (*Aeneid* 3.426 ff.):

A human face above, a maiden with beauteous bosom;
Below a monstrous mass, wolf's belly, dolphin's tails.

The beasts attached to Scylla are at least horrendous and fleet; but of what monstrosities has that school constructed wisdom! Man's prime art is virtue unqualified. Subjoined to it is useless and ephemeral flesh, fit only, as Posidonius says, for receiving food. Then divine virtue tapers off to vileness, and to the revered and celestial portions above there is mortised a sluggish and nerveless beast. Repose, the other factor, does not of itself serve the soul, but it eliminates obstacles; pleasure actually unstrings the soul and blunts all its force. Can you imagine a union of such inharmonious bodies? The most nerveless is built onto the most strenuous, the frivolous onto the most austere, the intemperate and even the iniquitous onto the most sacred.

"Well then," says the opposition, "if virtue is not impeded by good health and repose and freedom from pain, will you not seek these things?" Of course I shall, not, however, because they are goods but because they are in accordance with nature and because I shall avail myself of them judiciously. And what good will they involve? Simply this: proper choice. When I put on clothing that is appropriate, when I walk as I should, when I dine as becomes me, it is not the dinner or the walk or the clothing that are good but my own program of observing in every act a measure which conforms to reason. I must add that choice of becoming clothing is a desideratum, for man is by nature a tidy and well-groomed animal. Becoming clothing is therefore not a good per se, but the choice of becoming clothing is; the good lies not in the thing but in the quality of selection. Our modes of action, not the things we do, are honorable. My remarks about clothing you may apply to the body, for it is a sort of garment with which Nature has clothed the soul; it is the soul's sheath. But who has ever valued clothes by the rack? The scabbard does not make a sword good or bad. In regard to the body, then, my response will be the same: If I have the choice I shall take health and strength, but the good involved will not be these things per se but my choice of them.

"Granted that the wise man is happy," says the opposition, "yet he does not attain the supreme good unless the natural appliances for it are available to him. The possessor of virtue may not indeed be wretched, but neither can he be very happy if he lacks such natural goods as health and soundness of limbs." You concede the point which seems harder to believe, that a man beset by acute and unremitting pain is not wretched and even happy, but deny the easier point, that he is very happy. But if the efficacy of virtue keeps a man from being wretched, it is certainly capable of making him very happy, for the interval between happy and very happy is less than between wretched and happy. If a force is strong enough to snatch a man from disaster and set him among the happy, it is surely capable of adding the touch which will make him very happy. Will its strength fail at the top of the rise? There are commodities in life and discommodities, both outside our control. If a good man is not wretched despite the presence of all discommodities, will he not be very happy if a few commodities are missing? Just as the pressure of discommodity cannot sink him to wretchedness, so the lack of commodities cannot deprive him of being very happy. He is very happy without commodities in the same degree as he is not wretched under discommodities. Else, if his good can be diminished it can be taken from him altogether.

A little while ago I said that a tiny flame adds nothing to the light of the sun, for any light other than the sun's is eclipsed by the sun's brilliance. "But there are things which obstruct even the sun." Yet even amidst obstructions the sun is undiminished, and though some intervening object may block our view of it, it continues to function and travel its course. When it shines through a rift in the clouds it is no smaller or tardier than in a cloudless sky; there is a vast difference between an obstruction and an impairment. Similarly, obstructions do not detract from virtue; it retains its stature, only its light is dimmer. For us, perhaps, it is less conspicuous and luminous, but for itself it is unchanged, and like the sun in eclipse it continues to exercise its function. Against virtue, therefore, disasters and losses and injuries have no more power than a cloud has against the sun.

One opinion holds that a wise man with physical affliction is neither wretched nor happy. This, too, is a fallacy, for it puts what is fortuitous on a par with the virtues and assigns no higher value to the honorable than to what is devoid of honor. Could anything be more sordid or scurvy than to equate the venerable and the contemptible? Justice, piety, loyalty, steadfastness, and prudence are venerable; but sturdy legs and sound and solid biceps and teeth, on the other hand, are worthless and often occur in fuller measure in the most worthless characters. Moreover, if the wise man with physical affliction will be regarded as neither wretched nor happy but left somewhere between, his life will be an object of neither aspiration nor avoidance. But is it not the height of foolishness to say that the life of a wise man is not to be aspired to? Or is it credible that any life is neither to be aspired to nor avoided? Again, if physical infirmities do not make a man wretched, they allow him to be happy. What has no power to change his status for the worse cannot interdict it from being the best.

"We know cold and we know hot," it is objected, "and what is between is tepid; similarly, one man is happy, another is wretched, and a third neither happy nor wretched." I must get to the bottom of this figure which is aimed at our position. If I add a little cold water to the tepid it will become cold, and if I pour in more hot it will eventually become hot. But however much misery I pile on to your man who is neither wretched nor happy he will not, according to your statement, be wretched; the figure is therefore not apposite. Again, I give you a man who is neither wretched nor happy. I add blindness; he is not made wretched. I add lameness; he is not made wretched. I add intense and unremitting pain; he is not made wretched. If so many calamities cannot shift him to wretchedness, neither can they dislodge him from happiness. If, as you say, the wise man cannot fall from happiness to wretchedness, he cannot fall into non-happiness. If a man has begun to slip he cannot stop at any particular point. The thing which keeps him from rolling to the bottom holds him at the top. Can a happy life not be pulled to pieces? It cannot even be loosened, and that is why virtue per se is sufficient for a happy life.

"But look you," it is objected, "is not the wise man happier if he has lived longer, if no pain has distracted him, than if he had always had to wrestle with misfortune?" Tell me, is he better or more honorable? If not, then neither is he happier. To be happier he must be more upright; if he cannot be more upright then neither can he be happier. Virtue cannot be stretched, and neither can the happy life, which is the issue of virtue. So great a good is virtue that it is impervious to such visitations as shortness of life, pain, and assorted physical infirmities. Pleasure does not even earn its attention. What is the outstanding characteristic of virtue? Indifference to the future and disregard of the calendar; in an instant of time virtue consummates good everlasting. To us these things seem incredible, seem to transcend human nature; that is because we gauge its grandeur by our own puniness and bestow the title of virtue upon our failings. It is equally incredible, surely, that a man subjected to exquisite torture should say, "I am happy." But the very workshop of voluptuousness heard that exclamation. "This day and that other were my happiest," said Epicurus; one of the days he was tormented by strangury and the other by an incurable stomach ulcer. Why should men who cultivate virtue find qualities which even the votaries of pleasure exhibit incredible? The Epicureans too, for all their ignoble and unaspiring mentality, assert that in extreme pain and distress the wise man will be neither wretched nor happy. This too is incredible, even more incredible. I do not see how virtue will not be precipitated into the abyss once she is dislodged from the height. Either she must keep a man happy, or, if she is evicted from this function, she cannot prevent him from becoming miserable. She cannot be dismissed while she stands; she must either be conquered or conquer.

"Only to the immortal gods," an opponent says, "are virtue and the happy life allotted; ours is but a shadow and a semblance of their goods. We approach but never reach them." But reason is shared by gods and men; in them it is perfected, in us it is perfectible. But it is our vices that reduce us to despair, for the junior partner in reason is of lower rank, too unstable for surveillance over choice wares, with judgment still unsteady and unsure. He may desiderate the faculties of sight and hearing, good health, a physique not repulsive, and in addition a longer span with faculties unimpaired. Through reason he can lead a life beyond reproach, but in the man imperfect there persists a certain malignant force, because his mind is susceptible to distortion. The badness has shown up and been exercised and is now gone; he is not yet a good man but is being molded into one. Anyone who falls short of good is bad.

But where "virtue and spirit are present in his frame" (*Aeneid* 5.363) a man is equal to the gods. He remembers his origin and makes it his goal. It is never wrong to attempt to regain the heights from which you have descended. Why should you not believe that there is an element of the divine in what is part of god? The totality in which we are contained is one, and it is god; and we are his partners and his members. Our spirit is capacious, and its direction is toward god, if vices do not press it down. Just as our bodily posture is erect and looks toward heaven, so our soul, which may reach outward at will, was fashioned by Nature to desire equality with the gods. And if it utilizes its powers and expands outward into its own reaches, it is by no alien path that it makes its way to the heights. A pioneer journey to heaven is a great task; the soul is retracing its path. When it has found its road it marches boldly on, disregarding all distinctions. It casts no backward glance at riches; gold and silver, which are most appropriate to the darkness in which they had been buried, the soul values not by the glitter which overwhelms the eyes of the ignorant, but by the primal muck from which our greed separated them and dug them out.

The soul knows, I declare, that riches are stored elsewhere than in vaults; it is the soul which needs to be filled, not the money chests. The soul we may raise to sovereignty over all things, to the soul we may commit ownership of nature, to limit its sway by boundaries of east and west and possess all things by divine patent, to look down from its treasures on high upon the rich below, not one of whom is so pleased with his own wealth as he is disgruntled at his neighbor's.

When the soul has raised itself to this sublimity it regards the necessary burden of the body not as a lover but as a steward, and it does not submit to its ward. No man that serves his body is free. Even if you pass over the other masters that excessive solicitude for the body has contrived, its own lordliness is imperious and touchy. From the body the soul springs forth, now calmly and now with elation, and never thereafter does it ask what is to befall the husk that it has left behind. Just as we are unconcerned about the clippings of beard and hair, so upon its departure from man's mortal frame the divine soul judges that its receptacle's final destiny—whether fire shall consume it, or stone shut it in, or earth cover it, or beasts rend it—is of no more relevance to itself than the afterbirth is to a newborn child. Whether it will be thrown to the birds to tear apart or whether it be consumed, "a prey offered to the hounds of the sea" (*Aeneid* 9.485), how can it concern a no-body? Even when it was among mankind the soul did not fear the threats of post-mortem terrors held out by people who thought it too little for terror to stop with death. "I am not terrified by the executioner's hook," says the soul, "or by the disgusting mutilation of a cadaver exposed to the scorn of spectators. I ask no one to see to my funeral. I commend my remains to no one. Nature has provided that none shall be unburied; if savagery cast a body out, time will dispose of it." Maecenas has put it deftly: "I care for no tomb; Nature buries the forsaken." You would suppose this was said by some stalwart; Maecenas did indeed possess imposing and virile gifts, but prosperity relaxed them. Farewell.

It is provoking to be aroused from an agreeable dream; the pleasure which is lost may be specious but it produces the effect of truth. Your letter has been just such a rude awakening; it brought me up short when I was sunk in comfortable meditation and on my way to further musing if I had been left alone. My pleasure was induced by investigating, or rather, by Hercules, by believing, the doctrine of the immortality of the soul; I gave easy credence to the opinions of distinguished authorities who promised rather than proved so great a boon and adopted the high hope for myself. I was already bored with myself, already contemptuous of the broken odds and ends of my life, and ready to pass over into the timelessness where I would inherit all eternity, when I was shocked into wakefulness by the receipt of your letter and lost my charming dream. But I shall woo it again, if I can come to terms with you, and redeem it.

The opening of your letter objected that I had not fully explained the proposition I was endeavoring to prove, to wit, that posthumous fame is a good, because I had not resolved our opponents' objection that "no good can be comprised of disparate elements, and fame is so comprised." Your query, my dear Lucilius, belongs to another aspect of our theme, and I had therefore postponed it, along with other kindred aspects. As you know, certain ethical questions involve logical elements. What I dealt with was the central part of the theme, which has to do with ethics: whether it is foolish and useless to be concerned for our posthumous future, whether our goods perish with our bodies and nothing can belong to a person who is non-existent, or whether, out of the state of which we will not be sensible when we reach it, we may anticipate the enjoyment of or aspiration toward some profit.

These questions all pertain to ethics, and have therefore been given their proper place. The objections raised by the dialecticians had to be sifted out, and I therefore put them aside. Now, at your insistence, I shall take a summary view of their whole position and then address myself to individual points. But without a preamble the refutations will not be intelligible. The essential preamble is this: some entities consist of a continuous body, as for instance man; some are composite, as for instance ship, house, or any structure where disparate members are joined to form a unity; some are comprised of units otherwise discrete, as for instance an army, a populace, a senate. Discrete units cohere to form such entities by law or function, but in nature they are disparate individuals. The remainder of my preamble is this: we Stoics hold that nothing composed of discrete parts is good. A single good must be defined and regulated by a single soul, and the essence of a single good must be single. This can be demonstrated without external proof whenever you like; it had to be relegated for the present because we were being attacked with our own (Stoic) weapons.

"You maintain," our opponent says, "that nothing composed of discrete parts is good. But the fame you are discussing is the favorable opinion of good men. Fame is no more the approval of one good man than rumor is the conversation of one man or notoriety the bad opinion of one man. For fame the consensus of many esteemed and respectable men is essential. But this involves the judgment of several, that is, of discrete, persons, and therefore it cannot be a good. You maintain that fame is praise rendered to a good man by good men. Praise is speech, the utterance of significant sound. But sound, even uttered by good men, is not necessarily good, for not everything a good man does is good. He may applaud or hiss, yet no one will call his applause or hissing good, however admirable and praiseworthy the man may be, any more than he would call his coughs and sneezes good. Fame is therefore not a good. And finally, tell us whose the good is, the praiser's or the praised's. If you say that it belongs to the man praised, you are as absurd as if you asserted that my neighbor's good health belongs to me. But to praise deserving men is an honorable act; the act, and therefore the good, belongs to the man who praises, not to us who are praised. Yet this was the subject of our inquiry."

I shall now address myself briefly to the individual objections. First, the question whether good can be comprised of discrete parts is still unsettled, and each side has its supporters. Next, does fame require many votes? The judgment of one good man can be sufficient, for a single such judgment establishes that we are good. "What?" says my opponent. "And will fame be the opinion of one man and notoriety the malignant conversation of one man? Glory, too, I regard as something more widely broadcast; it requires the consensus of many men." But these "many" and that "one" are in different categories. Why? Because a good man thinking well of me is tantamount to all good men thinking well of me, for if they knew me all would think alike. The judgment would be alike in every case because it would be equally shaped by truth; there could be no disagreement. The decision of one is as good as unanimous if there can be no different decision. "For glory or high repute," you say, "one man's opinion is not enough." In the former case one good man's suffrage is virtual unanimity because a complete canvass would yield the same result; but here dissimilar men give diverse judgments. You will find intransigent emotions, equivocations, inconstancy, suspicion. Do you imagine that all men can hold to one opinion? Even one man cannot hold to one opinion. The good man is guided by truth, and the force and aspect of truth is single. What these others agree upon is false, and the false are never consistent but variable and at odds.

"But praise," my opponent says, "is nothing else than utterance, and utterance is not a good." When Stoics say that fame is praise of good men rendered by good men they refer not to the sound but to the sentiment. Though a good man remain speechless, if he judges a person worthy of praise that person is praised. Praise and laudation are different things; the latter does require utterance. We do not say "funeral praise" but "funeral laudation," for it involves discourse. And when we say that a person is worthy of praise what we are vouchsafing him are not men's kind words but their judgments. "Praise" may therefore denote speechless and private high opinion and approval of a good man.

Praise, as I have remarked, refers to a mentality, not to words, which only formulate the praise the mind has conceived and advertise it to the many. Whoso judges a man praiseworthy praises him. When our tragic bard (Naevius) says it is magnificent "to be praised by a man bepraised" he means "by a man worthy of praise." And when an equally venerable poet says, "Praise nurtures the arts," he does not mean laudation, for that corrupts the arts. Nothing has had so deleterious an effect upon oratory and other professions which depend upon hearing as has popular approval.

For reputation utterance is requisite, but fame is content with judgment and can come to a man without resort to speech. It is unimpaired not only amid silence but even amid denigration. I shall tell you the difference between fame and glory: glory implies the judgment of the many, fame of the good. "But to whom," it is objected, "does this good, this praise rendered a good man by good men, belong? To the praised or the praiser?" To both. It belongs to me who am praised, because Nature has begotten me to love all mankind, and I am happy to have done good things and to have found appreciative exponents of my merits. The good belongs to the many, because they are appreciative, but is mine also. My mental constitution is such that I can judge the good of others my own, especially where I am myself the cause of the good. The good belongs to the praisers because the operation is virtuous and every act of virtue is good. This good could not have come to them if I were not the man I am. The just rendering of praise is therefore a good for both parties, as much so, by Hercules, as a righteous judgment is a good both of the judge and of the party who wins the suit. You must surely admit that justice is a boon to its possessor and likewise to the man who receives his due. To praise the deserving is justice, and therefore the good belongs to both.

This should be answer enough for those quibblers. But our task is not an exercise in casuistry or in degrading philosophy from its lofty majesty to such hair-splitting. How much better it is to go by the open and direct road rather than to set up a maze which requires great trouble to thread through! Disputations of that kind are nothing else than a sleight-of-hand game. Tell us rather how natural a thing it is for a man to project his mind into the infinite. A great and noble thing is the human mind; it brooks no limitations other than god's universals. It acknowledges, in the first instance, no lowly fatherland, no Ephesus or Alexandria or any ground even more populous or more lavishly built over. Its fatherland is all the arch that encompasses the height and sweep of the firmament, this whole dome within which lie sea and land, within which the ether separates human and divine and also joins them to one another, which is spangled by luminaries which keep their vigils in their proper turns. Neither will the mind tolerate a restricted time span. "All centuries are mine," it says; "no era is closed to great intellects, no epoch impassable to thought. When that day comes which shall separate this mixture of human and divine I will leave the body here where I found it and betake myself to the gods. Even now I am not without them, but I am held back by the heavy and the earthy." These delays of mortal existence are a prelude to that better and longer life.

Just as the mother's womb holds us for ten months not in preparation for itself but for the region to which we seem to be discharged when we are capable of drawing breath and surviving in the open, so in the span extending from infancy to old age we are ripening for another birth. Another beginning awaits us, another status. We cannot yet bear heaven's light except at intervals; look unfalteringly, then, to that decisive hour which is the body's last but not the soul's. All that lies about you look upon as the luggage in a posting station; you must push on. At your departure Nature strips you as bare as at your entry. You cannot carry out more than you brought in; indeed, you must lay down a good part of what you brought into life. The envelope of skin, which is your last covering, will be stripped off; the flesh and the blood which is diffused and courses through the whole of it will be stripped off; the bones and sinews which are the structural support of the shapeless and precarious mass will be stripped off.

That day which you dread as the end is your birth into eternity. Lay the burden aside, why delay?—as if you had not already left the covert of your body and gone forth! You stick, you resist; at your other birth, too, it required a great effort of your mother to thrust you forth. You weep and wail; weeping, too, is incidental to birth, but then it was pardonable, for you came with no knowledge or experience. When you issued from the warm and soft shelter of your mother's womb a freer air breathed upon you, then the touch of coarse hands impinged upon you, and in your newness and total ignorance you lay stunned in an unfamiliar world.

But now it is no novelty for you to be separated from what you have previously been a part of. Dismiss with serenity limbs now useless, and lay down that body you have so long occupied. It will be pulled apart, covered over, got rid of. Why repine? This is the normal way; the fetal sheath always perishes. Why stay attached to it as if it were part of you? It was only your hull. There will come a day which will wrest you from the foul and noisome quarters of the belly and set you at large. Withdraw even now, so far as you can, and from pleasure too, except where it is inherent in necessary and serious pursuits. Dissociate yourself from your body and contemplate loftier and sublimer things. Eventually the arcana of Nature will be uncovered to your sight, the mist will be dispersed, and bright light will radiate from all sides.

Fancy the brilliance when all the stars mingle their radiance and there is no shadow to disturb the heaven's calm. All its expanse will shine with equal light; alternations of day and night belong to the lowest atmosphere. Then will you say that you have lived in darkness when you in your totality have surveyed light in its totality, light that you now behold but darkly, through the tiny passages of your eyes. Even so you admire it, though it is yet so far away; how divine will that light appear when you behold it in its proper seat?

Thinking at this level allows nothing sordid to find lodgment in the soul, nothing base, nothing cruel. It maintains that the gods are witnesses of all things. It bids us win their approbation, prepare to be with them in future, set our sights for eternity. And the man who has conceived eternity in his mind cringes from no army, is alarmed by no trumpet blast, is intimidated by no threats. How can a man not be free of fear if he hopes for death? Even the school which holds that the soul abides only so long as it is held captive by the body believes that it disperses at once, to be of use even after death. Though he is taken from our sight, still "thoughts of the hero's virtue come often to mind, thoughts

of the glory of his race" (*Aeneid* 4.3 f.). Reflect upon the
profit good examples bring us, and you will realize that
great men's presence and their memory are alike useful.
Farewell.

I could teach thee wisdom by the ancients' rule
Wert thou not truant to so humble a school.
—Vergil, *Georgics* 1.176–7

But you are not truant, nor does subtlety deter you. You are too precise a mind to deal cavalierly with weighty subjects. You insist that study must make some contribution to progress and object only when refined subtlety produces no yield. I shall endeavor to avoid useless subtlety in the present inquiry. Our subject is whether the good is apprehended by the senses or by intellect; the corollary to the latter alternative is that it does not exist for dumb animals or children.

The school which makes pleasure its ideal holds that the good resides in the senses; we Stoics hold that it resides in the intellect, which is the domain of the mind. If senses were the criteria for the good, there is no pleasure we should reject, for there is no pleasure which does not attract and titillate; and on the other hand there is no pain we should willingly undergo, for pain always offends the senses. Besides, no blame could justly attach to persons excessively devoted to pleasure or fearful of pain. We do in fact disapprove of persons addicted to appetite and lust, and scorn those whom fear of pain deters from any manly venture. How are they to blame if the senses they serve are the criteria of good and evil? It is to the senses you have assigned the decision on what a man is to aim for and what to avoid.

But the presiding judge is, of course, reason; reason holds jurisdiction over good and evil just as it does over virtue and honor. The Epicureans give the worst element authority over the better; the good is arraigned before the senses, which are blunt and dull and less alert in man than in other animals. And the absurdity of making fine distinctions by touch rather than sight! Our subtlest and keenest faculty for distinguishing good and evil would be eyesight. You see in what abysmal ignorance of truth a man involves himself, how he treads sublime and divine ideals underfoot, when he makes touch the ultimate criterion for good and evil. "Just as every art and science," he says, "should have a tangible element which can be apprehended by sense and receives its origin and growth from sense, so the happy life draws its basis and inception from a tangible element which is subject to sense perception. Surely you too assert that the happy life takes its inception from tangible elements."

We assert that "happy" is what is in accordance with nature, and what is in accordance with nature is directly obvious, just as wholeness is obvious. The endowment according to nature which comes to us at birth I call not a good but the inception of good. You assign the highest good, because you define it as pleasure, to infancy, so that the baby at birth begins where man consummates his journey. You put the treetop where the root belongs. If a man should say that a fetus in its mother's womb, weak, unformed, amorphous, its sex not yet determined, already participated in goodness, he would manifestly be wrong. And yet how little difference there is between a newborn babe and the unseen burden in a mother's inward parts! As far as perception of good and evil is concerned both are equally mature; an infant is no more capable of the good than is a tree or some dumb animal.

And why is the good not present in tree or dumb animal? Because reason is not. Hence the good is not present in an infant because it lacks reason. It will attain to the good only when it attains to reason. There is the irrational animal, the not yet rational, and the imperfectly rational; in none of these is the good present, because the good comes with reason. What are the distinctions between the degrees I have mentioned? In the irrational there cannot be good ever; in the not yet rational there cannot be good now; in the imperfectly rational there can be good now, but there is not.

What I mean, Lucilius, is this: the good is not to be found in any person whatever or in any age whatever; it is as remote from infancy as last is from first, or as consummation from inception. It is therefore not present in a weak and tiny body just knitting together—how should it be?— any more than in the seed. If you argue that we recognize a certain good in a tree or plant, the good is not present in the first shoot, when the plant has just begun to emerge from the soil. There is a good of wheat, but it is not present in the burgeoning stalk or when the soft spike is thrusting out of its husk, but when summer's heat and the requisite processes have ripened the grain. Nature in general does not bring forth her good until her process is complete. And so in the case of man, there is no good in him until his reason is matured. And what is this good? I will tell you: It is a free and upstanding mind which subjects other things to itself and itself to nothing. So far is infancy from being capable of this good that even boyhood cannot hope for it and young manhood is wrong to hope for it; old age can be thankful if it attains it after long study and application. By this definition the good is a matter of intellect.

"You said," the opposition objects, "that there is a certain good of trees and of shrubs; hence there can be a good of infants also." True good is present neither in trees nor in dumb animals; good as applied to them is a borrowed term. If you ask what their good is, it is their individual conformity to nature. True good cannot possibly occur in a dumb animal; its nature is richer and superior. Where there is no place for reason there is no good. There are four natures for us to consider: the tree's, the animal's, man's, and

god's. The latter two, being rational, possess the same nature; the distinction between them is that one is immortal
and the other mortal. Of these two the good of the one—
god—is perfected by nature, of the other—man—by application. The others, because reason is missing, are perfect only
in their own nature, not truly perfect.

Only what is perfect in accordance with nature as a
whole is truly perfect, and nature as a whole is rational.
Other things can be perfect according to their species. A
being not capable of the happy life is not capable of the
efficient cause of the happy life, and the efficient cause of
the happy life is the good. A dumb animal is not capable
of the happy life or of the efficient cause of the happy life;
a dumb animal is not capable of the good. A dumb animal
apprehends the present by the senses. He recalls the past
only when something comes up to jog the senses. A horse,
for example, remembers the way when he is started upon
it; standing in his stall he had no memory of it, no matter
how often he may have trodden it. The third tense—the
future—has no relevance to dumb animals.

How can the nature of beings who have had no experience of perfected time be perfect? Time is comprised of
three parts—past, present, and future. Animals know only
the present, which is the weightiest factor in their limited
orbit. There is an occasional recollection of the past, but
only at the instance of a present encounter. The good of
perfected nature cannot therefore exist in imperfect nature,
or if imperfect nature possesses the good so also does plant
life. I do not deny that dumb animals have strong and ex-
citable impulses towards conduct which seems to be according to nature, but these impulses are unsorted and
confused.

"Do you mean to say," you object, "that dumb animals
move in a confused and unregulated fashion?" I would say
that they do move in a confused and unregulated fashion
if their nature were capable of order; as it is, they move in

conformity with their nature. Confusion is applicable only where non-confusion can also occur, as anxiety is applicable only where serenity can obtain. No man is vicious unless he is capable of virtue. In dumb animals their movement is a function of their nature. Not to detain you overlong, the dumb animal does possess a certain good, a certain virtue, a certain perfection, but not absolute good or virtue or perfection. This is the prerogative of rational creatures, who are endowed with the capacity of knowing why, how far, and how. Good can therefore exist only where reason exists.

Do you wish to know the objective of my argument and the benefit it can bring your mind? I will tell you. It exercises and sharpens it and by worthy occupation constrains it to achievement. Any brake upon the race to iniquity is worth while. But I will go further: there is no way I could serve you better than by pointing your true good out to you, by separating you from dumb animals, by classing you with god. Why, tell me, do you nurture and exercise your physical strength? Nature has made cattle and beasts stronger. Why do you cultivate your beauty? When you have done all you can the dumb animals still score higher in handsomeness. Why do you dress your hair with such exquisite care? Wear it loose as the Parthians do or tie it up in the German style or ruffle it in the Scythian fashion, you will still find a thicker mane tossing on any horse and a handsomer on any lion. Train as you will for speed, you cannot match a hare. Will you not abandon competition in fields that belong to others and betake yourself to your own true good?

And what is this? A mind flawless and pure, which emulates god and raises itself above ordinary humanity, allowing nothing outside to impinge upon itself. You are a rational creature. What, then, is your peculiar good? Perfect reason. Will you exploit this to its fullest limits, to its maximum potentiality? Pronounce yourself happy only when all your satisfactions are begotten of reason, and when, having surveyed what men struggle for, pray for, watch over, you find nothing to desire let alone prefer. I give you a rule of thumb to assess yourself and ascertain your perfection: You will come into possession when you understand that the "successful" are least successful. Farewell.